Effective Document and Data Management

Effective Document and Data Management

Unlocking Corporate Content

BOB WIGGINS

GOWER

Published by
Gower Publishing Limited
Wey Court East
Union Road
Farnham
Surrey
GU9 7PT
England

Gower Publishing Company
Suite 420
101 Cherry Street
Burlington
VT 05401-4405
USA

www.gowerpublishing.com

Bob Wiggins has asserted his morals right under the Copyright, Designs and Patents Act, 1988, to be identified as the author of this work.

British Library Cataloguing in Publication Data
Wiggins, Bob.
  Effective document and data management : unlocking
  corporate content. -- 3rd ed.
  1. Business records--Management. 2. Business records--
  Management--Data processing. 3. Information storage and
  retrieval systems--Business.
  I. Title
  651.5-dc23

ISBN: 978-1-4094-2328-7 (hbk)
ISBN: 978-1-4094-4625-5 (ebk)

Library of Congress Cataloging-in-Publication Data
Wiggins, Bob.
  Effective document and data management : unlocking corporate content / by
  Bob Wiggins. -- 3rd ed.
   p. cm.
  Includes bibliographical references and index.
  ISBN 978-1-4094-2328-7 (hardback) -- ISBN 978-1-4094-4625-5
  (ebook) 1. Business records--Management. 2. Business
  records--Management--Data processing. 3. Information storage and retrieval
  systems--Business. I. Title.
  HF5736.W733 2011
  651.5--dc23

2011045650

Printed and bound in Great Britain by the
MPG Books Group, UK

Contents

List of Figures

Selective Glossary

'Human nature insists on a definition for every concept'. Henry Mintzberg

The definitions are drawn or adapted from various glossaries and are intended to be most appropriate for the way topics are treated in this book. References are provided where the source definition is stated verbatim.

Activity	Measurable amount of work performed to convert inputs into output; a piece of work; a task that forms one logical step within a process.
Archive (noun)	A place in which collected public or corporate records are kept; a repository for documents etc.; a databank. (OED 2001).
Business process	A set of one or more linked procedures or activities which collectively realize a business objective or policy goal, normally within the context of an organizational structure defining functional roles and relationships. (WFMC 2009).
Content Management System (CMS)	A system for managing the life cycle of an organization's information content. Usually taken to refer to unstructured information. (CMS can also refer to Case Management System, reference to which is made clear in the text).
Data	Facts, esp. numerical facts, collected together for reference or information. A piece of information, a statistic. The quantities, characters, or symbols on which operations are performed by computers and other automatic equipment. (OED 2001).
Document	Recorded information or object which can be treated as a unit. (ISO 15489-1 2001).
Document type	Categorization of documents into mutually exclusive groups to aid the designing of document templates, and facilitate subsequent retrieval. See also Record Type.
Electronic Document and Records Management System (EDRMS)	A type of content management system which provides document management and records management functionality in an integrated system. ERMS will refer to an Electronic Records Management System and DMS to a Document Management System (EDRM also refers to Electronic Discovery Reference Model, reference to which is made clear in the text).
Entity	Something about which you wish to hold information, for example document, employee, equipment or supplier.

File	A set of data available from within a computer system that is capable of being manipulated as a whole. Its use in the computing industry to indicate a means for holding a collection of records has diminished with the advent of databases.
Folder	A folder is a digital or physical container for related records. Folders (segmented into parts) are the primary unit of management. (TNA 2007a).
Function	A particular type of action or operation undertaken by a person or other entity. A set of related activities.
Information	Communication of the knowledge of some fact or occurrence; knowledge or facts communicated about a particular subject, event, etc.; intelligence, news. (OED 2001).
Knowledge	The fact of knowing a thing, state, person, etc.; acquaintance; familiarity gained by experience; acquaintance with a fact or facts; a state of being aware or informed; awareness, consciousness. (OED 2001).
Metadata	A set of data that describes and gives information about other data.
Mission	The purpose for which an organization is established.
Objective	A specific thing aimed at or sought; a target, a goal, an aim.
Ontology	The study of the representation and categorization of entities, ideas, and events, along with their properties and relations.
Operational function	Functions that establish the identity of an organization and the reasons for its existence, for example the manufacturing function of a car maker or the research function of a pharmaceutical company.
Organizational structure	The pattern of arrangement of responsibilities, authorities and relations to enable the organization to perform its functions. Typically exemplified by departmental and management hierarchies.
Policy	A course of action or principle adopted or proposed.
Procedure	A statement that prescribes specific actions to be taken to implement established policies. More specifically, fixed, step-by-step sequence of activities (with definite start and end points) that must be followed in the same order to correctly perform an activity.
Process	see Business Process.
Record	Information created, received and maintained as evidence and information by an organization or person, in pursuance of legal obligations or in the transaction of business. (ISO 15489-1 2001).
Record series	A group of logically-related records, irrespective of format, that support a specific activity.
Record type	Categorization of records into mutually exclusive groups so that a different management policy (e.g. retention scheduling, security category) can be applied to each record type. See also Document type.
Routine	A repetitive procedure.
Strategy	The overall plan and direction to achieve an objective or vision.

Support function	Functions that are common to most organizations and provide underlying administrative or other support for their day-to-day existence, for example managing staff and finance and providing information technology services.
Task	See Activity.
Transaction	An event or process initiated by a user or computer program, regarded as a single unit of work and requiring a record to be generated.
Vision	The aspiration of the organization as regards what it would like to achieve or accomplish in the future. It is intended to provide clear guidance for courses of action.

Preface

The technical, commercial, political and social landscapes have changed dramatically in the decade since the publication of the second edition over a decade ago, for example:

- mobile technology and social networking are creating both opportunities and challenges for managing personal and corporate information
- economic activity has increasingly gravitated towards the east with China as a manufacturing power house and India as a supplier of outsourcing skills
- there have been changes in the structure and focus of the information professions and further consolidation in the supplier market as well as the emergence of new players
- system development methodologies such as Agile and object-oriented approaches are gaining ground as organizations demand more rapid realization of benefits based on improved data and ways of working
- more information-related standards have appeared and the regulatory environment relating to information access has become more complex.

This edition is therefore extensively revised to take into account the impact of such changes and to give greater consideration to data and the business processes involved. I would like to thank all those who commented on the last edition.

From Papyrus to Pixels

'Plus ça change, plus c'est la même chose'. Les Guêpes. Jean-Baptiste Alphonse Karr

A brief canter through the history of recorded information offers some credence for Jean-Baptiste's belief and provides a backdrop to the matters covered in this book.

Paper is still an important medium on which to record or convey information, whether between individuals or organizations. Why this reliance on paper in the age of IT? Various factors combine to explain this situation. Readily produced, easy to handle and with a history harking back to the use of papyrus some 5,500 years ago, paper is a familiar, uncomplicated medium on which to record information. It requires no special technology or skill to use, and facilitates review and browsing of information.

In early days communication of information (other than by word-of-mouth) required manuscripts to be transcribed to enable wider distribution, thereby providing the first example of a 'copy'. The invention of the printing press by Gutenberg in the fifteenth century overcame this problem and hence the publishing industry was born.

The coming of the typewriter in the late eighteenth century was a major 'information technology' development. It enabled a much wider population to record or capture information and, from a social perspective, greatly influenced female employment prospects and social and physical arrangements in the office; the word 'typewriter' originally referred to the female operator rather than the machine itself. Its impact was certainly greater than that which would be encountered later with the introduction of computer-based word-processing (Delgado 1979).

Carbon paper used between two sheets of ordinary paper to make one or more copies of an original document was developed in the early 1800s and was initially used to copy hand-written private or business documents. Its use expanded greatly with the availability of typewriters. Together with stencil technologies such as the mimeograph, it enabled small numbers of copies to be reproduced automatically for distribution, reference or safeguard against loss. Although the later development of the photocopier caused the demise of carbon paper and its later derivatives in most offices and businesses, it has survived in the world of emails as 'cc' (carbon copy) to indicate additional copies for distribution.

The late nineteenth century saw the invention of microfilm by Rene Dagron, who was granted the first patent for microfilm in 1859. By the early part of the twentieth century microfilm was being adopted commercially to save space and costs, and this usage increased greatly on into the 1980s using a variety of formats – roll film, aperture cards (microfilm image mounted in a punched card) and microfiche (rectangular sheets of film). Microfilm is not primarily a substitute for paper and hence the 'all-paper' world was virtually unassailable until the coming of computers, the development of which, like many advances, was largely boosted by the Second World War.

Early applications of computers were not focused so much on replacing paper but rather on producing paper documents more effectively. Allied technology such as fax machines and photocopiers did little to dampen the enthusiasm for paper. Computers initially needed manual intervention to undertake calculations. Punched cards were then used, these having the digital information represented by the presence or absence of holes in predefined positions. Then came the ability to store the required actions as programs and execute them from the computer's memory, thereby eliminating the need for manual intervention or the cards.

The miniaturization of components and advances in manufacture made computers increasingly affordable. However, a major attraction for users was the introduction of standardized software for the production of text documents, tabular material in the form of spreadsheets and graphical output, as exemplified by Microsoft and its Office suite. The ability of individuals to control what they produced and to manage their output in electronic form, rather than solely on paper, was liberating. However, effective management of information was now more challenging given the proliferation of electronic records and the need to organize these along with paper versions and perhaps microfilmed archives.

Communication networks, higher capacity storage systems and the birth of email provided the opportunity to share electronic records, but also highlighted the need to agree on ways to organize electronic folders (whether private or public) to facilitate finding the required information. These were embryonic document management systems using the basic metadata of electronic files and folders and of the office software to organize and classify the records.

The development of scanners from early telephotography input devices in the 1920s enabled the conversion of paper documents, and later microfilm itself, into an electronic form. Initially using dedicated screens and imaging software, scanners came into greater prominence as storage systems and computer hardware were able to offer the required capacity and speed, and as imaging standards were put in place. Although document image processing, subsequently embedded in document management systems, fostered the vision for managing all recorded information in electronic form, in reality this vision has not been fully realized and must await technology that matches the alluring nature of paper as a medium.

Arguably the more significant advances have centred around communication technology. The development of the text-based internet arising from US military requirements in the early 1970s was followed by the creation of the World Wide Web in the 1990s which allowed multimedia communication and the creation of new forms of mediated interaction as well as commercial opportunities.

On the software front, the relational database designed by IBM in the 1970s was a major advance, as structured data about the information and the means to manage it could be readily stored, accessed and extended without requiring all the existing applications to be altered. Relational technology remains at the heart of modern electronic document, records and content management systems.

The major challenge has been to process and enable the searching of unstructured information contained in text documents and emails. The automatic indexing of content can be traced to Salton (1989). It involves mechanical analysis of the words in a document and typically the creation of a 'book-type' index providing a pointer from a search term in the index to where it can be found in the document. Although such 'inverted files' are still used to find 'keywords', great strides have been made to understand the idea behind a search term or phrase and the context in which they appear – so–called conceptual searching. Software technology is now available to enable searching across all types of information system in or available to an organization. This federated searching capability is important as increasingly organizations must be able to demonstrate that a search has covered every nook and cranny to find relevant information.

Despite the importance of paper as a convenience medium rather than as the master record, digital information has long predominated. A survey undertaken by IDC (2008) estimated that the digital universe – information that is either created, captured, or replicated in digital form – amounted to 281EB (exabytes) in 2007 and was projected to reach nearly 1,800EB by 2011. Furthermore because of the growth of technologies such as internet phones and Automatic Identification and Data Capture devices, by 2011 there will be more than 20 quadrillion (20 thousand million million) of these information containers, thereby creating a tremendous management challenge for both businesses and consumers. Of that portion of the digital universe created by individuals, less than half can be accounted for by user activity. The rest constitutes a digital 'shadow' of surveillance photos, Web search histories, financial transaction journals, mailing lists and so on.

Pixelated papyri are likely to be included in this digital universe!

Acknowledgements

Special commendations to my wife Traudi for her support in the back office and to Nils Lofmark for his forensic review of key parts of the text. Also thanks to my publisher Jonathan for his enthusiastic support.

Introduction

Why the Need to Consider Both Documents and Data in this Book?

The effective and efficient management and use of information can be major contributors to improving the business performance of an enterprise.

In the context of this book 'information' embraces that which is:

- structured – data, facts and figures in some organized form; those that are alike are grouped together and have defined format and length; similar ones have formal relationships to one another
- unstructured – data that can be of any type and does not necessarily follow any defined format, sequence or rules. It can be considered as the direct product of human communication.

Examples of structured data are found in line-of-business (LIB) computerized systems such as finance, personnel and marketing, and in systems that are specific to the organization's operations such as litigation case information for a law firm, or well sample databases in the oil industry.

Examples of unstructured data are text documents, emails, video, sound or images. A 'compound document' is defined as a document that combines multiple document formats either by reference, by inclusion or both (W3C 2010) and exemplifies the complexity of these types of information. Thus a spreadsheet and picture embedded in a word-processed document is a compound document, as is an email with attachments. An email without its attachment is likely to be useless to the recipient. When managed by records management processes this integrity is maintained. A document management environment, however, is unlikely to guarantee this.

Enterprise content covers all information used or handled by an organization. These two worlds of structured and unstructured data continue largely to be dealt with independently as regards their management – for example, information system (aka computer) departments dealing with the former and records departments managing the latter. This occurs despite the fact that there can be considerable overlap between the two as regards the data they contain and the processes that manage them.

For example, information that appears in a management report on the outcome of litigation cases will be incorporated in a document which may pass through several drafts before becoming final. However, this outcome data may have been extracted from the organization's commercial case management system. There are therefore two places where such outcomes are recorded:

- in a management report document – which may exist in both electronic and paper form with drafts and duplicates spread around the organization, often as attachments to emails
- in the system as data entries linked to the individual cases – the data will usually be backed up for security and continuity and may be retained for longer periods to provide a history.

This situation raises several questions, for example:

- what is the 'master' information?
- in what format will the formal record of this information be held?
- what retention is to be applied?
- how can duplicates be controlled?
- how can data quality be improved?
- what risks may arise concerning statutory or regulatory compliance?
- what processes need to be in place to manage the agreed creation, storage, retention and disposal of this information and the access to it?
- what integration is needed between the various 'information systems'?
- who has responsibility for addressing these questions?

It should be evident from the foregoing that 'documents' and 'data' ('unstructured' and 'structured' information) need to be dealt with together in a coherent and consistent manner, particularly where data appears in unstructured formats. Without this approach the efficiency and effectiveness of an organization will be undermined by less-than-optimal management and use of its information.

As regards the technology systems designed to satisfy this need, many of the solutions consist of a variety of products integrated in various ways and providing different components or services, including records management, document management, content management, workflow and other processes and supporting technologies. For example, a content management system can provide a repository for records and documents and other artefacts such as website snapshots. This book is not focused on any particular technology, but rather aims to address the functions that such technology is required to support.

How this Book Can Help

The book aims to provide an understanding of the following topics:

- the make-up of organizations, areas of similarity and difference between organizations and the challenges faced, whether in the public or private sectors
- ways in which organizations can seek to improve their performance and the measures that are applied to monitor that performance
- the nature of information and the role of information professionals
- ways in which information is captured for subsequent management
- the management of captured information, including document and records management and storage

- methods of information retrieval and information use
- data management and its use for ensuring quality of data
- general project management approaches from initiation through procurement to sign-off
- aspects of an information management project.

How this Book is Structured

The foregoing topics are grouped into the following parts and chapters which can, if required, be consulted individually by those with a greater interest in one subject as compared with another.

Part 1 – Context

Chapter 1 – The Organizational Context

Chapter 2 – Improving Organizational Performance

Chapter 3 – The Information Context

Part 2 – The Information Life Cycle

Chapter 4 – Information Capture

Chapter 5 – Manage Information

Chapter 6 – Information Retrieval and Use

Chapter 7 – Data Management

Part 3 – Projects

Chapter 8 – Undertaking a Project

Chapter 9 – Information Management – the Project Focus

A short glossary of the main terms relevant to the topics is provided at the beginning of the book and a bibliography and detailed index at the end.

Software used in the information life cycle is discussed, but any specific products cited should only be considered examples of what was available at the time of writing. They should not be considered recommendations on which readers should base their decisions.

The main changes from the second edition of the book are:

- a major restructuring of the topics around context, life cycle and projects

- inclusion of data management as a topic in its own right, including data analysis and process analysis
- expanded coverage of information storage and capture devices; less emphasis on general information technology.

Who this Book is For

As with the earlier edition, it is hoped that the book will be helpful to readers from across the organization. This will facilitate attaining a common framework of understanding between those who may be affected by the introduction of new information systems, policies and procedures. Particular targets are noted below.

BUSINESS MANAGERS

Managers responsible for line functions need to be sufficiently aware of technological or specialist developments and the way that these can impact and support their business information requirements.

TECHNICAL STAFF – SYSTEM DESIGNERS, DEVELOPERS AND IMPLEMENTERS

Those concerned with the technology aspects of a project need to understand the management and relevance of information in the organizational context and not merely the technology that holds or manipulates it.

RECORDS MANAGERS, LIBRARIANS AND INFORMATION MANAGERS

Information professionals, particularly those who have long been concerned with managing mainly paper-based documents, need an appreciation of the impact of the technology and of how their particular areas of expertise can best be applied. Such professionals have a key role to play in the management or operation of document management systems.

END-USERS

The user who is seeking information is generally only concerned with receiving the right information in the right form and at the right time (irrespective of the method of access or delivery). Nevertheless if a new information system is to be introduced, the user must be suitably involved in the appropriate system project stages, including such aspects as the specification and agreement of requirements. An appreciation of the significance and potential of such systems and of the scope of their facilities provides the user with confidence in dealing with system designers at the outset, and with system implementers towards the end of the project.

EDUCATORS

Those involved in running courses may find the broad subject coverage of the book to be a useful introduction to many aspects of information management.

Further Resources and Keeping Up-to-date

References to sources of information used are provided, as are locations where further information on particular topics is available. A companion website – www.cura.org.uk – complements the book's coverage by providing web pages relating to each chapter where supplementary information, updates, copies of some of the figures and links to Web sites and pages including system, software and service suppliers relevant to the each chapter's topics are provided.

1 *Context*

1 *The Organizational Context*

'We cannot meet 21st Century challenges with a 20th Century bureaucracy'.
Barack Obama, Nomination Acceptance Speech, 28 August 2008

This book covers a wide range of issues relating to information management in the context of organizations. Having some understanding of what comprises an 'organization' places anyone in a better position to deal with change, whether as the initiator of change or the recipient of the outcomes. Without this knowledge, inferior managerial decisions may result and staff may be poorly placed to adapt to new situations. This chapter deals with some of the broader issues that need to be considered to help ensure that innovation enables rather than disables improvement.

1.1 What Constitutes an Organization?

At its simplest, an organization is a group of people working together. It may range in complexity from ad-hoc local community groups to businesses, governments and international bodies. Each will have – to varying degrees – objectives, rules and structures. They may produce goods or services, or generate other outcomes as in the case of legal institutions, trade unions or religious bodies. They will aim to employ resources effectively and efficiently and need to operate within the law.

Detailed consideration of organization theory is outside the scope of this book; for further information see Handy (1993) and Crowther and Green (2004). However, there is merit in viewing an organization as a dynamic human system consisting of four basic elements (Leavitt et al., 1973).

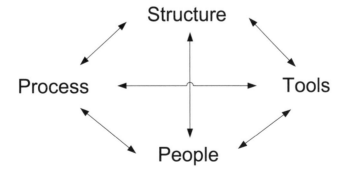

Figure 1.1   Organizational model

- processes (Leavitt referred to 'Tasks' here):
  - the organization builds or designs things or provides services by undertaking an organized assembly of activities that transform inputs into outputs, subject to particular controls
- structure:
  - the organization has some broad, more or less permanent framework; some arrangement of processes and material resources and people in some sequence and hierarchy
- tools:
  - the organization utilizes technological advances and provides tools that enable people or machines to perform tasks and to effect administrative control
- people:
  - the organization is populated by, as Leavitt expressed it *'these sometimes troublesome, but highly flexible doers of work'*.

These elements serve as organizational levers of change and are interdependent in that any change in one will affect the others. Thus the introduction of a content management system will change the way people work, outsourcing tasks will change the structure and staffing elements and introducing a new product or service will require changes or additions to existing processes.

While other elements will be considered in more detail in later chapters, the structural aspect of organizations merits attention here.

1.2 Organizational Structures

When planning improvements in managing information, consideration needs to be given to the organizational context of the intended target area and to answering the following types of question:

- is the venture to be undertaken on an organization-wide scale, or departmentally?
- where are the decision makers located in the management structure?
- what professional and specialists need to be involved and where are they located?

To address these questions it helps to understand the type of management structures that exist in the organization.

As noted (Handy 1993), structure includes the allocation of formal responsibilities as depicted in the typical organization chart. It also covers the linking mechanisms between the roles i.e. the coordinating structures of the organization, if any are needed. Organizations change their design as they grow, based on what they would like to be – their mission and objectives.

Where a range of different products is produced or the enterprise operates over a large geographical area, the management structure will usually decentralize into divisions, each with its own supporting functions such as sales and marketing.

New organizations, especially entrepreneurial ones, tend to be heavily centralized, informal and lacking in bureaucracy with a flat structure. As they grow they need to introduce a certain degree of standardization and official routine as exemplified by a functionally structured hierarchy. Such bureaucracy is prevalent in most government organizations.

Information-intensive organizations such as those concerned with information technology or pharmaceutical research require approaches to management that differ from the traditional style of 'command and control' arising from manufacturing industries. Staff are highly educated, work will be less structured and emphasis is placed on teamwork and collaboration.

Matrix organizations are an example of a task structure which is job or project oriented. Personnel are grouped by product and function with the aim of gaining the benefits of both approaches. Thus a project manager has responsibility for a project, while a functional manager provides the necessary resources. The degree to which one manager has greater authority over the other can vary depending on the organizational culture, aims and objectives, for example.

1.3 Why Organizations Exist

An organization is formed, or comes about, for a purpose. That purpose may or may not be well defined, indeed, it may sit there as an aspiration with little to enable it to come into being. Visions and objectives are promulgated, but will have little relevance if there is no means to determine whether they have been achieved.

As organizations grow, the need for clarity of shared objectives becomes greater. For example, the records manager's concern with managing emails is far removed from the worries of the transport manager about enlarging the lorry fleet to meet demand. However, the catering department's desire to source ingredients locally may conflict with finance's aim to reduce costs.

There are also differences in purpose between profit-making and government and not-for-profit agencies. While the former may place good financial performance as the prime objective, public sector organizations will place greater emphasis on the customer perspective.

1.4 What Organizations Do

In order to operate, an organization has a range of *functions*; that is, sets of related activities. 'Functions' are not to be equated with organizational structures such as the 'finance department', 'personnel department' or 'production section', as is discussed further below. While functions generally remain unchanged, managerial structures are less stable and may centralize, decentralize, devolve or otherwise restructure over time.

There are two types of function – operational and support – and it is important to know the distinction between the two.

OPERATIONAL FUNCTIONS

Every organization will have core functions that establish its identity and the reasons for its existence and thereby differentiate it from organizations in other fields of activity. Thus for a vehicle manufacturer, design and production functions are important, exploration is key for an oil company and providing sheltered housing is the focus of a housing association. These are referred to as *'operational functions'*.

SUPPORT FUNCTIONS

An enterprise cannot survive with operational functions alone. It has to exist within legal, regulatory, commercial and social environments which require it to have a range of other functions to support its day-to-day activities and longer term objectives. These are *'support functions'* that are common to most organizations and provide the underlying support; for example, managing staff and finance.

As will be seen later in Chapter 5 relating to business classifications, it is important to understand the difference between these types of function. Consider the United Kingdom's economics and finance ministry, 'The Treasury'. It is responsible for developing and executing the British government's public finance and economic policies. This 'financial' activity is an 'operational' function as it embodies the reason for the organization's existence. However, The Treasury also has to manage its internal finance, such as expenditure on office supplies, repairs, salaries, and so on. This 'financial' activity is a 'support' function, vital for supporting day-to-day operations, but not one that will be core to driving the economic strategy of the country.

While functions will remain relatively unchanged as compared with managerial structures, there will be exceptions, particularly for operational functions. For example, Nokia was originally involved in wood pulp and paper manufacture and changed direction radically, moving into electronics. This will have required the introduction of new operational functions relating to the design and production of mobile phones. Nevertheless, Nokia will have continued to rely on its existing support functions before, during and after the change in strategy.

BUSINESS PROCESSES

A function is defined as a set of related activities and does not in itself deliver a specific output. This is achieved by a business process which is a set of one or more linked procedures or activities which collectively realize a business objective or policy goal. Processes will cross functions to deliver the required output as exemplified in Figure 1.2 – based on Hatten & Rosenthal (1999).

Here five generic business functions (technology, marketing, operations, human resources and finance) and four principal customer-focused business processes (new product development, order acquisition, order fulfilment and post sales service) are identified. It provides a framework for the first step in an enterprise audit.

Capabilities are measures of the performance of business processes. Competencies are measures of the organization's potential to conduct business at state-of-the-art level. Capability gaps are the inability to do things, and incompetencies are gaps in know-how. Detailed examination of these interfaces allows alignment and misalignment of functional competencies and process capabilities to be identified.

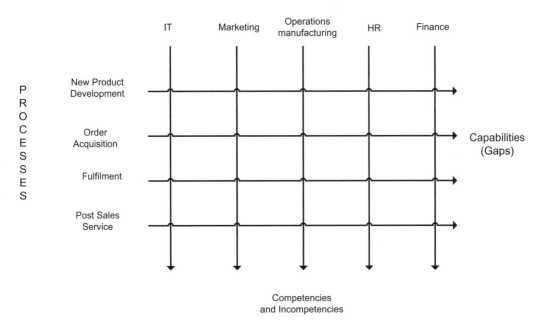

Figure 1.2   Aligning processes to functions

Source: Reproduced with permission of Elsevier

To complete the first step, one determines which of the various functions makes the largest contribution to the success of each business process. In Figure 1.2, each node or nodes (intersecting points) between processes and functions should prompt the questions: 'is this particular interaction of function with process important to the performance of the enterprise'? and 'if so, how and why?

1.5 Strategic Planning

The development of a strategy should progress according to some form of planning process. This process can be divided into the following stages:

- strategic analysis
- strategic choice
- strategic implementation.

Together they form a three-stage hierarchy as depicted in Figure 1.3 with the lower levels defining 'how' the preceding levels are achieved and the preceding levels defining 'why' the following activities are being undertaken.

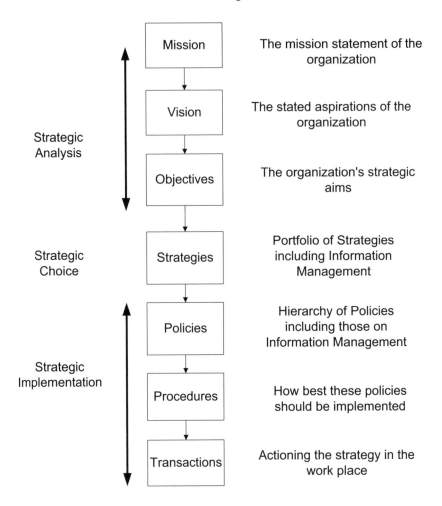

Figure 1.3   Strategic planning hierarchy

The following meanings are employed for the terms used:

- *mission* is the purpose for which the organization is established
- *vision* is the aspiration of the organization as regards what it would like to achieve or accomplish in the future. It is intended to provide clear guidance for courses of action
- *objective* is a specific thing aimed at or sought; a target, a goal, an aim
- *strategy* is the overall plan and direction to achieve an objective or vision
- *policy* is a course of action or principle adopted or proposed (the term is not used to denote what is actually done, which is referred to as a procedure)
- *procedure* is a statement that prescribes specific actions to be taken to implement established policies
- *transaction* is an event or process initiated by a user or computer program, regarded as a single unit of work and requiring a record to be generated.

1.5.1 STRATEGIC ANALYSIS

Strategic analysis helps to define the vision of the organization and the objectives that will enable the vision to become a reality; other terms such as 'mission', 'goals' and 'aims' relate to the same concept of looking forward to a future state. The objectives are a statement of what must be done well in order to implement the strategy.

While there are different definitions of strategic analysis, they generally feature the following elements:

- identifying and evaluating information relevant to strategy formulation
- defining the external and internal environment to be analyzed
- employing a range of analytical tools.

Figure 1.4 includes examples of analytical techniques that can assist strategic and planning initiatives. Each has its own particular focus, some being oriented towards business data and their processing, others look out from the organization to the customer and their needs, while others look inwards at the human resources to see how their contribution to success can be maximized. The use of some of these is described more fully in later chapters.

Techniques	Description
Balanced Scorecard	An integrated framework for describing and translating strategy through the use of linked performance measures in four balanced perspectives, typically: Customer, Internal Processes, Employee Learning and Growth, and Financial. These perspectives are often substituted with alternatives to suit the application
Benchmarking	A process by which an organization evaluates and compares itself in chosen areas against other reference points, for the purposes of monitoring and improvement
Benefit realization	Ensuring the achievement of defined benefits through planned organization and management
Boston Square	A means for balancing high and low risk with high and low return for proposed investment or project
Business Excellence	Using a business excellence model (such as EFQM, Baldrige, or other national excellence model) for assessment and improvement
Business Modelling	Typically involves construction of models for business functions, major entities and information flows. Can be the basis for systems development using structured methodologies
Business Process Re-engineering	The fundamental rethinking and radical redesign of business processes to achieve dramatic improvements in critical, contemporary measures of performance such as cost, quality, service and speed
Business Systems Planning (BSP)	Developed by IBM it provides a data-oriented view of the organization

Figure 1.4   Techniques for business improvement

Techniques	Description
Critical Success Factor Analysis	A method developed at MIT's Sloan school by John Rockart to guide businesses in creating and measuring success. A top-down methodology that is especially suitable for designing systems as opposed to applications
Directional Policy Matrix	Summarizes the competitive strength of a business's operations in specific markets
Five forces analysis	Identifies the forces which affect the level of competition in an industry
Lean management	A way of working which identifies and eliminates waste to deliver improved value and service, based on identified customer requirements
PEST analysis	Helps gain a better understanding of the organization's environment viewed from a Political, Economic, Social and Technological (PEST) viewpoint
PESTLE	A development of PEST with the addition of Legal and Environmental factors
Plan-Do-Check-Act	A four step process for continuous improvement
Portfolio Analysis	Typically based on the Boston Square (see above) it assists obtaining the best result from an evolving number of products in a competitive environment
Prince 2	Project management method developed initially for UK Government organizations
Root Cause Modelling	Discovers the points of leverage where patterns of behaviour originate and can be changed
Scenario planning	Builds various plausible views of possible futures for a business
Six Sigma	A measured and fact-based approach to reducing process variation and improving performance
Soft Systems	Aimed at addressing 'fuzzy' ill-defined problem situations, it involves conceptual modelling and comparing the results with the real world to identify areas for improvement
Stakeholder Analysis	Identifies the major external influences, their likely perceptions of the organization, and their potential interactions with it
SWOT Analysis	Strategic analysis of internal strengths and weaknesses, and external opportunities and threats
Total Quality Management	A management approach for long-term success through improving customer satisfaction, processes, products, services and culture
Value chain analysis	Describes the activities that take place in a business and relates them to an analysis of the competitive strength of the business
5S	Workplace organization methodology to improve efficiency and effectiveness. Uses a list of five words starting with the letter 'S'

Figure 1.4   *Concluded*

1.5.2 STRATEGIC CHOICE

This stage involves identifying, and then evaluating and selecting strategic options. Several options may present themselves; for example, related to the organization's products or services or driven by external events such as new legislation. The options may overlap or be interrelated in some way.

Making a choice is not a purely logical process of identifying the options, evaluating them against selected criteria, choosing the best option and then putting it into action. For example, selecting which mix of options to pursue has to take into account the organization's politics, as the final choice has to be capable of endorsement by those who are key to implementing the strategy.

The need to relate the strategic intent ('vision') with assessment and the available options is shown in Figure 1.5 (Macmillan and Tampoe 2000).

The chosen strategy requires that it satisfies the organization's vision, comes from the set of available options and is derived from the assessment process. As is clear from Figure 1.5 it is possible to have feasible options which do not align with the vision and options that are aligned but are shown to be infeasible.

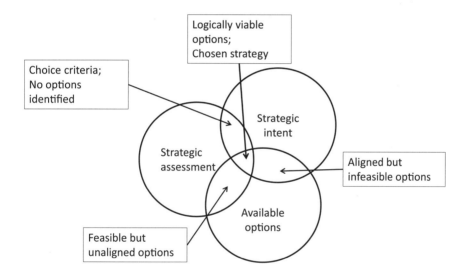

Figure 1.5   Selecting a strategy from various options

Source: Reproduced with permission of Oxford University Press www.oup.com from *Strategic Management – Process, Content and Implementation* by Macmillan and Tampoe (2000) Fig. 11.2, p. 134

1.5.3 STRATEGIC IMPLEMENTATION

To deliver the agreed strategic approach, a hierarchy of policies is needed and, at the working level, supporting procedures and transactions. This stage is concerned with realizing the chosen strategic option by determining how best the policies should be implemented.

Strategies set directions over the medium to longer term and are therefore intended to be unchanged over these periods. However, policies and more particularly procedures will evolve and change and new ones will be introduced as more efficient and effective ways of working are identified; for example, with the introduction of new software and associated systems. Also, the success (or otherwise) of the strategy needs to be tracked.

Various surveys have shown that the implementation stage has proved to be the weakest link in the chain with the defined strategy rarely giving rise to the expected performance improvement. It is fundamentally easier to talk about strategy than to do it. According to Kaplan and Norton (2005) this is partly due to the fact that 95 per cent of a company's employees are not aware of or do not understand their organization's strategy. Also 66 per cent of corporate strategy is never implemented, according to Johnson (2004). This can be explained in part by managers having to focus on day-to-day matters and problems in which context corporate visions and strategy plans take a back seat.

Research reported by Hrebiniak (2006) identified (see Figure 1.6) the following main obstacles to executing the strategy, with change management being identified as by far the most critical capability required to make strategy work:

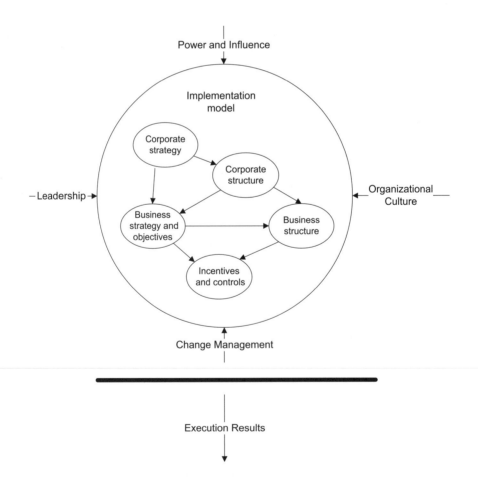

Figure 1.6   The context of implementation decisions

Source: Reproduced with permission of Elsevier

- an inability to manage change effectively and overcome resistance to change
- poor or vague strategy
- not having guidelines or a model to guide implementation efforts
- poor or inadequate information sharing among individuals or units responsible for strategy implementation efforts
- working against the organizational power structure
- unclear responsibility and accountability for implementation decisions or actions.

To place this in the organizational context Hrebiniak (2006) highlighted the factors of change management, organizational culture, power structure and leadership that require attention in order to deliver the output from the strategy implementation model shown in the centre of Figure 1.6.

1.6 Conclusion

It is interesting to ponder the extent to which the following predictions made nearly two decades ago about the future of the organizational world have largely come true (Handy 1993):

Assumptions that appear to be losing their value:

- *That concentration plus specialization = efficiency*
- *That hierarchy is natural*
- *That labour is cost*
- *Than an organization is a property*

Four clues to the future:

- *The communications revolution*
- *Fees in place of wages*
- *Tools in place of machines*
- *The economics of quality*

These will produce new challenges for organizations, including:

- *The idea of federalism*
- *Spliced careers*
- *New patterns of planning*

These predictions all involve change and ideally change should not take place without effecting improvements. This is the topic of the next chapter.

2 *Improving Organizational Performance*

'Management means, in the last analysis, the substitution of thought for brawn and muscle, of knowledge for folklore and superstition, and of cooperation for force'. Peter Drucker, People and Performance

The strategic planning and execution processes discussed in the previous chapter are not ends in themselves. They are used to help achieve corporate or more localized visions or objectives, thereby bringing about change and improving efficiency and effectiveness; that is, to improve performance. This chapter focuses on a range of quality, process and people-oriented approaches for improving performance (Sections 2.1 to 2.7) and introduces ways that can help deal with problematic situations (Section 2.8).

Any method for addressing poor performance needs to answer the following questions (although they may be couched in other terms by the different approaches):

- what is the scope of the investigation?
- where are we now?
- where do we want to be?
- how do we get there?

To answer these questions appropriate information needs to be available to allow informed conclusions to be reached, as exemplified in Figure 2.1.

Some of the required information, such as that relating to the vision of the organization, will reside in existing documents. Other information, such as the use made of existing computer systems, is likely to be recorded as structured data within databases. Customer survey findings, however, may well be found in written documents as well as databases. Where the information does not exist, work needs to be undertaken by knowledgeable people to generate it, aided by a variety of business improvement techniques such as those contained in Figure 1.4. Having up-to-date and reliable information about the present situation and the 'best possible' information about future scenarios is key to the success of organizations, and, for that matter, is equally important to individuals. The topics of information, data and knowledge, the role they play in organizations and the contribution of information specialists requires more detailed consideration. This is provided in Chapter 3, which also introduces the concept of the information life cycle.

Returning to ways of effecting improvements, organizations can easily fall into a cycle of 'paralysis by analysis' if such approaches are applied without prior informed consideration of their merits and of their appropriateness to the situation in mind; the survey undertaken by the Global Benchmarking Network (GBN 2010) throws some light on this matter.

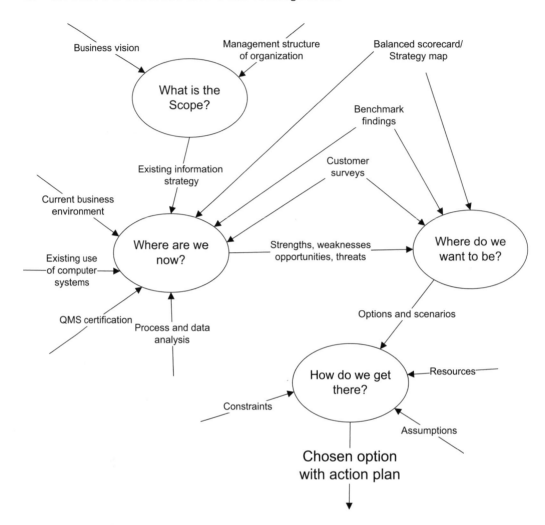

Figure 2.1   Key questions for effecting improvement

To gain awareness of the techniques, and of their usage, effectiveness and future adoption, twenty business improvement and benchmarking techniques were surveyed. The findings are shown in Figure 2.2.

The top five most used techniques were Mission and Vision statements, Customer (client) surveys, Strengths, Weaknesses, Opportunities and Threats (SWOT), Informal Benchmarking, and Quality Management Systems (QMS). Of these, Customer (client) surveys and QMS were also in the top five as regards effectiveness.

The three forms of benchmarking and Balanced Scorecard and SWOT were thought likely to become more popular over the next few years. More detailed consideration of the major techniques and some other improvements approaches is provided in the following sections. 'Mission and Vision statements' is not included, however, as arguably it does not truly constitute an improvement mechanism. Statements alone are not enough; they need to be followed through with a strategy plan to deliver benefits. Their place in strategy planning was considered in Chapter 1.

Improvement technique	Awareness %	Usage %	Effectiveness %	Future adoption %
Global average	65.0	50.2	68.2	30.5
Informal benchmarking	75.2	69.2	64.2	41.0
Performance benchmarking	66.2	49.1	63.1	50.0
Best practice benchmarking	60.0	39.6	64.3	45.1
Balanced scorecard	67.7	43.4	66.3	37.9
Business Excellence	59.5	39.8	71.7	29.0
Business Process Reengineering	56.9	45.6	73.3	26.4
Corporate Social Response System	46.9	37.0	56.9	26.0
Customer (client) surveys	85.8	77.0	74.4	29.8
Employee suggestion scheme	76.8	63.7	60.8	31.7
Improvement teams	73.5	64.8	74.7	29.7
Knowledge management	59.5	47.4	62.2	32.8
Lean	51.8	35.8	70.4	24.8
Mission and vision statement	82.3	77.2	68.2	29.1
Plan-Do-Check-Act	70.6	57.7	73.2	28.8
Quality function deployment	42.7	23.9	63.0	16.9
Quality management system	81.4	67.3	76.6	30.4
Six Sigma	47.6	21.9	62.6	19.8
SWOT analysis	83.2	72.1	70.9	37.6
TQM	67.3	40.7	74.5	24.3
5S	45.8	30.3	72.3	19.0

Figure 2.2   Usage of improvements techniques

Source: Reproduced with permission of the Global Benchmarking Network

2.1 Benchmarking

The improvement journey cannot commence without a clear understanding of the state in which the organization finds itself. This can be aided by the use of benchmarking – a process by which an organization evaluates and compares itself in chosen areas against other reference points, for the purposes of monitoring and improvement.

There is no standard method of benchmarking although it can be applied to any assessable factor; that is, something that can be measured either quantitatively or qualitatively. Having relevant data and the ability to measure are therefore vital prerequisites for demonstrating performance improvement.

Examples of benchmarking are:

- strategic benchmarking – usually focused on the overall performance of an organization
- process benchmarking – focuses on similar processes undertaken by others
- product benchmarking – may involve dismembering or reverse engineering a rival's product
- financial benchmarking – comparing financial performance with competitors
- standards benchmarking – assessing conformance to a standard or code of practice.

These and other types of benchmarking can be categorized as informal or formal (GBN 2010) with the latter split again into performance and best practice benchmarking.

> Informal benchmarking is that which is undertaken unconsciously day-to-day; for example, learning from the experience of work colleagues, networking or consulting experts.

> Performance benchmarking involves the comparison of performance data obtained by studying similar processes, whether or not of a financial nature. It can be undertaken against other organizations or other parts of the same organization. An advantage of the latter is that sensitive data can usually be shared, something that may not be possible with external bodies.

> Best practice benchmarking is viewed by the GBN as a project involving not only the comparison of performance data obtained from similar processes and then identifying the best, but also proceeding to adapt and implement the best performance results.

All benchmarking requires the involvement of another 'partner', the type of which can be categorized as:

- internal – within the same organization or group
- external – a different organization or group
- best practice – irrespective of industry sector or location.

The relative advantages and disadvantages of these are summarized in Figure 2.3 (Codling 1992).

INTERNAL	EXTERNAL	BEST PRACTICE
Functions, departments, projects, businesses in the same company or group at the same or another location	Other companies in a similar sector	Any organization, regardless of sector or location
ADVANTAGES	**ADVANTAGES**	**ADVANTAGES**
• Similar language, culture, mechanisms and systems • Ease of access to data • Existing communications • Low profile, low threat • Relatively quick returns possible • Good test bed	• Similar structure and constraints • Relative ease of access to data • Relatively low threat • Helps to overcome complacency and arrogance	• Less sensitive to ethical and political reservations • Possibility of breakthroughs • Broaden corporate perspective • Stimulates challenge
DISADVANTAGES	**DISADVANTAGES**	**DISADVANTAGES**
• Might inhibit external focus and foster complacency	• Legal, ethical and political considerations	• Relatively difficult to access data
• Possibly results in returns that are merely adequate	• Sector paradigms might restrain creativity	• Change ramifications are greater • Higher profile

Figure 2.3   Benchmarking partners

Source: Reproduced with permission of Gower Publishing

2.2 Strengths, Weaknesses, Opportunities and Threats (SWOT)

SWOT analysis arose from research funded by the Fortune Magazine Top 500 companies and conducted at Stanford Research Institute from 1960–1970 into why corporate planning failed.

SWOT is used to evaluate the **S**trengths, **W**eaknesses, **O**pportunities, and **T**hreats impacting some planned or existing venture. It is typically employed at the first stage of planning. Strengths and weaknesses relate to factors internal to the organization, while opportunities and threats are external factors. The findings are recorded in the relevant square of a four square grid. Following the analysis an action plan is drawn up, a summary of which can be included below the grid as shown in Figure 2.4.

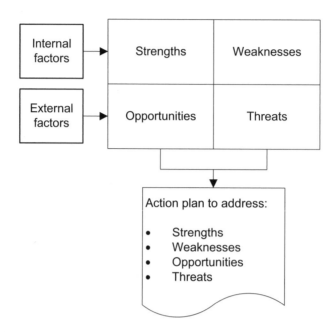

Figure 2.4   SWOT grid

A workshop environment is recommended for its use (CIPD 2010a), possibly preceded by a PESTLE analysis (see below).

2.2.1 POLITICAL, ECONOMIC, SOCIAL AND TECHNOLOGICAL, LEGAL, ENVIRONMENT (PESTLE)

PESTLE is a variant of PEST with the addition of the Legal and Environment aspects. Its origins date back to the work of Aguilar on scanning the business environment (Aguilar 1967). It appears under different guises with acronyms such as SLEPT and ETPS; all are used to assess a variety of external influences over which the organization has no control but which have a bearing on its ability to survive and prosper (CIPD 2010b).

Examples of the types of influence that may need to be considered are provided in Figure 2.5. The headings do not have precise meanings, hence the same entry may be placed under different labels by different users.

As with SWOT, a workshop or team approach is recommended. Additionally, the effect of each factor can be rated according to its potential impact and time frame when the impact might be felt.

2.3 Balanced Scorecard

Financial measures may well provide much information about an organization's past actions, but they reveal little about the future and do not address intangible assets such as human resources, innovation and the goodwill (or otherwise) that the organization has engendered. To counter this, the Balanced Scorecard was developed at the Harvard

PESTLE Influence	Examples
Political	Tax policy Trading policy Political instability
Economic	Inflation Interest rates Wage rates Unemployment trends
Social	Populations growth trends Cultural differences Health Age distributions
Technological	Impact of social media Mobile communications Internet trading Outsourcing of services
Environment	New planning laws Stakeholder values Recycling policies
Legal	Consumer protection Data protection Employment law Regulatory bodies

Figure 2.5   Some external factors

Business School (Kaplan and Norton 1996) to translate vision and strategy into objectives and measures that would answer questions from four perspectives:

- customer perspective – how do customers view us?
- financial perspective – how do we look to shareholders?
- internal business process perspective – what must we excel at?
- learning and growth perspective – can we continue to improve and create value?

Vision and strategy are at the heart of the four perspectives.

The Balanced Scorecard is distinct from other strategic measurement systems as it contains outcome measures and the performance drivers of outcomes, linked together in cause-and-effect. It is also intended to align departmental and personal goals to overall strategy. The scorecard has been subject to criticism, one being that there is not always a causal relationship between the areas of measurement suggested, another that being a hierarchical top-down model it is not easily embedded in a dynamic environment (Nørreklit 2000).

The concept has been refined over the years in part to address these concerns. Thus the method was subsequently adapted for government and not-for-profit bodies (Niven 2003), and alternative or additional perspectives were employed to meet the particular needs of those applying the technique. Also, the developers of the scorecard provided additional levels of granularity to depict the time-based dynamic of strategy in a strategy map and enable objectives and measures to be established and managed (Kaplan and Norton 2004). The aim was to provide the missing link between strategy formulation and strategy execution.

2.4 Customer Surveys

Being knowledgeable of the expectations and degree of satisfaction of customers helps ensure that an organization's services and products satisfy customers. Customer surveying is an essential technique for eliciting such views. Data obtained from surveys can also inform strategies for improving production, delivery and marketing aspects, whether they relate to commercial or non-profit organizations or government bodies.

Knowing the levels of customer satisfaction has been shown to be important. Regardless of how they feel, customers of companies with reasonably good product or service quality tend to find it difficult to respond negatively to a customer satisfaction survey. Research by Xerox showed that the firm's totally satisfied customers were six times more likely to repurchase Xerox products in the 18 months following the study than were its satisfied customers. Merely satisfying customers who had the freedom to make choices was not enough to keep them loyal. Xerox found that the only truly loyal customer is the totally satisfied customer (i-Sight, 2011).

The concept of the customer is wide-ranging. It may be a member of the public or another business to whom a product or service is supplied. Hence surveys may be business-to-business or business-to-consumer, or the customer may be internal with one department providing a service such IT or records management across the organization. The surveys may cover general relationship aspects such as price and service levels, or concern a specific product or service.

To be effective, a survey must elicit the type of information required and be easy to respond to. In the past the use of focus groups has been popular, involving a group of people chosen to be representative of the wider population and brought together to take part in guided discussions so that their attitudes and opinions can be studied. However, interest in them has waned for a number of reasons, one being the expense of establishing and running them. They may, however, be more useful as a precursor to more widespread survey techniques such as mail shots or telephone interviews.

The main media used for conducting surveys are:

- telephone
- mail (postal)
- email
- internet.

Telephone surveys are akin to face-to-face interviews and are likely to be more effective when dealing with the public than with businesses unless times to receive calls have been agreed.

Compared with phone surveys, mailshots will reach a far larger audience at the same time. Although only a small percentage of those surveyed will respond, the numbers will be much larger than can be achieved over the phone.

Email provides the most effective way to reach the largest number of potential respondents and obtain the highest response rate. It has the advantage that recipients can deal with the survey when they wish and if late in replying they can be sent an email reminder.

Many suppliers end their interaction with a consumer over the Internet by asking them to assess their experience in using their online service. This typically consists of a short number of questions with tick boxes for the response and often an option to respond later or more fully.

The concept of the customer should also include the stakeholder, that is 'a person who has an interest or concern in something, esp. a business' (OED 2001). Engagement with such persons goes beyond simple surveys and needs to follow a managed process as exemplified by Bourne (2008) in Figure 2.6.

This layout is not intended to imply a strictly linear process starting at step 1, as the organization may well have identified the relevant stakeholders and can therefore commence the process from a later step.

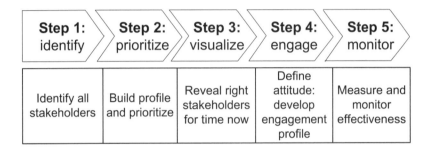

Figure 2.6   Steps to manage stakeholder relationships

Source: Reproduced with permission of Gower Publishing

2.5 Approaches Based on Quality

The word 'quality' accompanies many words in the organization world – quality systems, quality management, quality standards, quality awards, to name but a few – but the status that it merits can easily suffer due to circumstances where its use is not justified. For example, some businesses which have successfully had their Quality Management Systems certified to ISO 9000 give the impression that their products have been accorded this certification. However, a clear distinction must be drawn between conformance to a product standard and conformance to a quality system standard. A business may have a superb quality system, but such a system may be supporting the manufacture of a poor, non-standard product, albeit consistently.

Many of the analytical techniques listed in Figure 1.4 can help improve quality within organizations. In the following sections the main focus is on:

- management approaches using quality management (Section 2.5.1)
- quality management specifications (Section 2.5.2)

- business excellence models (Section 2.5.3)
- quality in service organizations (Section 2.5.4) and
- quality management tools (Section 2.5.5).

2.5.1 QUALITY MANAGEMENT

Quality management once meant simple inspection and rejection or acceptance of a worker's output, often based on inappropriate criteria and undertaken by someone with inadequate knowledge of the task. The introduction of statistical theory, the work of early pioneers such as Deming and the adoption in Japan of quality management practices in the 1950s led to the concept of 'total quality' appearing in the late 1960s. Since then, quality management has become a more holistic approach in the form of Total Quality Management (TQM) and more recent incarnations such as Six Sigma developed by the Motorola company (Pande and Holpe 2002).

TQM (Oakland 2003) has developed around a number of key factors which can be categorized as 'soft' and 'hard'. The former includes the management systems such as leadership, planning and human resources. The hard or technical elements include analytical tools and systems based on international standards such as ISO 9000. Overall the aim of TQM is to improve the competitiveness, performance and flexibility of the organization and to embed the notion of continuous improvement as exemplified by the 'plan-do-check-act' cycle (ASQ 2004) shown in Figure 2.7.

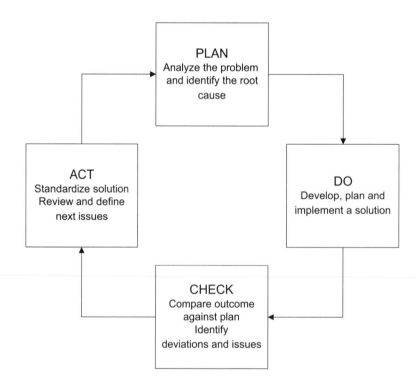

Figure 2.7   PDCA cycle

TQM has not been codified, although it is founded on the following 14 points attributed to Deming (Deming 1986):

- create constancy of purpose
- adopt the new philosophy
- cease dependence on mass inspection to achieve quality
- improve the quality of supplies
- improve constantly and forever the system of production and service
- train and educate all employees
- institute leadership
- drive out fear
- eliminate barriers between departments
- eliminate slogans and exhortations
- eliminate work standards that prescribe numerical targets
- let people be proud of their work
- encourage self-improvement
- everybody to commit to accomplish the transformation.

The introduction of TQM needs to be undertaken as part of a quality plan which documents quality practices, resources and sequence of activities relevant to a particular product, service, contract or project or conformance to a quality system standard such as ISO 9000 within a specified timeframe. Suggested steps for developing a quality plan are shown in Figure 2.8 (Oakland 1992).

It is important that audits are undertaken to ensure that the programme of work is in line with the agreed objectives. However, auditing should not be so frequent or detailed so as to disrupt normal work activities.

2.5.2 QUALITY MANAGEMENT STANDARDS

A quality management system (QMS) is a set of interrelated elements that organizations use to direct and control how quality policies are implemented and quality objectives are achieved. Such elements will include management structures, roles and responsibilities, processes and resources. The QMS is documented in a Quality Manual which defines the scope of the QMS and includes justifications for any exclusions.

In conducting business many organizations require their suppliers (and often encourage their customers) to have their QMS conform to the requirements of an

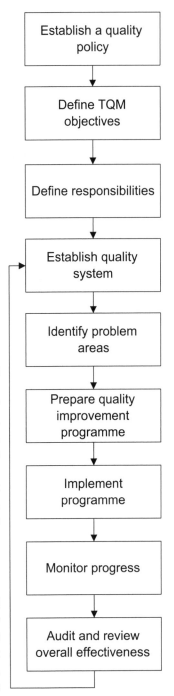

Figure 2.8   Elements of a quality plan

Source: Reproduced with permission of Gower Publishing

international QMS standard. ISO 9000 is the generic name given to the most commonly used family of standards that provide a framework for effectively implementing a quality management system, the requirements for which are contained in ISO 9001 (2008). It is also worth mentioning the ISO 14000 family of standards which address environmental management and, like ISO 9000, provide a means to assess conformance, this time of an environmental management system. The requirements for environmental management are contained in ISO 14001 (2004).

Although ISO 9001 (2008) states the requirements for a QMS, it does not dictate how they should be met in any individual organization; similarly ISO 14001 (2004) does not specify levels of environmental performance for any specific business sector. The standards complement one another in that the application of ISO 14000 can, for example, help ensure that products and services produced within the framework of an ISO 9000 QMS are done so within an approved environmental management system that should avoid environmentally damaging circumstances.

Having a QMS in place is not sufficient in itself. There needs to be a way to assess that it is operating as planned. This can achieved by one, or more, of the following:

- conducting an internal audit using the organization's own auditing function
- using an external auditor, possibly from the organization's client base, thereby enabling the latter to be assured that quality management is in place
- contracting with an independent quality system certification body to acquire a certification of conformity.

Of the three options the use of a certification body provides more credibility as it is viewed by others as being the most independent means of assessment. A large number of such bodies exist and selection from those that belong to a recognized accreditation organization such as the United Kingdom Accreditation Service (http://www.ukas.com) is recommended.

When initially introduced ISO 9000 was seen as overly bureaucratic and costly for small and medium-sized enterprises (SMEs) to implement and operate. To address this issue a guide book aimed at small business was produced (ISO 9001 2010) and provides an example of the steps that they can take to introduce a QMS. Following these steps (ISO Mgt Sys 2004) as shown in Figure 2.9 can also inform the introduction of business process improvements irrespective of whether a QMS is to be formally linked to ISO 9000.

2.5.3 BUSINESS EXCELLENCE MODELS

Beyond quality standards there are business excellence models which organizations can use to measure their activities against 'best practice' and 'best in class' performance and use as a guide to TQM implementation. The models form the basis of quality awards such as the Malcolm Baldrige National Quality Award (MBNQA) and the European Foundation for Quality Management (EFQM) Excellence Model. For a few companies, obtaining quality awards presents the opportunity for national or international recognition. For most, however, applying the quality award process itself has been seen as worthwhile because it requires a thorough examination of the company's strengths and identifies opportunities for continuous improvement.

Many quality awards exist; some are offered at the international level, while others are national, regional or specific to a trade or professional body. Some examples are provided in Figure 2.10 and two are described further below.

STAGE	STEP	
DEVELOPMENT	1	Consider what your main business activities are
	2	List your business activities
IMPLEMENTATION	3	Get people involved by writing down what their jobs cover
	4	Collate this in sequences relevant to the list of business activities (Step 2)
	5	Identify where the standard and this list of your business activities link together
	6	Apply the standard and the quality management system
	7	Keep the quality management system simple, functional and relevant to the business operations
MAINTENANCE	8	Consider the feedback of information from the quality management system to lead to improvement in ideas and activities
	9	Monitor and measure the changes so you know what you have gained

Figure 2.9   Introducing a QMS in small businesses

Source: Reproduced with permission of Gower Publishing

Committed to Excellence	A practical way to begin your organization's Excellence Journey http://excellenceone.efqm.org/Default.aspx?tabid=463
Recognized for Excellence	A standard recognized all over Europe for organizations that demonstrate high levels of performance http://excellenceone.efqm.org/Default.aspx?tabid=375
European Excellence Award	The most prestigious competition for organizational excellence in Europe http://excellenceone.efqm.org/Default.aspx?tabid=376
Scottish Awards for Business Excellence	Recognizes Scottish organizations that have achieved a level of excellence comparable to the best in Europe http://www.qualityscotland.co.uk/scottish-awards-for-business-excellence.asp
UK Excellence Award	National recognition of organizations which have excelled http://www.bqf.org.uk/awards/uk-excellence-award
Malcolm Baldrige National Quality Award	The Baldrige Program's mission is to improve the competitiveness and performance of U.S. organizations http://www.nist.gov/baldrige/

Figure 2.10 Quality awards

Malcolm Baldrige National Quality Award (MBNQA)

The award is for United States of America organizations that demonstrate quality and performance excellence (http://www.nist.gov/baldrige/). It is presented annually in each of six categories ranging from manufacturing to non-profit making. Recipients are chosen based on achievement and improvement in the following seven areas, known as the Baldrige Criteria for Performance Excellence:

- leadership
- strategic planning
- customer focus
- measurement, analysis, and knowledge management
- workforce focus
- process management
- results.

Many organizations begin their improvement efforts by using the criteria for self-assessment for which a range of tools is provided by the National Institute of Science and Technology (http://www.nist.gov/baldrige/enter/self.cfm).

European Foundation for Quality Management Excellence Model

The basis for the Foundation was to increase the competitiveness of European organizations and so the founding members joined forces to develop a management tool, the EFQM Excellence Model. Membership of the Foundation (http://www.efqm.org) provides access to a range of assessment tools, assessor and leadership training courses, benchmarks and means of communicating with others at various stages along the business excellence route.

The basis of the Foundation is the EFQM model which is used to assess and help attain business excellence. It incorporates the following nine criteria as shown in Figure 2.11:

1. Leadership
2. Strategy
3. People
4. Partnerships & Resources
5. Processes, Products and Services
6. Customer Results
7. People Results
8. Society Results
9. Key Results.

The model aims to inform a logical, systematic review of how an organization performs and to define what skills and resources are required to reach strategic objectives. The review focuses on the nine criteria comprising five enablers concerned with what is done to run the organization and how it is operated and four results concerned with what the organization has achieved and is achieving as seen by its stakeholders i.e. customers,

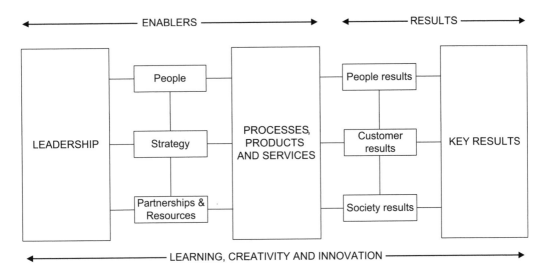

Figure 2.11 EFQM model

Source: Reproduced with permission of the European Foundation for Quality Management www.efqm.org

employees, the community and those who fund the organization. It will be noted that this approach is similar to the plan-do-check-act cycle in Figure 2.7.

2.5.4 MANAGING QUALITY IN SERVICE ORGANIZATIONS

Quality improvement has largely been associated with manufacturing-type enterprises where the concept of measurement is well embedded in their nature. This concept is less evident in service organizations where perceptions on quality relate more to qualitative factors, these being less amenable to 'counting'. Examples include:

- reliability
- access
- communication
- security
- responsiveness
- competence
- courtesy
- credibility
- understanding.

Identifying key determinants of quality for such factors needs careful thought. For example, the determinants for a railway station caterer will differ depending on whether the customer is in a hurry or has time to spare.
    Other actions to take include:

- managing customer expectations
- managing impressions

- customer education
- developing reliable support systems
- soliciting feedback, and addressing the needs of dissatisfied customers
- providing unconditional service guarantee over areas in your control.

A distinction also needs to be made between seeking technical efficiency and achieving functional quality. Economies of scale do not necessarily deliver improvements. Thus a lone typist may not be technically efficient, but could provide functional quality. A typing pool is likely to prove efficient but not deliver the required quality of output.

The key role of front line staff needs to be recognized. They represent the organization and have to manage the potentially volatile customer interface since they are the first to deal with crises. This aspect is particularly important for government organizations as they are the quintessential service organizations. People aspects of quality improvement are covered in more detail below with regard to Investors in People.

2.5.5 QUALITY MANAGEMENT TOOLS

Improving quality in all its aspects has to involve the ability to measure. A large number of measurement tools exist (Tague 2005) which can make selection difficult. Kaoru Ishikawa, the then head of the Japanese Union of Scientists and Engineers, identified in the 1960s seven key quality control tools as summarized in Figure 2.12.

These tools use statistical techniques and their effective use needs people who operate or fully understand the tasks under investigation.

TECHNIQUES	DESCRIPTION
Cause and effect diagram	Analysis of relationships to assess possible causes of defects. Also called fishbone or Ishikawa diagram.
Check sheet	Shows the history and pattern of variations; used at the beginning of the change process to identify the problems and collect data easily.
Control charts	Monitor performance of a process against a statistical background to help set and assess improvement actions.
Graphs	Displays logical relationships of elements to identify root causes. Data can be depicted graphically using bar graphs, line charts, pie charts and control charts.
Histograms	Display of data to show variables against a common background.
Pareto diagram	Display of data ranking significant factors in priority order.
Scatter diagram	Graphical technique for assessing data to establish a relationship.

Figure 2.12 Quality management tools

Concluding Comment on Quality Approaches

There needs to be a substantial investment in time and effort to plan for and undertake such quality initiatives and it is often the case that 'models' are not applied according to the 'instruction manual', but rather are adapted or formed through a 'pick and mix' approach to suit the organizational culture or the views of those adopting them. This is not necessarily to be decried as the models are not prescriptive.

The degree to which these approaches are successful in producing the required outcomes is sometimes questioned. MacLeod and Baxter (2001) cited some wide-ranging studies of quality initiatives, some showing success, whilst others failed to produce the required outcome. Their own research indicated, however, that the use of quality models as frameworks can be of material assistance in reviving quality improvements where previous failures had occurred. This emphasizes the need to maintain continuous improvement.

2.6 Process Reengineering

Process reengineering in the guise of Business Process Reengineering (BPR) was coined by Hammer (1990) and involves the analysis and redesign of workflow within and between organizations around seven principles:

- organize around outcomes, not tasks
- identify all the processes in an organization and prioritize them in order of redesign urgency
- integrate information processing work into the real work that produces the information
- treat geographically dispersed resources as though they were centralized
- link parallel activities in the workflow instead of just integrating their results
- put the decision point where the work is performed, and build control into the process
- capture information once and at the source.

The main differentiating factor between BPR and other improvement approaches is the emphasis it places on achieving 'step changes'; that is, dramatic, shorter term improvements. It is probably this factor more than any other that caused BPR to catch the imagination of business managers and executives in the early days and also of consultants, some of whom recast existing methodologies to fit.

BPR has been viewed as a complementary approach to TQM with benefits of applying them together in an integrated way (Figure 2.13).

For example, Hammer and Champy (2003) consider that TQM should be used to keep a company's processes tuned up between periodic process replacements that only reengineering can accomplish. Furthermore, TQM once built into corporate culture can, they state, go on working without much day-to-day attention from management. Reengineering, in contrast, is an intensive, top-down, vision-driven effort that requires nonstop senior management participation and support.

TECHNIQUE	USED FOR	IMPACT	SCALE	STYLE	FOCUS	PERIOD
Total Quality Management	Problem-solving	Incremental	Wide-spread	Analytic	Bottom-up	Longer-term
Business Process Reengineering	Re-inventing	Dramatic	Project-teams	Creative	Top-down	Shorter-term

Figure 2.13 Comparison of TQM and BPR

On reaching a peak in the late 1990s, the use of BPR *per se* fell away somewhat partly because of the incorporation of much its features in other guises with titles like 'Business Process Management', 'Business Process Redesign' and 'Business Process Improvement'. Also, 'reengineering' soon became synonymous with 'downsizing' which does not generate a spirit of cooperation within the workforce. This emphasis on 'reengineering' rather than 'process' caused the good things about BPR to be lost in hype and the proliferation of consultancy assignments that did not deliver what was expected (Davenport 1995). Some of these issues are considered in the UK context by Graham et al. (2000) who noted that, although BPR is no longer the currency of corporate change programmes, it does have life in other techniques and in the continued stress on process within these methodologies.

Having an understanding of process flows in organizations is a vital first step in effecting improvements, and is considered in more detail in Chapter 7.

2.7 People Approaches

Suitably trained and motivated people are needed for the smooth running of any enterprise and are vital resources for effecting change and improvements. They are one of the key levers of change in Leavitt's four-element model encountered in Figure 1.1.

In recognizing that the UK lagged internationally in terms of both competitiveness and training and development expenditure, the 'Investors in People' (IiP) standard was developed with UK government support by a partnership involving the Confederation of British Industry and the Trades Union Congress. This endorsement by the trade union body in the UK (Monks 2010) makes this performance improvement approach stand out from others like BPR that have often engendered fierce opposition from organized labour.

The standard was launched in 1991 and more recently underwent a major review with the aim of providing a more flexible framework that users can adapt to meet their local needs (http://www.investorsinpeople.co.uk). The UK Commission for Employment and Skills (UKCES) took strategic ownership of the IiP from April 2010. The standard, although based in the UK, has been licensed for use in other countries.

The three core principles of IiP (which echo the improvement cycle of Figure 2.7) are 'Plan', 'Do' and 'Review'. The principles are broken down into ten indicators as follows:

Plan – develop strategies to improve performance:

- business strategy
- learning and development strategy
- people management strategy

- leadership and management strategy.

Do – take action to improve performance:

- management effectiveness
- recognition and reward
- involvement and empowerment
- learning and development.

Review – evaluate and improve performance:

- performance measurement
- continuous improvement.

The intention is that organizations can pick and mix which combination of principle and indicator they wish to focus on to achieve improvement. To gain an idea of how the standard operates, an online business support tool, 'Interactive', poses 20 questions for users to answer. In so doing it also gives an idea of how the organization is performing.

IiP is also used as an award scheme involving external assessment by a network of UK training agencies. The levels of recognition acknowledge organizations that perform beyond the standard through the award of bronze, silver or gold awards and a long service award for those accredited for ten or more years.

According to Bourne et al. (2008), almost forty thousand organizations were working with Investors in People in 2008. Their research found that adopting IiP set up a chain of impact ending in better financial performance. This indicates that IiP is more than a mechanism for improving the skill base of employees, but is one that creates changes that deliver performance improvement. They conclude that linking business goals to employee objectives is key to improving business performance.

The standard is not, however, without its critics. In a review of evidence based on available research and analysis, Higgins and Cohen (2006) concluded (amongst other observations) that:

- there is little evidence that Investors in People accreditation leads to tangible commercial benefit
- the process of assessment raises questions around the degree of consistency and quality in the award of Investors in People status, particularly around underlying assumptions, definitions, and individual assessor interpretation
- given the dynamic nature of organizations and people management, the three-year assessment cycle is overly long and inappropriate
- in terms of medium to large employer organizations, there is a heavy bias towards the public sector.

CONCLUDING COMMENT ON PERFORMANCE IMPROVEMENT APPROACHES

Some means for improving performance have been outlined; many more exist and others will certainly emerge in the future. Not one of them will provide all the answers to an organization's problems and it is incumbent on those seeking assistance to consider dispassionately what is available and not be disposed to jump on the next 'bandwagon'. Be wary of anything that purports to provide all the answers; if it looks too good to be true, it probably is.

One of the first steps to take along the road to improvement is to understand the nature of the problem that requires attention. Some may seem clear at the outset, others may need to be teased out. The last section in this chapter introduces a way to help deal with fuzzy, imprecise situations which require clarification before substantive action can be taken.

2.8 Problem Solving

The focus of most methods and methodologies is on objective and quantitative aspects of a problem area, often to the detriment of subjective and qualitative issues. These latter may be the more important factors in deciding the success or otherwise of a project. This problem is compounded if, for example, there is uncertainty in the first place about what issues and concerns need to be addressed. Two methods that can be applied to assist in such problem solving are:

- Soft Systems Methodology (SSM)
- Concept mapping.

These two methods are described further below.

2.8.1 SOFT SYSTEMS METHODOLOGY

An overview of SSM is provided in Figure 2.14 comprising various stages, some being in the 'real world', others in the 'abstract world' of systems thinking (Checkland 1981).

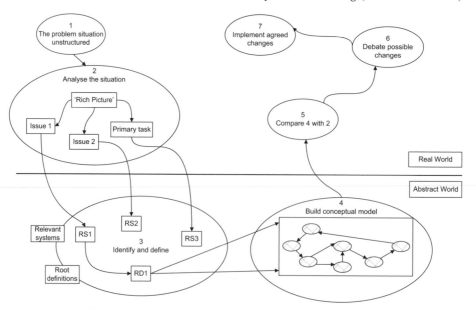

Figure 2.14 Soft systems methodology stages

The stages are usually undertaken iteratively rather than in series and comprise the following:

Stage 1 (Real World): The Problem Situation: Unstructured

The first stage involves recognition of a 'messy' situation, identifying elements of relatively slow-to-change *structure* and of continuously-changing *process*. It is important to avoid imposing a particular form to the situation; it is necessary to think about the roles of the client, problem-owner and problem-solver.

Stage 2 (Real World): The Problem Situation: Expressed

Here a 'Rich Picture' (usually a hand drawn cartoon) is produced which incorporates 'hard' factual and 'soft' subjective information; structure and processes and their interaction; people and players involved; tensions and conflicts. The aim of the Rich Picture is to help identify new ways of viewing the situation and to identify *primary tasks* (these being tasks that the organization in question was established to perform, or tasks which are essential for survival) and *issues* (matters of concern or which are the subject of dispute).

The information professionals and their relationships shown in Figure 3.6 in the next chapter gives an idea of what can be included in a Rich Picture, although in a real life study individuals and organizational structures and the tensions that might exist would be identified.

Stage 3 (Systems World): Relevant Systems and Root Definitions

Here the aim is not to identify what systems need to be engineered or improved, but rather what are the names of notional systems which from the analysis phase seem relevant to the problem. Having identified such *relevant systems* they are defined more formally by way of *Root Definitions* (a concise, tightly-constructed description of a human activity system which states what the system is).

Stage 4 (Systems World): Conceptual Models

A graphical model is built on the basis of the chosen Root Definition and comprises a structured set of activities expressed as verbs. They are justified purely on logical terms, not by mapping on to the real world.

Stage 5 (Real World): Comparison of Conceptual Model with Reality

Back in the real world one now looks for similarities and differences between the conceptual model from Stage 4 and the Real World situation from Stage 2; the results of the comparison are recorded and topics are identified for discussion.

Stage 6 (Real World): Debate Feasible and Desirable Changes

A structured discussion is undertaken with those involved – such as the client, problem-owner(s) and problem-solver(s) – with the aim of identifying ideas which are both systemically desirable and culturally feasible.

Stage 7 (Real World): Implement Agreed Changes

Changes may involve changes in structure, procedures or in attitudes and are implemented if agreed.

It is important that the identification of relevant systems at Stage 3 is undertaken divorced from the real world so that choices are not swayed by day-to-day concerns. For example, when considering a problem situation relating to prisons, the question of the role of these institutions may need to be addressed. Thus are they:

- means for providing employment for prison management, staff and the neighbourhood?
- ways of locking away offenders to protect the public?
- places for the rehabilitation of offenders?
- ways to boost the construction industry by building new establishments?

Adopting such different viewpoints can often expose areas for further investigation which might otherwise have been neglected or missed altogether.

It is recognized that the methodology does not provide explicit advice concerning implementation as the 'problem areas' that may be the subject of study can be completely different in nature. Thus one problem may relate to human conflicts in an organization, while another may be to identify the most suitable business area for piloting a document management project. The actions that need to be taken following agreement at Stage 7 will therefore differ widely.

SSM is a well-established methodology with an assembly of principles applied at different stages. It is perfectly possible to utilize parts of the process in isolation, such as drawing a Rich Picture to clarify issues, or formulating a Root Definition (RD) to firm up on the scope of a software development project. The intellectual process of devising a Root Definition is worth considering further.

The Root Definition is a concise, tightly-constructed description of a human activity system which states what the system is. It needs to contain certain elements these being:

- customer(s) of the system – those who will benefit (or be the victim of) the system's activities
- actor(s) – person(s) who carry out one or more of the activities in the system
- transformation – this is the key feature of the definition and refers to the core transformation process of the human activity system, i.e. the process of converting input(s) into output(s)
- weltanchauung (or world view) – the unquestioned image or model of the world which makes the particular human activity system a meaningful one to consider
- owner(s) of the system – those who have sufficient power over the system to cause its demise

• environment – constraints which the system has to take as given.

The initial letters of these elements form the mnemonic CATWOE to identify these six crucial characteristics which should be included in a well-formulated Root Definition.

An example of a conceptual model is provided in Figure 2.15 and relates to the role of an information and library service department (ILSD) (Checkland and Scholes 1990).

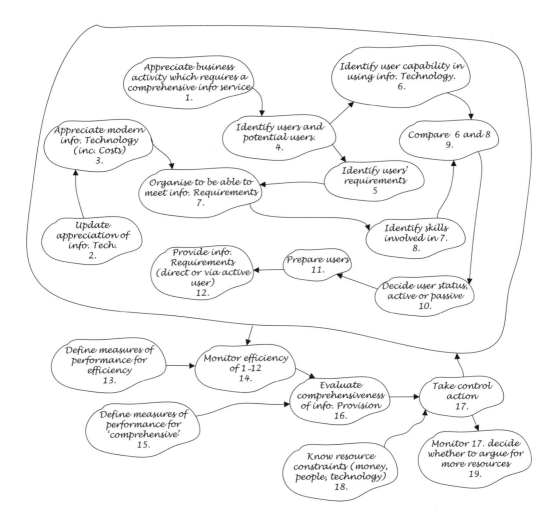

Figure 2.15 Conceptual model for an ILSD

Source: Reproduced with permission of John Wiley & Sons

The associated Root Definition is:

A system organized by ILSD, which provides comprehensive information to active and passive users employing technical and other skills, assisted by modern technology, so that the service is regarded as comprehensive.

C = User

A = ILSD, some users

T = User transforms to user helped by information provision

W = Modern technology and local culture make this feasible, useful

O (implied) =The company using ILSD as agent

E = Existing structure, modern technology, company resources.

It will be noted that the model is normally drawn by hand and text is handwritten. There is merit in avoiding computer-based tools for the analysis stage as otherwise one may focus on formatting issues and the peculiarities of a tool with which one is not familiar and thereby fail to concentrate fully on the problem situation.

2.8.2 CONCEPT MAPPING

A concept map (Figure 2.16) is a downward-branching hierarchical structure showing the relationships between concepts connected by arrows labelled with linking phrases (http://en.wikipedia.org/wiki/Concept_map). The technique has been applied in a number of fields for problem solving and mapping concepts (Moon et al., 2011) and is supported by a free mapping tool available from http://cmap.ihmc.us/download/.

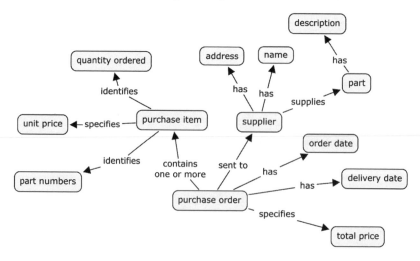

Figure 2.16 Concept mapping of a purchase order

It can be used as the initial stage of data modelling as the diagramming conventions are likely to be more readily comprehended by non-IT staff than traditional data models as described later in Section 7.2.2. An example of mapping to tease out the attributes relating a purchase order is shown in Figure 2.16.

This example of a purchase order will be developed further in Chapter 7 when discussing data analysis and data modelling.

2.9 Conclusion

This chapter concerned ways in which improvements can be brought about in organizations by focusing on such aspects as quality, business processes and the people involved. It also outlined approaches for tackling 'messy' problem areas that are not immediately amenable to the 'mechanical' techniques discussed. No single method is likely to be appropriate for tackling the range of uncertainties that organizations face. Often a method needs to be tailored to fit an organization's culture, or a portfolio of compatible approaches adopted to address the particular mix of problems.

The information used and generated by these various techniques provides the basis for decision making and for future action. Achieving the required outcomes from applying these techniques depends on having an understanding of the nature of information and data and the role of information in organizations. It also depends critically on harnessing the knowledge and expertise of information specialists, whether they are staff members or need to be brought in to assist. These aspects are dealt with in the following chapter, which introduces the concept of an information life cycle covering creation, management and utilization.

3 *The Information Context*

'The challenge of the Information Age lies not in building bigger and faster machines or in designing more and more complex automata; it lies in learning to analyze arguments we can't support, to handle data we don't understand and to see what we may not believe'. Burns (1985)

Information is arguably the life blood of an organization. It permeates the organizational elements of structure, processes, people and tools which were discussed in Chapter 1. It is a vital resource when there is a need to tackle problems, assess current performance and effect improvements, as was considered in the previous chapter.

Systems that help to address the information problems facing organizations are increasingly computer-based. Humans are necessary parts of these systems as designers, maintainers, information providers or as users of the system outputs. However, all too often technology-oriented personnel are seduced by the technology and their familiarity with it. Hence they fail to properly take account of the real business needs and the business information which the system stores and processes. In contrast, many who utilize information in their day-to-day activities may have a cavalier attitude to the systems and data management aspects.

As Burns (1985) stated in his article, what went wrong at the Three Mile Island nuclear plant was a classic information management collapse:

'The crisis at Three Mile Island dramatically illustrates how disaster can result if information quantity is used as a substitute for information quality [and] if information systems are considered merely mechanisms for producing disparate, unrelated data without any thought given to how the data will be used or to the information-handling processes of the people who will use it.'

Have the lessons been learnt? As Bradford (2011) noted, while the level of computerization and information transfer available to Japanese officials at the Fukushima nuclear reactor disaster in March 2001 gave much more insight to what happened – at least in theory – 'They've got so much more going on in terms of the earthquake and the tsunami that we didn't have at TMI, that I'm sure that the situation is every bit as confused'.

This chapter delves further into the topic of information by considering the:

- nature of information and its relationship to data and knowledge
- concepts of information management and knowledge management
- the contribution of information specialists
- life cycle of information from creation through management to utilization.

3.1 Data, Information and Knowledge

We now enter murky waters where it has long been difficult to agree on what the terms in the information world mean. As is often the case, it largely depends on the viewpoint of those expressing an opinion. For now, the following definitions will suffice (OED 2001):

- Data:
  - facts, esp. numerical facts, collected together for reference or information
  - a piece of information, a statistic
  - the quantities, characters, or symbols on which operations are performed by computers and other automatic equipment
- Information:
  - communication of the knowledge of some fact or occurrence
  - knowledge or facts communicated about a particular subject, event, etc.; intelligence, news
- Knowledge:
  - the fact of knowing a thing, state, person, etc.; acquaintance; familiarity gained by experience
  - acquaintance with a fact or facts; a state of being aware or informed; awareness, consciousness.

These definitions imply a form of hierarchy comprising elements of information (data) leading to assemblies of data being communicated as information (human involvement) and thence to collections of data and information gathered by and familiar to individuals. An example of such a hierarchy is shown in Figure 3.1. Numerous variations on this theme are to be found in academic, commercial and consultancy literature.

From these definitions many will be able to agree on what data and information means, and will acknowledge that they can reside in tangible form as electronic or physical messages or records that can be managed as 'information resources' along with other corporate resources (capital, human and so on). Nevertheless, information has some differentiating and unique characteristics, for example its utility can vary with time and furthermore it may be:

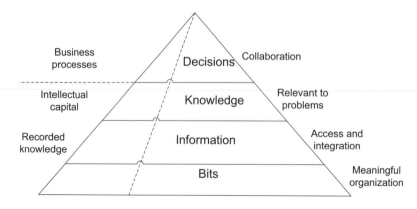

Figure 3.1   KM hierarchy

- used simultaneously by interested parties
- converted to, and exist in a variety of forms
- expressed in different languages (computer- or human-based)
- open to different interpretations and degrees of acceptability, depending on such factors as social and cultural background, gender and one's state of motivation.

'Knowledge', however, has no such tangible form. The only way it can be made a manageable information resource is for the knowledgeable person to output their experience or the facts with which they are acquainted into forms that can be recorded and reused. On this basis 'knowledge management' has no meaning; one cannot manage what an individual knows. Nevertheless, a whole industry has built itself around 'knowledge management' (KM), often simply replacing the word 'information' by 'knowledge' or rebranding products so that today's 'search engine' becomes tomorrow's 'knowledge manager'. So it is necessary to consider in more detail aspects of information and knowledge management.

3.2 Information Management and Knowledge Management

So who are the winners in the 'knowledge', 'information' and 'data' debate? An advanced search on Google on 1st August 2011 obtained the following number of hits for the phrases indicated:

- 'data management' – 65,600,000
- 'information management' – 75,000,000
- 'knowledge management' – 46,000,000.

As regards roles associated with these 'disciplines' the hit results were:

- 'Chief Data Officer' – 246,000
- 'Chief Information Officer' – 13,600,000
- 'Chief Knowledge Officer' – 304,000.

Note that repeating the search does not provide nearly the same results, a fact that is indicative of the vagaries of search engines. The topic of quality of information is covered in Chapter 6, Section 6.8.8.

Various definitions exist for information management and knowledge management as exemplified in Figure 3.2 (access to the websites was made on 3 February 2012).

As will be seen, some of those for knowledge management refer to it as a discipline, a management activity or one that relies on technology. Those for information management often emphasize collection, organization and storage, but sometimes note its use to aid decision making, an attribute linked to some definitions of knowledge management. There is therefore extensive overlap in the definitions.

Definitions of Knowledge Management	Source
A range of strategies and practices used in an organization to identify, create, represent, distribute, and enable adoption of insights and experiences	http://en.wikipedia.org/wiki/Knowledge_management
The discipline to enable individuals, teams, organizations and communities, more collectively and systematically capture, store, share and apply their knowledge, to achieve their objectives	http://www.knowledge-management-online.com/what-is-Knowledge-Management.html
A managerial activity which develops, transfers, transmits, stores and applies knowledge, as well as providing the members of the organization with real information to react and make the right decisions, in order to attain the organization's goals	http://hosteddocs.ittoolbox.com/KKRR41106.pdf
The process through which organizations generate value from their intellectual and knowledge-based assets	http://www.cio.com/article/40343/Knowledge_Management_Definition_and_Solutions
The set of professional practices which improves the capabilities of the organization's human resources and enhances their ability to share what they know	http://www.processrenewal.com/files/def-km.doc
A discipline that uses technology to share and leverage information for innovation	http://www.computing.co.uk/ctg/analysis/1825228/knowledge-management-fountain-knowledge
Definitions of Information Management	
Uses technology for information collection, storage and control	http://www.computing.co.uk/ctg/analysis/1825228/knowledge-management-fountain-knowledge
Application of management techniques to collect information, communicate it within and outside the organization, and process it to enable managers to make quicker and better decisions	http://www.businessdictionary.com/definition/information-management.html
The discipline that analyzes information as an organizational resource. It covers the definitions, uses, value and distribution of all data and information within an organization whether processed by computer or not	http://www.pcmag.com/encyclopedia_term/0,2542,t=information+management&i=44948,00.asp
The collection and management of information from one or more sources and the distribution of that information to one or more audiences	http://en.wikipedia.org/wiki/Information_management
All processes and technologies that help create high quality information, where all elements are clearly defined and can be combined with each other in a meaningful way, in order to support the management processes	http://www.oracle.com/us/products/middleware/bus-int/064320.pdf

Figure 3.2   Definitions of information and knowledge management

Knowledge management is often taken to subsume all things 'information'. For example, Desouza and Paquette (2011), in their book on *Knowledge Management*, provide no index entries for 'information management' or 'data management', but extensive entries under 'knowledge management'. These lead to topics referred to as classification for knowledge organization, metadata of knowledge and relationships between knowledge artefacts. Substituting the words 'information' or 'data' for 'knowledge' might render these more meaningful given that the definition of knowledge provided by the authors ('the beliefs of an individual based on the meaningful accumulation of information') does not logically allow for classification or metadata to be applied to 'knowledge'.

Reverting to terminology, consideration also needs to be given to the words 'tacit' and 'explicit' in relation to knowledge, as these terms occur frequently in 'KM' literature. Turning again to the OED (2001) we have:

- Tacit: unspoken; silent, emitting no sound; noiseless, wordless; implied without being openly expressed or stated; understood, inferred.
- Explicit: distinctly expressing all that is meant; leaving nothing merely implied or suggested; unambiguous; clear.

'Tacit' indicates that no form of communication is involved, hence 'tacit knowledge' is actually not capable of being 'downloaded' and captured. The phrase 'tacit knowledge' originated from the work of Polanyi (1966) who coined the much quoted statement 'we can know more than we can tell'. As an example Polanyi noted that we can recognize a face we know, yet we usually cannot tell how we recognize a face we know. The concept of 'tacit knowledge' was taken up by Nonaka (1991) but on the basis that such knowledge could be captured. As Wilson (2002) points out, 'implicit' is a more suitable word to use than 'tacit' as then 'implicit knowledge' becomes something that, although not expressed, is capable of expression. The OED (2001) definition of 'implicit' is 'implied though not plainly expressed; necessarily or naturally involved (in); able to be inferred'.

Finally, we have 'explicit knowledge' which can be equated more directly with recorded information and data.

For clarity, this book is solely concerned with information (including data) that is available in some recorded form independent of humans. Thus oral communication directly between individuals, although important in the context of spreading knowledge about processes or technology, is excluded, as there is no permanent record to 'manage'.

This is not intended to suggest that 'knowledge capture' is unimportant. Much is being done within organizations to encourage sharing of know-how and experience and to record this knowledge for the benefit of others. But 'knowledge is power', and in the uncertainties of the organizational world employees may not willingly share their knowledge, as this may put their position at risk. The organization's culture needs to be supportive and encouraging for knowledge sharing to flourish.

Although considered by some as being over-hyped, 'knowledge management' cannot be ignored. If one can clarify what colleagues, suppliers or customers mean when they refer to 'KM', and a common understanding is reached, all to the good.

If 'knowledge' is information that an individual knows and holds in their brain, 'information' is that which is available in recorded form independent of humans, and 'Enterprise Content Management' (ECM) is 'recorded knowledge' in the corporate context, then the relationship between these elements is shown in Figure 3.3.

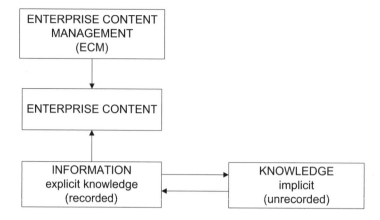

Figure 3.3   Knowledge and Enterprise Content Management

Given this viewpoint, one can identify the key constituent elements of ECM based on those of Leavitt et al. (1973) – namely 'process', 'people', '(organizational) structure' and 'tools' (Figure 3.4).

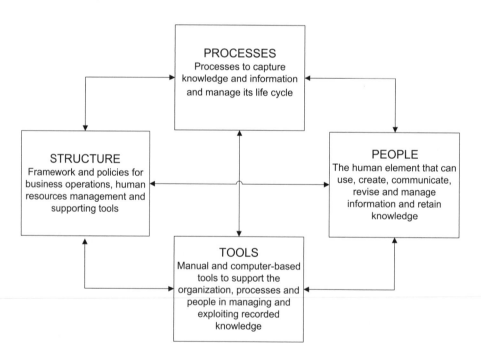

Figure 3.4   Constituent elements of Enterprise Content Management

3.3 The Role of Information

In order to function according to its intended purpose, an organization needs information about:

- itself
- its customers (however they may be defined)
- its suppliers
- its environment.

Such information can be broadly categorized into that required for:

- day-to-day functioning (operations) of the organization
- managerial control and monitoring
- planning.

Information required to enable the organization to operate from one day to another tends to be short-term and detailed and is typically delivered through automated means. In contrast, that required by management will generally be selective and summarized and may not need to be immediately available (but when it is required it has to be available promptly). Planning information tends to be more diverse and outward-looking. It also often relies more on qualitative judgement than is the case for control and operations.

Clearly one type of information will often rely on another. For example, control cannot be exercised without access to operational information, while planning for the future is impossible without knowledge of current performance derived from monitoring. Nevertheless, being able to consider information types in this way can help address questions of information management at different levels in the organization.

There is also the aspect of the source of the information; it may be internally generated and therefore unique to the organization, or be sourced externally and potentially be available to others, unless subject to some contractual or exclusive arrangement. Planning needs knowledge of the organization's environment and hence great reliance is placed on external information concerning such matters as competitors and government regulations.

Monitoring and control is more inward-looking, although there will be a need to consider supply chains, customer satisfaction and so on. Day-to-day functions will tend to rely most on internal information, but again there may be key operational links to suppliers and customers. While clear dividing lines cannot be drawn to delineate the roles played by internal and external information and the three categories of information, one can picture the relationship between these aspects in general terms as shown in Figure 3.5.

The way the diagram is drawn shows a large proportion of the internal information falling outside the categories of operations, control and planning. This represents archives and other records that are, for example, held for historical reasons and are not usually utilized for the core activities of the organization.

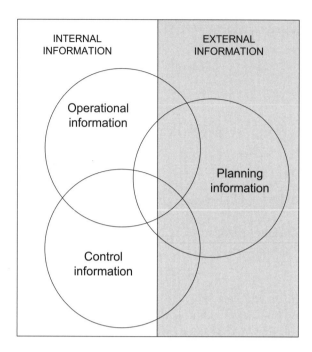

Figure 3.5   Information needs of operations, control and planning

For some organizations the role of information will have particular significance because their productive activities are information-intensive, as is the case for pharmaceutical companies. Others such as metal fabricators will be more focused on the day-to-day manufacturing processes, although clearly information is needed to ensure smooth day-to-day running.

3.4 The Contribution of Specialists

A wide range of expertise needs to be available to ensure proper management of information throughout its life cycle. Some of this expertise has been around for centuries in those safeguarding the records of human existence in the form of papyri and other ancient manuscripts, for example. The coming of new technologies for information creation, representation, manipulation, communication and storage provided vastly increased opportunities for recording and disseminating knowledge. It also introduced the need for new skills in such areas as computer design, software programming and linguistics. Such wide-ranging and demanding skills are rarely to be found in a single individual and hence new breeds of 'specialists' emerged, coalescing around associations or societies created to foster their common interests.

An attempt to capture the richness of this 'specialist' landscape is provided in Figure 3.6, with the more traditional and long-standing expertise of records and library management to the right and the more recent technologically-based specialists to the left. A more detailed version of this figure is provided at the book's companion website www.cura.org.uk.

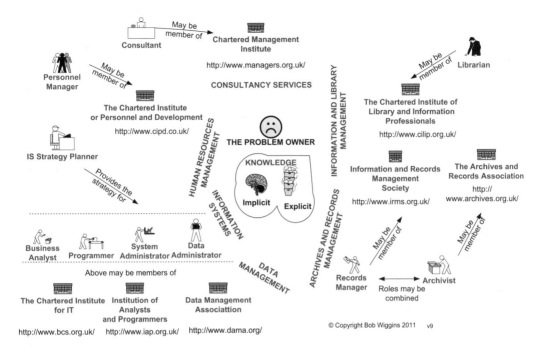

Figure 3.6   Information specialists

Examination of the version of this 'rich picture' in the previous edition of this book would show that several 'professional' societies or associations no longer exist, some having merged with others or simply folded, while others have renamed to better reflect their membership or direction. For example:

- The Institute of Information Scientists merged with the former Library Association to form the Chartered Institute of Library and Information Professionals in 2002
- The Institute of Management Consultancy (IMC) merged with the Chartered Management Institute in 2005
- In 2011 the Society of Archivists amalgamated with the National Council on Archives (NCA) and the Association of Chief Archivists in Local Government (ACALG) to become the Archives and Records Association (United Kingdom and Ireland), otherwise known as the ARA
- The UK Records Management Society was renamed in 2011 as the Information and Records Management Society
- The British Computer Society now refers to itself as BCS, the Chartered Institute for IT.

It is interesting to note that the major changes have occurred in the traditional disciplines relating to information, records and libraries – an indication perhaps of the vagueness of the intellectual boundaries between them. Some members of the extinct bodies will have been uneasy or even hostile to the changes – however, information science lives on, for example, albeit as a discipline rather than a society (IIS 2008).

This fluidity is also indicative of the uncertainties concerning who should have responsibility for records management. A survey undertaken by the Association for

Information and Image Management (AIIM 2009a) in the United States failed to find any definite trend as to where records management responsibility lies. This was underlined by the cross-organizational nature of records management with different parts of the organization taking responsibility, for example:

- Chief Records Officer – this role has started to appear within the executive team
- legal and compliance function – demonstrating compliance relies on records and hence lawyers and the like are taking a greater role in records management
- IT function – this function continues to maintain its dominant position as regards managing electronic records despite not fully appreciating the application of retention to data. As the AIIM report states 'giving the electronic records management responsibility to IT because records reside on IT-managed systems is akin to giving the facilities manager control of paper records because they are stored in his basement'
- line of business – assigning records to responsibility to those who use the records is not uncommon, but records management is often viewed as something to be delegated rather than being an integral part of their use.

The division of labour shown in Figure 3.6 may be effective in delivering the 'specialist' outputs, but it has also led to difficulties in understanding and collaborative working between the various groups. Thus practitioners in such fields as computing, records management and libraries may be aware of each other's existence within organizations, but are not necessarily clear as to their respective roles, functions and inter-relationship.

This situation has been accelerated by the convergence of data processing, telecommunications and office technologies. No longer can individual 'experts' such as data analysts, system designers, records managers or librarians afford to isolate themselves in watertight service compartments. An example is the need to consider records retention and freedom of information principles when designing and implementing document or case management systems. There is a need to capitalize on the skills and experience of all such 'information' specialists and the services they can provide when undertaking broad-based information-related initiatives.

Studies have shown (Ang and Pavri 1994) that if both IS specialists and users heighten awareness of their respective power bases this can facilitate the parties working in unison for the development of effective systems. Furthermore, it is important to recognize that 'IS development and politics are inextricably intertwined. An IS specialist who approaches the systems development process in a clinical, methodological and completely detached manner is not being constructive'.

Although there needs to be this inter-working, specialists will still be concerned with particular information aspects. Consider the famous quote 'In a culture like ours long accustomed to splitting and dividing all things as a means of control, it is sometimes a bit of a shock to be reminded that, in operational and practical fact, the medium is the message' (McLuhan 1964) – you can equate 'message' to information as understood by (most) users and 'media' as the storage medium. If you accept this analogy then data can be considered to be the 'elements' (words, phrases, numbers, even characters) which make up the message. Given this somewhat artificial basis, the following suggests the contribution of specialists to information management based on the activities which make up the information life cycle – see Figure 3.7.

SPECIALIST:	IS strategy planner	Business analyst[4]	Programmer	System administrator	Data administrator	Records manager	Archivist	Librarian[1]	End user[2]
INFORMATION	**TYPE**								
'Message'	P	P	S	N	S	P	P	P	P
'Elements'	N	P	P	S	P	S	N	N	N
'Media'	N	S	N	S	N	P	P	S	N
Ext. information	P	S	S	S	S	S	S	P	P
Int. information[3]	P	P	P	S	P	P	P	S	P
ACTIVITIES									
Determine business strategy	P	N	N	N	N	N	N	N	P
Identify relevant information	P	S	N	N	P	S	S	P	P
Acquire	S	N	N	N	S	N	N	P	S
Create	N	S	N	N	N	N	N	N	P
Review/approve	S	S	N	S	P	P	P	S	P
Assign value	N	S	N	N	P	P	P	P	P
Access/utilize	N	S	N	N	S	S	S	P	P
Disseminate	S	S	N	N	S	N	S	P	P
Process/file	S	S	N	S	S	P	P	P	S
Archive	N	S	N	P	S	S	P	P	N
Destroy	N	S	N	P	P	P	P	S	N
Monitor and control	S	S	N	P	P	P	P	P	S
Organize	S	S	N	P	P	P	P	P	S

Key: P= Primary concern; S= Secondary concern; N= Minimal if any concern

[1] Many 'librarians' are more proactive than is indicated here. The 'title' given to a post-holder is not necessarily descriptive of their information activities.

[2] The answers provided will depend on the seniority of, and activities undertaken by a particular end-user.

[3] 'Brought-in' external information is typically integrated with internal information. Thus it is not always possible clearly to distinguish between the two.

[4] The role of the Business Analyst may be restricted to specific activities depending on the scope of the study. That shown here indicates a wide-ranging brief

Figure 3.7 Contribution of specialists

Clearly the categorization is merely indicative of the inputs that these specialists might provide to an information-related project.

Having responsibility for records management requires a range of skills which are not often possessed by one person. In its study AIIM (2009a) proposed that the required skills are:

- political and cultural adeptness – necessary to obtain buy-in and finance
- understanding of information processes and context – knowledge of process and data analysis
- records management competence – importance of classification, retention and records disposition
- awareness of legal and regulatory environment – not just data protection and freedom of information but also the regulatory environment of the organization's business sector
- information technology skills – sufficient to judge the suitability of what IT exists or is proposed.

3.5 The Information Life Cycle

The organization and management of information is a challenge, given the range of its characteristics as discussed in the previous sections. However, there is merit in considering the main types of process that make up an information life cycle from cradle to grave, as depicted in Figure 3.8.

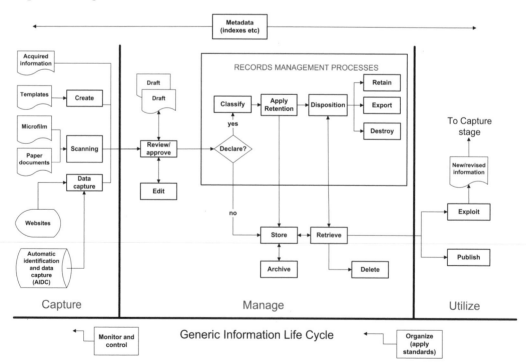

Figure 3.8   Information life cycle

The stages are set out in a linear arrangement which clearly do not reflect the more dynamic and feedback nature of real life. The stages are dealt with in more detail later, including:

- 'records management', whose management processes are delineated in the figure
- 'document management' which can be considered to cover the remaining processes from and beyond the creation of electronic formats via templates and the conversion of hard copies into electronic form using scanners, and
- 'data management' concerned with data from line-of-business applications; for example, a finance or human resources database.

CAPTURE

Acquired or received information may be in a variety of formats (for example, electronic, paper or in physical forms such as exploration drilling samples) and from a variety of sources (such as customers, suppliers, internal line-of-business applications, external databases, Internet sites, and from social media such as Facebook and Twitter). Where possible, electronic formats are created (for example, paper documents are scanned), so that onward management is made easier.

Where the information does not exist, or its acquisition is too difficult or costly, it may need to be created through intellectual effort by knowledgeable people. This stage is under the complete control of the organization and enables information to be produced from the outset in electronic form according to internal standards, including those relating to document layout and content as may be defined in templates.

EDITING, REVIEW AND APPROVAL

Created, acquired or revised information will need to pass through some approval or authorization procedure before it is processed or distributed further. The makeup of these procedures will depend on the type of document (for example, correspondence or engineering drawing) and its intended usage and promulgation. Internally-created information will usually need to be edited to bring into some agreed order. This may also be required for externally-received information, for example where extracts are to be incorporated within internal documents (subject to intellectual rights). The output of this stage will be draft or final versions of recorded information. Means to control document versions will be applied here so that an audit trail is available covering superseded versions, and users may only see the latest, current version, for example.

DECLARE – ASSIGN ORGANIZATIONAL VALUE

The decision as to whether a piece of recorded information is to be 'declared a record' is a vital one, as such declaration provides a special status which is aimed at preventing unauthorized destruction of or changes to the recorded information (whether data or document). The terminology is one that is well known to records managers and their staff, but tends to be opaque to others, hence reference to the process as 'assigning organizational value', as this is more readily understood by others and has a wider connotation that just 'record declaration'.

CLASSIFY

When is it decided to declare a record it is necessary to place the record (logically if not physically) within some form of classification scheme (or file plan), both to facilitate subsequent searching for the record and assist with assignment of a retention period.

APPLY RETENTION

As has already been noted, information's utility can change with time. How many times is information destroyed on a whim, only to find one needs it soon after? Nevertheless, there needs to be some idea as to how long a piece of recorded information is to be retained and for what reason. This stage involves applying retention schedules, which are often informed by legal and regulatory requirements. This ensures that information which is needed is not destroyed and that redundant information can be weeded out of the system.

DISPOSITION – RETAIN, EXPORT, DESTROY

In line with agreed retention policy and the assigned retention periods, records are reviewed to determine if they are to be retained, permanently destroyed or transferred to another authority such as a National Archive. Care needs to be taken to ensure that effective techniques are available to completely destroy digitally stored information.

STORE AND ARCHIVE

Created or acquired information will need to be stored using suitable media and storage systems once it has passed through the editing, review, approval and value assignment stages. Thought should be given to the location of the stores, the need for conversion between media, storage life, the legal acceptability of the various media and provision for making security copies (backups) of the information in case the main store of information is destroyed.

RETRIEVE

Ready means of access to the stored information is a prerequisite for its utilization, subject to any security that may restrict such access.

DELETE

Hitting the delete button in a word processing program will not permanently destroy a document. This process as depicted in the diagram relates to recorded information which has not been declared a record and is therefore under the control of the user. A declared record should not be capable of being deleted or permanently destroyed by anyone other than an authorized person – typically the organization's Records Manager.

UTILIZE

Retrieved information may be required for a variety of purposes, each of which will need the information communicated by suitable means and in appropriate formats. The information may be reused in some way, with the resulting output passing through the life cycle to be captured and managed. Alternatively, the information is published or replicated in some form but its essential content remains unchanged.

METADATA (INDEXES ETC)

Everyone is familiar with the idea of a book index or telephone directory and most people are now used to employing Internet search engines. Within organizations, more specialized search and retrieval tools will be available, such as corporate intranets, personnel databases and case management systems. These tools typically enable users to enter search terms or browse through hierarchically-arranged subject directories to home in on the required information. Very broadly in this sense they are information indexes and represent one type of metadata – this being 'a set of data that describes and gives information about other data'.

Other types of metadata will record such matters as 'document version', 'retention schedules', 'approver details', 'electronic file formats' and 'access rights for individuals'. These are necessary for the day-to-day management and operation of the system.

MONITOR AND CONTROL

Irrespective of how efficiently and effectively the individual processes have been undertaken, the overall life cycle has to be managed as a whole and this requires that its operation and performance are monitored and controlled. Performance measures must be established appropriate to the activity to be monitored. Typical measures might be the speed of response of the information retrieval system, the degree of satisfaction of users with the answers to their queries, the number of documents accessed per week or the percentage of projects completed on time and within budget.

ORGANIZE (APPLY STANDARDS)

The total life cycle must be properly organized as regards people, technology, policies, procedures and tasks and their inter-relationship (recall Figure 1.1). Appropriate standards need to be applied (for example, quality systems) and regulatory and legal matters (such as Freedom of Information) adhered to. The application of such measures enables compliance to be monitored.

3.6 Conclusion

When information-related problems are being addressed it is vital, when dealing with others, to have mutual understanding of what meaning is ascribed to terms such as information, data, knowledge and their 'management'. It is confusing, and in fact erroneous, to use 'knowledge' to mean anything that is recorded independent of an individual and therefore potentially available to others. Certainly have policies and procedures to encourage the sharing of knowledge and have systems to allow those with the knowledge to voluntarily record that which they are able to put into words or figures. However, this is not knowledge management; one cannot manage what an individual retains in their head.

Having reached agreement on such topics, progress can more easily be made in marshalling the necessary expertise, whether from traditional disciplines such as records management and librarianship or from those that arose with the coming of computing technology such as software programmers and data analysts.

Finally, when addressing issues around managing information and data, it is helpful to use the concept of an information life cycle, from creation through management to utilization, following which new information may arise and need to be managed. The life cycle forms the basis of Chapters 4, 5 and 6 which are concerned respectively with information capture, managing information and information retrieval and use. Dealing with data (structured information) rather than documents (unstructured information) poses some unique aspects and these are dealt with in Chapter 7.

2 *The Information Life Cycle*

CHAPTER 4

Information Capture

'I only ask for information'. Miss Rosa Dartle in 'David Copperfield', Charles Dickens

Information capture requires a conscious decision to create, acquire or accept received information into some form of organized and managed system. This chapter describes the main processes by which information is captured and includes user-created documents, electronic imaging (for example, scanning of paper documents), and automated data capture from bar codes, tags, computer systems or web-based sources. The inputs that comprise the capture stage are shown in Figure 4.1. The elements of this figure are described during the course of the chapter.

The extent to which the captured information might be managed is dealt with in Chapter 5.

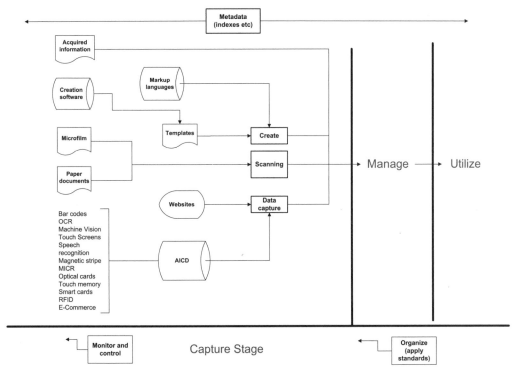

Figure 4.1 The capture stage

4.1 Document Creation

Document creation can be divided into three main categories – general office work, publishing and long-document production, and web publishing. The first category includes text, tabular and presentation ('slide') material which most office workers will have the basic ability to produce using ubiquitous office software programs. The second category is often called desktop publishing, the software for which requires more training than that for general office document production. The content and structure is usually of greater complexity and is focused on composing text and graphics into page layouts for publishing. The third category concerns either replicating existing documents to the web or creation specifically for the web.

Irrespective of the category, there should be a standard layout and content for the type of document being produced. Adopting such practice lays the foundation for effective management of the generated document throughout its life cycle. Today's office programs provide a vast range of functions, most of which the average user will never need or use. They also offer considerable flexibility in the way they can be utilized, with many of the options providing support for improved management of the created document. Unless the user has had appropriate training and, importantly, the organization has the necessary document and records management policies and procedures actively in place, the availability of such functionality will be of little consequence.

Failure to standardize at the outset may have other consequences such as undermining the organization's 'brand' to the outside world or providing conflicting information where standard content (such as names, contacts and references) is not controlled.

When creating new information, whether structured data or unstructured documents, you need to consider its possible future use. If it is to be reused in any way, aim for single sourcing of the information, that is, content reuse, and select creation software that will provide the output format to facilitate this.

4.1.1 CREATION SOFTWARE

Where you are dealing with a wide range of organizations and document interflow is extensive, it is worth maintaining the highest degree of compatibility in terms of document styles and formats. Without this rigour, you risk wasting considerable time reformatting documents. It is therefore no surprise that the software company providing the most popular product in its field will tend to dominate. For office software, Microsoft currently holds this position.

Increasingly, however, its dominance has been challenged principally on the basis of costs and accessibility. Microsoft, like most software companies, jealously guards its products and does not release the software for others to adapt or enhance. The concept of Open Source (2011) has challenged this and is 'a development method for software that harnesses the power of distributed peer review and transparency of process. The promise of open source is better quality, higher reliability, more flexibility, lower cost, and an end to predatory vendor lock-in'.

An example of Open Source office software is OpenOffice.org (2011) which provides packages – Writer, Calc, Impress, Draw and Base – that aim to match those offered by Microsoft – Word, Excel, PowerPoint, Visio and Access. This software was managed under the wing of Oracle until April 2011 when the company announced that it would no longer support the product commercially. As members of the 'open' community wanted a vendor-neutral alternative (Paul 2011) they founded a non-profit organization called The Document Foundation (TDF) – http://www.documentfoundation.org – in order to create a truly vendor-neutral governance body for the software which is called LibreOffice. Most of the major companies that have historically been involved in 'open' development moved to support TDF and LibreOffice, including Red Hat, Novell, Google and Canonical.

However, in June 2011, Oracle announced that it was donating OpenOffice.org's code to The Apache Software Foundation's Incubator. Created in 1999, the all-volunteer Apache Software Foundation oversees over one hundred Open Source projects. A preliminary OpenOffice.org incubator http://incubator.apache.org/openofficeorg/ site was established as of June 13, 2011 for the transition and has IBM support. So, at the time of writing, there is uncertainty as to which 'open' products will emerge on top.

Office software has traditionally been provided for use on an organization's existing network. This involves the expense of loading, supporting and upgrading the software locally. Now users can use web-based software (commonly called cloud computing) as an alternative to access office functions and store and share documents.

Cloud computing is 'a (pay-per-use) model for enabling ubiquitous, convenient, on-demand network access to a shared pool of configurable computing resources – e.g., networks, servers, storage, applications, and services – that can be rapidly provisioned and released with minimal management effort or service provider interaction' (Mell and Grance 2011). Suppliers of cloud computing include Google, with the Google Docs suite of applications, and Microsoft, with some of its Office software. Google has advantages over Microsoft's offerings in that no desktop software needs to be installed and the application is plug-and-play. With all cloud-based applications there is the issue of security to be considered. Is an organization content to have its key documents held elsewhere other than on its internal systems?

As regards desktop publishing software the choice will depend largely on the complexity of the intended output. At the professional end of the spectrum are products such as Adobe InDesign, QuarkXPress and Corel Ventura. For those requiring less sophistication there is, for example, the open source Scribus and proprietary products exemplified by PagePlus, Print Artist, The Print Shop Professional and Microsoft Publisher which were the top 5 in a 2011 software review (DTP 2011).

For publishing to the web most creation software has export or save as options to create web-friendly versions, for example as HTML. However such on-the-fly conversions may not conform to the current and developing standards for markup languages. The use of markup languages such as XML or HTML is discussed in Section 4.1.5.

4.1.2 TEMPLATES

While it is necessary to have written guidelines for layout and content, adherence to them is facilitated by the use of document templates. Templates are a special type of electronic document that can store text, document styles, macros (a set of instructions that can, for example, indent a paragraph or insert a data value), keyboard shortcuts, custom toolbars and automatic text entries. Much of the effort to create a document is avoided by using a template, although it is not necessary to use every feature it may offer.

Using Microsoft Office software as an example, any newly-created document is based on a template. If the user has not selected a specialized template, the software automatically bases the document on the 'Normal' template which is a standard feature of the software.

On creation, a document inherits the following elements from its parent template:

- styles
- content
- page settings.

Following creation of the document the template provides:

- macro functionality
- a way to store parts of a document for re-use (termed AutoTexts or Building Blocks depending on the version of Microsoft Office)
- toolbars
- keyboard shortcuts.

Although some of the items controlled by a template, such as house style, are generally not of great relevance to a seeker of information or a records manager, other data may be, examples being addressee's name, email address and originating organization. Such data can be gathered using macros which provide links to other systems in the organization such as a personnel database for details of staff and client databases for contact details of customers.

4.1.3 CONTENT DESIGN CONSIDERATIONS

Consider, for example, the requirements for documentation relating to litigation. The legal cases may vary in type from personal injury claims to immigration and employment, with each type requiring different types of document, or small but important variations from a standard for the responsible lawyers. It is quite possible that each team of lawyers or even each lawyer devises their own templates or plagiarizes existing ones, particularly if they maintain their 'master' case files as paper. In this environment it is difficult to enforce any long-lasting standardization of the templates.

Introducing a computer-based system inevitably requires some rigour as regards the analysis of the data to be stored. It forces those affected by the introduction of the system to consider the meaning of the terms they use and to agree standardization of terminology. For example, in a case management system which job title and spelling is to be used: case officer, case worker, caseworker, caseholder or case holder?

In this situation a review of existing and proposed templates needs to be undertaken and the desired template data matched to the appropriate data in the system so that macros can be written to fetch the system data as the document is created. This review can be helped by using a spreadsheet listing the teams involved, the templates they use (or plan to use) and the data items each template contains (see sample layout in Figure 4.2 where, for example data item 5 is common to Teams 1 and 3). This will help highlight areas where debate is required, for example where gaps or anomalies are identified. Further aspects of data analysis are considered in Chapter 7.

	Team 1	Team1	Team 2	Team 2	Team 3	Team 3	Team 3
	Template 1	Template 2	Template 3	Template 4	Template 5	Template 6	Template 7
Data item 1			x			x	
Data item 2						x	
Data item 3	x						
Data item 4			x			x	
Data item 5	x					x	
Data item 6		x				x	
Data item 7							
Data item 8				x			x
Data item 9					x		x

Figure 4.2   Template for data analysis

Beyond the user-centric data there is the range of document-related metadata needed for control and management. Some of this data is captured automatically, but may need to be modified to reflect reality. For example, the person who commences the typing of a new document will be recorded by the software, but may not be the document's author. Similarly the date of creation is captured, but this will not be the document date as entered on the final version. While for auditing and control purposes both these data need to be retained, additional fields are needed to store the name of the true author and the formal date of the document.

Largely hidden from the user there will be records management data which will need to be configured into the system concerning such aspects as:

- levels of confidentiality of the document content (protective marking)
- review and disposal dates and decisions relating thereto
- Freedom of Information and the degree to which the contents of the document can be disclosed.

Once a file is created it needs to be given a name before is it saved to store. The choice of format and content for the file name is important. This topic is covered in Section 4.6.

4.1.4 FORMS MANAGEMENT

Much of the cost and inconvenience in managing records arises from the creation of unnecessary records and the excessive duplication of others. Forms are one way in which the recording of information can be standardized to ease its capture and subsequent use.

However, form work itself can suffer from poor design and unnecessary proliferation and hence its creation and use needs to be managed along with other records. Good design and consistency in its use is particularly important in relation to electronic imaging and the use of optical character recognition (OCR).

In order to address this issue, an inventory of all forms in use (printed, hand-written and computer-generated) should be compiled and maintained, with the general aim of increasing productivity and reducing forms production and usage costs. All types of form for use in the organization should be registered and coded.

Specific aims are to:

- eliminate unnecessary forms, copies of forms and items on forms
- consolidate forms serving similar purposes
- prevent the creation of unnecessary new forms and revisions to existing forms
- design forms for maximum effectiveness
- ensure, as appropriate, proper reproduction, stocking and distribution
- maximize the appropriate use of computer-based systems for form generation, information capture, distribution and storage.

The elements of a forms management programme covering analysis and design are given in Figure 4.3.

STAGE	ACTIVITY
ANALYSIS	Identify the purpose of the form
	Specify how it is used in operation
	Estimate the time taken to complete it
	State the required number of copies and how they are distributed
	Indicate the filing and retention procedures
	Interview or survey the form's recipients
DESIGN	Eliminate redundancy and duplication
	Make them easy to complete
	Make them self-filing
	Ensure they are readily accessed and the contents easily analysed
	Aim to replace paper by electronic versions
	All forms should have: • a title • name of issuing authority • reference code • edition/version/update code and issue date • retention period

Figure 4.3   Forms management tasks

Electronic forms can provide data validation and enforce certain types of input, for example:

- data fields can be set up to accept only numeric values, and if needed only designated values
- text fields may be controlled to only allow permitted terms or phrases to be entered

- embedded macros will pick up additional details from external systems when, for example, a customer name is entered
- data entry may be made mandatory for some fields, but optional for others.

This approach provides an efficient and reliable way of collecting and manipulating information.

Where there has to be reliance on paper there is a mid-way application using digital pen and paper suited to those on site who need to record information in a structured way for subsequent computer-processing. It involves 'photographing' handwriting on a form and overlaying the captured images onto a blank copy of the same form on a computer, and then saving the image. When the software has been trained, handwriting can be converted to processable text.

4.1.5 MARKUP LANGUAGES

The markup of text has long been associated with the correction or annotation of copies or proofs for typesetting, printing and similar publishing production processes. With the coming of computing and communications the need to ease the interchange of electronic documents increased and led IBM to produce a prototype markup language. This enabled the separation of the logical content of a document from its presentation with formatting information held in separate files called style sheets and the document structure held in another file called Document Type Definition (DTD). This approach was developed further as the Standard Generalized Markup Language (SGML) which was adopted as an international standard in 1986 and widely used for data storage and interchange.

SGML offers the advantages of being a non-proprietary international standard independent of the technology on which it runs. Its use, however, requires extensive expertise, so creating DTDs is time-consuming and hence expensive. Its use was therefore principally limited to database and commercial publishing applications.

The need to produce a more flexible and simpler way to mark up documents for the web was recognized by Berners-Lee and Calliau (1990) and led to the development of the Hypertext Markup Language (HTML). HTML is based on SGML but eliminates little-used features and adds the ability to include hyperlinks for linking web pages which may contain images, videos or other digital media along with text.

HTML is concerned with what the information looks like on a page, that is, how the page is displayed. Further control can be exercised by the use of style sheets which separate the specification of style such as margins, from structure exemplified by section headings. HTML has no awareness of or control over the content of a document. To address this the eXtensible Markup Language (XML) was created, again based on SGML. Thus HTML will determine the font size and colour of this book's title, while XML will define the book title 'Effective Document and Data Management'. This means that XML can be used to represent data in a way that facilitates its communication and exchange. Thus XML, when applied, is a way to semi-structure unstructured information to make it more amenable to computer processing.

Work proceeds to produce a single language that can be written in HTML and XML with competing solutions, for example, HTML5 (http://html5.org/) and XHTML (http://xhtml.com/en/xhtml/reference/), vying for dominance.

XML enables a company, or more beneficially an industry group, to define a standard set of markup tags to describe data and thereby facilitate sharing between group members. The inclusion of data with these tags goes to form an XML document which can thereafter be used by other applications. XML is a recommendation of the World Wide Web Consortium (W3C 2008) and the subject of a range of ISO standards, for example relating to information interchange (ISO 19503 2005).

Various XML schema are available to describe types of XML documents, the principal ones being Document Type Definitions, XML Schema (note capitalization of 'S') also known as XSD, and RELAX NG. The use of DTDs has declined as XSD provides more functionality. A comparison of these schema is provided at Wikipedia (2011c).

To exemplify the use of XML, consider a database detailing purchase orders as shown in Figure 4.4.

Order Number	Supplier Name	Order Date	Purchase Item
1023	J.Smith and Sons	25/07/10	Purchase Item 1
			Purchase Item 2
			Purchase Item 3

Order Number	Supplier Name	Order Date	Purchase Item
1025	Construction Ltd	30/07/10	Purchase Item 1
			Purchase Item 2
			Purchase Item 3

Figure 4.4   Purchase order table

The columns store the kinds of data (Order Number, Supplier Number, Order Date and Purchase Item) while each row contains one order number, one supplier name, one order date and one list of purchase items for the order. The columns need to be defined in detail with regard to, for example, their name, the type of information they are allowed to hold and the maximum size of the data that is allowed to be entered. If this information is to be exchanged or shared with other systems the target system may need to be reconfigured to align with the data that is to be received. This is time-consuming and open to errors.

To illustrate the use of markup, the order details in Figure 4.4 are represented in XML form in Figure 4.5 which depicts a nested structure with the various levels representing the relationships between tags.

These tags consist of the following:

- <orders> contains information about all orders and is the parent of
- <order> contains information about individual orders and is the parent of
- <OrderNumber>, <SupplierName>, <OrderDate> and <PurchaseItem> provides information about an individual order.

Note the convention of using a slash to 'close' a tag as with </order>.

```
<orders>
        <order>
                <OrderNumber>1023</OrderNumber>
                <SupplierName>J. Smith and Sons</SupplierName>
                <OrderDate>25/07/10</OrderDate>
                <PurchaseItem>
                        Purchase Item 1
                        Purchase Item 2
                        Purchase Item 3
                </PurchaseItem>
        </order>
        <order>
                <OrderNumber>1025</OrderNumber>
                <SupplierName>Construction Ltd</SupplierName>
                <OrderDate>30/07/10</OrderDate>
                <PurchaseItem>
                        Purchase Item 1
                        Purchase Item 2
                        Purchase Item 3
                </PurchaseItem>
        </order>
</orders>
```

Figure 4.5   XML version of purchase order

As XML does not allow the element tags to contain any white spaces, the words such as Order Number must be joined in some way, for example by an underscore or, as here, by joining the two words together and capitalizing the words to make them readable – so-called camel writing.

4.2 File Formats

Electronic records can exist in a variety of formats depending on the software application that created them. Some of these formats will be proprietary and hence their use is protected in some way by the owners. Others are non-proprietary, often conforming to available standards and used to facilitate file conversion and interchange, for example.

File formats can broadly be divided into those relating to text and digital images.

4.2.1 TEXT FILE FORMATS

Computerized text is made up of encoded characters, where the latter is exemplified by letters of the alphabet, numbers, punctuation and other symbols created via a keyboard. The ubiquitous American Standard Code for Information Interchange (ASCII) standard is used to encode text. Initially developed for the English alphabet, the standard has been broadened to handle other languages. Due to limitations in extending it beyond its original brief, ASCII is increasingly being replaced by Unicode (http://www.unicode.org/) which is better suited to creating localized and cross-platform software.

The same encoding is at the core of all text files, be they word processed documents, emails or spreadsheets, for example. While the character coding remains the same throughout, the text files themselves do not conform to a single format since the nature of the format is determined by the software application that produced them. Many of the formats are proprietary which can restrict the interchange of information between different software packages. Some file formats exist to overcome this, the principal ones being:

- Rich Text Format (RTF)
- Open Document Format (ODF)
- ASCII text files (.txt)

RTF is a proprietary format developed by Microsoft and promulgated via a published specification to enable cross-platform interchange of documents. New releases of Microsoft's products may exhibit variations in the RTF specification, so error-free interchange may not be guaranteed unless the same specification is employed.

ODF is a non-proprietary format developed by the Organization for the Advancement of Structured Information Standards (OASIS) and published as an international standard (ISO 26300 2006). It is based on XML formatting and is used by several 'open source' document creation applications as noted in Section 4.1.1.

ASCII text files represent the lowest common denominator as they usually have the majority of control characters, such as those relating to formatting, removed. As such the text itself can usually be relied upon to be transferred error-free from one software application to another. However, any formatting that is needed will have to be reintroduced in the receiving application.

Text files also play a role in importing or exporting tabular data as found in databases and spreadsheets. A comma separated values (CSV) format is used where the individual records are separated by carriage returns and the fields in the individual records are separate by commas. Other field separators may be used to deal with more varied content, hence different formats may be encountered.

4.2.2 DIGITAL IMAGES

Digital images can be created by a variety of software products variously named drawing packages, business graphics, desktop publishing, computer-aided design (CAD) and scanning software, for example. Due to the fact that these products have emerged over the years from various developers, different file formats exist to describe the structure of the digital data representation of the image as held on computer storage. More disturbingly, different implementations of the same format are often found. Knowledge of the file formats created and accepted by an imaging (or any other) product is an important factor in determining the ease with which it can be integrated with current and planned systems.

A file format comprises the data itself and a header section which typically includes the resolution, mode of compression and the image's dimensions which are required to ensure that the image can subsequently be recreated accurately.

Even if one format is acceptable for a particular application, it may not be suitable for another, and hence the need for conversion arises. For any pair of different image file formats, software may be available for effecting a direct conversion between the two.

If a large quantity of image data exists in the one format, and this is to be translated into a single target format, then these direct converters provide an effective and efficient solution. Where a variety of formats exist this method of conversion becomes cumbersome because of the need to utilize different direct converters for each unique combination of source and target formats. The alternative is to have a two-stage process where the source formats are first converted into a basic common format, edited (if necessary) and then output in the target format.

Digital images are either in raster (bitmapped) or vector form.

Raster Image

A raster image is made up of a grid of coloured pixels (dots) and is the type of image generated by scanners, fax modems and paint programs. The raster image of a bitonal document such as an engineering line drawing or a page of text is relatively simple in concept, as in visual terms it is formed of black dots arranged on a white background.

The commonly encountered format for raster images is TIFF (Tagged Image File Format) (ISO 12639 2004) which can deal with monochrome, grey scale, 8- and 24-bit colour. Bit-colour is the number of bits used to represent the colour of a single pixel in a bitmapped image. Thus for 8-bit colour each pixel is represented by one 8-bit byte and hence the maximum number of colours that can be displayed at any one time is 256 (2^8).

Although widely accepted as a *de facto* standard, variants of TIFF exist across different system vendors. Also, not every image editing software saves them with the same fidelity to the standards. Nevertheless the fact that it is ubiquitous makes it the first choice for many users as a transfer format and for commercial printing.

PNG (Portable Network Graphics) is a more recent bitmapped graphics file format endorsed by the World Wide Web Consortium and available as an international standard (ISO 15948 2004). PNG provides a range of new and advanced features including 48-bit colour and the ability to display at one resolution and print at another. It was developed to replace GIF (Graphics Interchange Format), although GIF is still widely used in web applications.

JPEG (Joint Photographic Experts Group) is a format principally intended for photographs and similar continuous tone images, and is covered by a series of standards (ISO 10918 1994). While it is extensively employed as an image format on the web, it is not best suited for print applications because during compression data is discarded and permanently lost. This is an example of lossy compression; that is, data is lost as a result of the compression process. In contrast, TIFF and PNG are lossless formats and do not suffer from the same degradation, hence their use by commercial printers.

Vector Images

Vector-based images, which form the basis of computer-aided design (CAD), are created using software which relies on mathematical representations of shapes such as curves and lines. The image is effectively created by drawing. The format is quite different from that for raster images and hence it is difficult to work on both formats in an integrated fashion without some form of conversion.

Storage sizes for vector images may be less than their raster equivalent, but as the information content, and hence complexity, of the drawing increases, the greater compactness of the compressed raster image becomes apparent.

A long-standing platform-neutral standard for vector data is IGES (Initial Graphics Exchange Specification) which caters for exchanging three-dimensional images. STEP (The Standard for the Exchange of Product Model Data) is a later initiative (ISO 10303 1994) and comprises several hundred parts which are regularly revised or added to. For two-dimensional images DWG, a proprietary format for the AUTOCAD software, is widely adopted as a de facto standard.

An international standard (ISO 8632 1999) for storing and exchanging two-dimensional graphical (vector) data is CGM (Computer Graphics Metafile). As it is not best-suited for web applications a variant WebGM has been specified (W3C 2011).

4.2.3 PAGE DESCRIPTION LANGUAGE

PostScript is a page description language from Adobe Systems that is used extensively across microcomputers, workstations, minis and mainframes. It is the *de facto* standard in commercial typesetting and printing houses. It comprises PostScript commands as language statements in ASCII text that is translated into the printer's machine language by a PostScript interpreter built into the printer. Fonts are scaled to size by the interpreter, thus eliminating the need to store a variety of font sizes on disk.

Encapsulated PostScript (EPS) is a file format for transferring a graphic image between applications, for example for importing into a page layout program. EPS files are larger than most other graphics file formats, but are readily compressed to around a quarter of their size as they are text files.

An international standard (ISO 10180 1995) for a Standard Page Description Language (SPDL) is based on work largely undertaken by Adobe and Xerox. It covers the interchange of documents or parts of documents in formatted, non-revisable final form ready for printing. It does not provide information about the logical structure of the document.

A summary of the main types of image file format is provided in Figure 4.6.

4.3 Document Viewers

One of the main problems facing recipients and users of computer-generated information is the ability to view and read information generated using application software which the recipient does not possess.

Despite the fact that Microsoft software is to be found on most desktop PCs, it can be difficult if not impossible to ensure that a document that has been created on one type of platform (such as PC, Apple or Linux) using one type of application software will be viewable and appear exactly the same when received by someone using a different platform and lacking the same application software. When it comes to reading information stored in spreadsheet, database or graphic formats, and the user only has word-processing applications, the problem is compounded further.

File	Name	Description	Advantages	Disadvantages
EPS	Encapsulated PostScript	Vector file. PostScript in a container	Importable and exportable from wide variety of programs	File format has evolved so is non standard; what is printed may not be the same as on screen
GIF	Graphics Interchange Format	Raster file. Lossless compression	Suitable for sharp-edged line art, such as logos, with a limited number of colours and small animations and low-resolution film clips	Rarely a good choice for print output. Single image format, not best for scanning multipage documents
JPEG	Joint Photographic Expert Group	Raster file. Lossy compression.	For web and digital camera storage and stock photos. Large number of colours (typically 24-bit/16 million colours) allows for photographic images. Compression allows for reduced file sizes	Many variants. JPEG compression always loses quality
PDF	Portable Document format	Captures and freezes appearance of document	Scalable without loss of information. More stable than PostScript	Not editable (but that's the reason it was created!)
PNG	Portable Networks Graphics	Raster file. Lossless compression	Improved file compression and better colour rendition than GIF. More features than GIF or JPEG	Single image format, not best for scanning multipage documents
PS	PostScript	Vector file	Standard format for prepress printing	Not all printers can print from this file
PSD	Photoshop Document	Used to create and edit images in Adobe Photoshop	De facto standard. Supports layers and many image types	Proprietary format. Not all features supported by other programs. Not suited to web browsing
RAW	RAW	Non-standard graphics file formats saved with no lossy compression	Format which captures exactly what a camera takes	A variety of camera-specific RAW formats exist
SVG	Scalable Vector Graphics	Vector file. XML derivative. Recommendation of the W3C	Being XML they can be edited and dynamically modified while matching open source vision	Broad recommendation. Not all graphic editors can read it
TIFF	Tagged Image File Format	Raster file. Prepress format for photos. Lossless compression	Best format for high level PostScript printing of photos. Can hold almost any resolution and colour scheme	Many variants. Cannot hold vector data. Large files sometimes slow to print

Figure 4.6   Image file formats

Software products usually have in-built conversion utilities, and third party software is also available to address this specific problem. However, 100 per cent conversion accuracy cannot necessarily be assured, hence the popularity of viewing software. Two main categories of viewers are:

- file format recognition viewers
- viewers for documents converted into a single format.

The former approach has the advantage that, given the viewing software, the user can quickly display information which has been created with other application software even though they do not possess the original application. The drawback is that the producer of the viewer has usually to re-program the software to deal with any new applications or upgrades to existing applications. Depending on the particular viewing software, features such as text searching, preservation of display formats and application launching are available.

Conversion to a single format is used by Adobe for its Acrobat product and is aimed at a somewhat different market, with a particular focus on document distribution and collaboration. The Adobe Acrobat family of software provides facilities for converting most computer-generated documents and file formats to a Portable Document Format (PDF) in which format the document retains all the look and feel of the original. Third party products are available to create PDF from existing documents.

Adobe provides a royalty-free reader (also available for downloading from the World Wide Web) which allows recipients of PDF documents to view and undertake searching of the text. Annotations and hyperlinks can be added to PDF documents which are fully compatible for use on the web. Paper documents can be scanned and converted to a PDF file using appropriate software, thereby providing means to integrate paper and existing electronic documents. PDF is the subject of a number of ISO standards including one as a portable format (ISO 32000 2008) and another (PDF/A) as a long-term preservation format (ISO 19005 2005).

4.4 Scanning for Image Capture

Electronic imaging involves the use of a scanner to convert the image of human-readable documents, be they on paper or microfilm, into a binary digital representation suitable for computerized storage, retrieval and transmission. Unlike a microfilm image, an electronic image is not human-readable, but has to be processed for output to a display or hard-copy device.

Many business documents are still in paper form, and some will not have readily accessible electronic equivalents, if they exist at all. Electronic imaging is a key technology which has contributed to the success of integrated document management projects that require the incorporation of existing or newly-received paper documents.

In a well-designed scanning application the desired functionality for scanning, coding and filing a document image should be built into the system. The application, supported by suitable scanning software, does the scan and processes the document, automatically undertaking such tasks as removing blank pages, converting text to machine readable form using optical character recognition and producing PDF/A file format for the long-term archiving of electronic documents. The system should also support some form of automatic import of individual files or groups of files as folders by using barcodes or similar coding devices on the documents and then naming the output files according to the barcodes, thereby avoiding manual intervention and costs.

Two main, but overlapping, markets exist for scanners. The first, and longer established, is that relating to publishing where scanners, in conjunction with image editing software, are used to capture and, as necessary, edit such features as line art work, photographs and text. These scanners range from relatively inexpensive hand-held units affordable for home use and capable of capturing images in black and white or colour, to sophisticated flat-bed colour units aimed more at the commercial printer.

The second market relates to document imaging. Here, the emphasis is on the information content of the material that is imaged, rather than its aesthetic appearance. Hence requirements will arise for such facilities as full text indexing, long-term high-capacity storage, backlog conversion and high bandwidth communication networks.

The capture stage is the most critical, as what can be achieved during any subsequent processing depends on the quality and type of image information initially secured. While this statement can be applied to micrographics applications, electronic imaging is a more complex process and differs from microfilming in that scanning time (as opposed to microfilm exposure time) is affected by such factors as resolution and the presence of continuous tone or colour in the documents. This demands that greater attention be taken during the scanning stage of the make-up of the document. This attention is needed, otherwise optimum use may not be made of the document's information in a computerized environment.

Documents can be rich in terms of the variety of information objects they contain. This richness can include, for example, text in various typefaces and sizes, line drawings, graphics, spreadsheets, tables, photographs and form work, some or all of which may be in colour rather than black-and-white. For the purposes of the scanning process images can be categorized under the headings:

- bitonal images – these require only two levels of intensity, as in line art work such as black and white engineering drawings, or pages of typed alphanumeric text
- continuous tone images – these exhibit indivisible transitions from dark to light (shades of grey) as in a black-and-white photograph
- colour images – these incorporate the three primary colours and shades of grey to register brightness. A colour photograph is such an image.

The output format for the resulting image is usually the Tagged Image File Format (TIFF).

4.4.1 SCANNER CONTROL SOFTWARE

There are two main scanner control software products – TWAIN and ISIS.

TWAIN is a de facto interface standard that lets applications communicate with scanner software to scan and acquire bitmap images. It was originally defined by a working group of scanner manufacturers and software publishers including Aldus, Caere, Eastman Kodak, Hewlett-Packard and Logitech, and was principally aimed at addressing the needs of desktop publishing. It is now managed by a not-for-profit organization, The TWAIN Working Group.

ISIS (Image and Scanner Interface Standard) was developed by Pixel Translations and is now owned by EMC. It was aimed principally at high-volume document image capture and processing systems.

Since ISIS is under the control of one organization and is the subject of a formal standard, EMC argue that they can offer better support than those using TWAIN (EMC 2011). To counter this the TWAIN organization introduced self-certification to improve the quality of TWAIN data sources and to provide more consistent integration for the application software providers (TWAIN 2009).

4.4.2 RESOLUTION IN ELECTRONIC IMAGING

Scanner resolution is normally expressed in terms of linear dots (that is, pixels) per inch (dpi). The number of pixels in a line and the number of lines used to create the bitmap indicate the resolution employed. The resolution chosen must be at least equal to that required for any subsequent processing and output. However, opting for too high a resolution may increase the size of the digitized documents to a level where storage space demands, or data transfer speeds over networks, or both, become unacceptable. It also increases scanning time.

The resolution chosen depends on the particular application (Figure 4.7). For bitonal images, the binary digital signals (bits) produced from scanning have only to represent black (bit set to 1) or white (bit set to 0), and not shades of grey, to create the required bitmap. Thus 1 bit per pixel is sufficient information to record bitonal images.

		Scanning resolution (dpi)					
		200	300	400	800	1200	2400
Bits per Pixel	36		Commercial colour					
	24		DTP colour					
	12		Commercial continuous tone					
	8	DTP continuous tone						
	1	Line art			DTP line art		Commercial line art	

Figure 4.7   Typical scanning resolutions for different applications

Photographs and specialized images such as X-rays achieve their rich, visual effect by the continuous range of tones they exhibit. The scanning process must ensure that any necessary subtleties are not lost. It is, in fact, unnecessary to fully capture and process the huge amount of data which this subtlety represents. For visual interpretation, 8 bits per pixel, which provide 256 levels of grey, is perfectly adequate for most applications. Use of grey scale does, however, increase the storage requirements. Examples of file sizes are provided in Figure 4.8; the actual sizes will depend on the amount of information contained on each item being scanned.

DOCUMENT compression	RASTER (MB)		
	200dpi	300dpi	400dpi
A0 Drawing bitonal uncompressed	7.74	17.43	31.00
A0 Drawing bitonal (25:1)	0.31	0.70	1.24
A4 bitonal uncompressed	0.48	1.09	1.93
A4 bitonal (10:1)	0.05	0.11	0.19
A4 256 grey scale 8bits per pixel uncompressed	3.87	8.70	15.47
A4 colour 32bits per pixel uncompressed	15.47	34.80	61.87

Figure 4.8   Typical file sizes

A scanning resolution of 200dpi is typically adopted for line art work such as engineering drawings. For most office applications 300dpi range is acceptable as it is well matched to the 300dpi output of laser printers. Scanning at 400dpi is usually only necessary where smaller typefaces (typically 10 point or less) are encountered so that they will be legible on the image and can be subjected to optical character recognition (OCR).

4.4.3 CONTRAST IN ELECTRONIC IMAGING

Most scanners capture information in a multi-bit per pixel, grey scale format, and this information would be retained for photographic or colour applications. However, to cater for line art, or to enable the grey scales of photographic material to be simulated on bitonal laser printers, the grey scale data must be processed to produce single bit per pixel images. This is effected by thresholding and dithering respectively.

The text or lines on a bitonal original may not be uniform in intensity. Hence a threshold, or contrast level, must be set to distinguish between black and white. This distinction can be made automatically by a scanner, based on such factors as the average density of the document's background and data from scanning the region surrounding individual pixels. Dynamic thresholding, available in some units, automatically adjusts the threshold level in relation to the quality of the document being scanned.

Dithering in scanning technology is akin to half-tone photographic reproduction in newspaper printing, in that both use accumulations of solid printed dots to give the overall illusion of shades of grey. In dithering, the pixels or printer dots are arranged in groups, or half-tone dots. The printer dots making up each half-tone dot are an appropriate mix of black or white to simulate the shade for that point on the original. Thus to cater for 256 grey scale levels, each half-tone dot comprises 16×16 (256) printer dots (pixels).

There is, however, a trade-off to be made between resolution and grey scale. For output on a 300dpi laser printer, the 16×16 printer dot would produce an effective half-tone dot pitch of 18.75 lines per inch (300/16), and hence an unacceptably granular image.

Depending on the scanner design, thresholding and dithering can be undertaken concurrently, if necessary on appropriate areas of the same page so that bitonal areas are subjected to thresholding and photographic areas are dithered.

4.4.4 DOCUMENT SCANNING

Optical scanners provide the means to capture the images of paper or microfilm documents. Such units are available in hand-held, sheet-fed and rotary designs and are operated in conjunction with a computer or microprocessor unit which processes the digitized product and prepares it for storage on suitable media.

Scanners for electronic document imaging generally need to cater for higher-volume throughputs and a greater range of document sizes and formats than are met in desktop publishing. In this context hand-held scanners are not suitable. Nevertheless, relatively inexpensive A4 flatbed monochrome scanners primarily intended for DTP are available for small-scale, low-volume electronic document imaging applications. Multifunction units that can scan, fax, photocopy and print are widely available for home and office use.

In general terms, a scanner incorporates a light source which illuminates the document page. Black areas on the page absorb most of the light, while white areas reflect it. For grey areas, light is reflected in proportion to shades of grey. During line-by-line scanning of the page, the light reflected from the document is detected by a charged coupled device (CCD) comprising a single, linear arrangement of individual photo-sensitive cells. The light falling on each cell during a line scan is converted into an electrical charge whose magnitude corresponds to the intensity of the light received. These analogue charges are then converted into digital signals for further processing. The image of the document page has thereby been captured as a two-dimensional grid of individual picture elements ('pixels') or raster image; a process termed 'bitmapping'.

For colour scanning, the light beam can be split into its red, green and blue (RGB) components which are each captured along with their associated grey scales by individual CCD arrays. The RGB elements may subsequently be converted into cyan, magenta, yellow and black (CMYB), a format usually employed for colour reproduction.

The throughput speed attained using a particular scanner depends on the scanning resolution which is chosen and whether colour scanning is adopted when coloured documents are encountered. Scanning at higher resolutions and for colour require more information to be captured in digital form.

Throughput speeds quoted for different scanners may be misleading in that they are not necessarily directly comparable from one model to another due to key factors being included in some instances but ignored in others. For example, scanning speeds are often based purely on the speed of transport of documents through a sheet feeder mechanism. However, in live systems the actual throughput speed must take the whole scanning process into consideration. Thus the speed with which documents can be processed includes not only other inescapable time elements associated with each scan, such as those relating to indexing, image quality checking and image compression but also ad-hoc occurrences such as removing that unexpected paper clip or re-scanning necessitated by document feeder jams or failures to meet quality control targets.

The mechanics of achieving relative movement between the document and the scanning light depend on the design of the scanner, each being suited to particular applications. Some scanners are produced by suppliers with experience of micrographics, hence designs often draw on those used for flat-bed or rotary cameras, although a precise distinction is not always possible as regards scanners. Generally scanners can be divided into flat-bed or sheet-fed designs.

In flat-bed units, documents are handled as if being used with a photocopier in that the documents are placed individually and usually face-downwards on a glass surface from beneath which they are illuminated. Relatively low throughput rates are achievable as they are not simply dependent on the speed of scanning, but also on the time taken to manually remove a scanned document and replace it with its successor.

Depending on the particular scanner model, automatic sheet feeding devices may be fitted to enable stacks of documents to be fed to, and ejected from the scanning surface with minimum operator intervention. This design resembles in many ways that found in facsimile equipment on whose technology scanners are based. As throughput speeds increase there is always the danger of misfeeds leading to the capture of a skewed image. This can reduce the accuracy or render impossible the use of OCR.

As with any mechanical paper-handling system, its smooth and continuous operation may be disrupted, for example by encountering staples, tears or creases. It is therefore important that documents are checked prior to scanning to take the necessary remedial action. Many of the defects that adversely affect mechanical handling also influence the quality and accuracy of the captured image as compared with the original, and hence their rectification is equally important when using flat-bed scanners.

Small hand-held scanners have become popular for incorporating portions of text or graphics from an existing document into one which is being word-processed. The scanners may be in pen form for moving across single lines of text or of greater width covering several lines. Both types will require several passes to be made to capture all the text. The fact that relative movement between page and scanner is achieved by hand can lead to unevenness in image capture and complications when using OCR software or joining the individual image segments. Nevertheless, compact handheld scanners are available which not only undertake OCR, but have in-built language software to provide 'instant' translation between different foreign languages.

4.4.5 MICROFILM SCANNING

Micrographics is the term generally applied to cover the creation and use of miniaturized, human-readable images of original documents which are held on film material. With its origins in photographic technology, microfilm is a long-established, well-proven medium for long-term storage of inactive records. However, the market for microfilm has declined in the last two decades as there is the desire to have information in electronic form along with all other organizational records.

The common storage formats for microfilmed images are:

* aperture cards (holding a single 35mm film frame)
* microfiche (sheets of film with images recorded in a grid pattern)
* microfilm jackets (rectangular flexible carriers with channels into which pieces of imaged microfilm are slid)
* roll film – 16mm.

The conversion of microfilm images to a digital format is complicated by the wide range of microfilm formats. Early scanners were limited to handling specific formats. Later designs were available with exchangeable or fitted attachments to cater for the full range of formats.

The condition of the microfilm will greatly influence the quality of the digital output. There is always the option to retain the microfilm versions as archives after their digitization.

4.5 Data Capture

Technologies for automatic identification and data capture have been described as 'a diverse family of technologies that share the common purpose of *identifying, tracking, recording, storing and communicating* essential business, personal, or product data' (AIM 2011).

The main types of technology are dealt with later. First capturing of information from websites is considered.

4.5.1 WEBSITE SNAPSHOTS

Given the relative ease with which a website can be created, updated and maintained its information content and structure may often be subject to change. If appropriate procedures are in place, the information intended for the site can be sourced from a system that monitors and controls information integrity, for example through document version control and logs for recording replication to the Internet server. This will not be possible for blogs and other immediate means of communication via the web. In this instance an organization may wish to capture information from its own websites as snapshots for which a range of software is now available. The reasons for undertaking this might include:

- to have a record before and after the site was updated
- to have a record of the site after new information has been added
- for quality control purposes
- to have evidence of what information was made available, when and in what format
- to have a historical record
- to compare what was available on its Internet site as compared with that on its intranet and/or extranet sites
- for submission to a web archive.

As regards the archiving of web sites, The National Archives is preserving digital government information by regularly archiving UK central government websites (http://www.nationalarchives.gov.uk/webarchive/). Also, the UK Web Archive (http://www.webarchive.org.uk/ukwa/) provided by the British Library is collecting website snapshots based on nominations from interested parties and following agreement of the site owners. The Legal Deposit Libraries Act 2003 in the UK was designed to facilitate digital archiving of digital content in the same way that printed works are deposited. However, the necessary regulation has, at the time of writing, yet to come into effect.

4.5.2 AUTOMATIC IDENTIFICATION AND DATA CAPTURE

Automatic Identification and Data Capture (AIDC) typically involves identifying an item by a reading device and feeding the captured data into some form of computer for subsequent use. The data may comprise anything from a simple identification code to more comprehensive information about the item. The reading devices typically decode as well as capture the data, which is then transmitted to the computer via a cable or radio transmission. The reading units may be hand-held or fixed, and the total system, both reader and computer, can be compact enough to be fully portable.

Several Auto ID technologies are available, and the choice depends on the intended application. The systems can be categorized by their technology base – namely, visual, voice, magnetic, optical and electronic as summarized in Figure 4.9 and described in more detail below.

A trade body concerned with AIDC is The Association for Automatic Identification and Mobility (AIM) (http://www.aimglobal.org/).

Useful fact sheets for many of the AIDC technologies are provided by the University of Glamorgan (AIDC 2011).

Bar Codes

Bar coding is a two-step technology as it first requires a code to be generated and printed out for subsequent reading and hence conversion into machine readable form.

Bar codes are familiar patterns on supermarket goods, but have a wider range of applications in areas such as stock control, version control for drawings and manuals, library lending and archive storage of company records as part of a records retention programme. Basic reference and indexing details of documents can be encoded and used to speed up index capture during document imaging and help manage the flow of batches of work. These bar codes are usually of linear design comprising rows of black and white bars of different thicknesses.

A range of international linear bar code standards exists and hence code generation software and bar code readers (both fixed and mobile) must be properly matched. The main standards are GTIN (Global Trade Item Number) and GS1 DataBar. GTIN comprises a range of data structures that employ 14 digits and can be encoded into various types of data carriers. Currently, GTIN is used exclusively within bar codes, but it could also be used in other data carriers such as radio frequency identification detectors. GS1 DataBar comprises two bar codes, one bar code placed above another (ISO 24724 2011). It can store more information than is possible with GTIN.

Two dimensional bar codes are a more recent development and offer faster data access and greater data storage capacity for the same space as compared with linear bar codes. There are two main variants. One holds information in both the vertical and horizontal planes, the other, PDF417, consists of a number of what are effectively small linear bar code rows. PDF417 is the subject of an international standard (ISO 15438 2006). Note that PDF417 does not relate in any way to Adobe's PDF which is a totally different technology.

TECHNOLOGY BASE	EXAMPLES	DESCRIPTION	EXAMPLE APPLICATIONS	ADVANTAGES	DISADVANTAGES
	Bar Codes	Printed patterns of parallel dark and light lines of varying width used to encode data based on largely standardized 'symbologies'. Codes read by contact or non-contact hand-held or fixed readers.	Goods receipt. Stock control. Document tracking. Document indexing. Goods despatch.	Well-established. Standardized symbologies for different applications. Low cost entry level.	Read-only capability. Reading accuracy may be affected by dirt, damage etc.
VISUAL	Optical Character Recognition (OCR)	Recognition of printed, handwritten (or digital images of) alpha-numeric characters to convert them to computer-readable form, e.g. for word-processing. Data capture often based on standardized fonts; text input (typically pages of text) requires ability to recognize virtually any font. Hand-held or fixed readers.	Desk-top publishing. Materials handling. Shelf labelling. Forms processing.	No coding needed. Readable by humans. Letters take up less space than equivalent bar code.	Read-only capability. Read accuracy more affected by dirt, damage etc than are bar codes. Accurate handwriting recognition depends on uniformity & consistency of script.
	Machine Vision	Shapes, features and positions of objects are recognized and any variations detected using a camera, image digitizer and processing equipment, often incorporating recognition algorithms.	Fault detection. Production line monitoring. Security systems. High-speed inspection.	May read bar codes & printed characters. Operable in 1 or 2 dimensions. Can initiate auto-rectification action.	Expensive.
	Touch Screens	Action initiated by directing a finger or a stylus onto a screen to issue a command, make a selection or respond to a question displayed there.	Ordering goods. PC monitors. Tablets. Process control.	Easy-to-use human-computer interface. Avoids keyboard use in dirty conditions.	Bespoke designs. Use of finger offers less precision than stylus.
VOICE	Speech Recognition	Recognition of the spoken word and conversion into computer-readable and processable form. May involve radio frequency or other communication links to central point.	Verification for access control. Placing orders. Car phone dialling. Help for disabled.	Hands-free operation. Supplements other ID methods. Easily used.	Systems may be speaker and/or vocabulary-dependent, and require "training".

Figure 4.9 Automatic identification and data capture technologies

Category	Technology	Description	Applications	Features	Limitations
MAGNETIC	Magnetic Stripe	Information encoded on stripe of magnetic material bonded to plastic, card stock or paper substrate depending on the durability required. Recording is effected by hard contact with the recording heads. Low- and high-energy media available depending on required immunity to accidental erasure.	Credit cards. Product tracking. Car park tickets. Identity cards. Transport tickets.	Well-tried system. Medium can be handled directly. Reasonably durable medium. Read/write capability. Established encoding standards.	Requires insertion into and intimate contact with reader unit. Fraudulent copying easy.
	Magnetic Ink Character Recognition (MICR)	Specially shaped characters are printed with magnetic ink which can be recognized by a magnetic reader.	Cheque printing. Financial documents.	Well-proven. Established character font standards.	Specialized equipment for printing and reading.
OPTICAL	Optical Cards	Optical storage media coated as strip on credit card size substrate. Information encoded in machine-redable form by low-power laser, and read using a specialized reader.	Maintenance logs. Medical records. ID systems. High security ID cards. Finance transactions. Digital images.	Offers very high-capacity storage in compact form.	Not re-writable.
	Touch-Memory	Button-like data storage device operated by physical contact with reader unit. Data transfer and communication possible to computers for further processing.	Personnel security. Asset tracking and management. Shipping manifests. Quality control.	Good storage capacity in compact form. Readily protected for harsh, dirty environments. Read only & read/write versions available.	Lacking standards. Limited number of established suppliers.
	Smart Cards	Credit-card size format incorporating solid-state memory chips, integrated circuitry and, at the higher end of the range, microprocessors.	Credit cards. Electronic cash. Security systems. Wireless communication. Loyalty systems. Banking. Satellite TV. Government identification.	Good storage capacity in well-accepted format. Improved security. On-board processing. Read and read/write versions.	Relatively expensive as compared with most other card formats.
ELECTRONIC	Radio frequency (RF) Tags	A tag holds the data. A separate reading unit reads the tag data. Tags available with or without batteries depending on the storage and read/write requirements.	Drill pipe tagging. File tracking. Records management. Access control. Vehicle access. Asset tracking. Freight handling. Vehicle identification. Vehicle toll booths.	Non-contact, remote sensing. Does not need 'line-of-sight' from tag to reader. Withstands harsh, environments. Suits moving, mobile objects or those 'in a crowd'. Read and read/write versions.	Technology well established. Tagging standards lacking (but being developed in vertical markets). RF entails licensing considerations. Health and safety concerns re. electromagnetic radiation. [Not sure there are any real H&S concerns re. RFID out there because of low power used.]

Figure 4.9 *Concluded*

Online services are available for generating bar codes, for example:

- online bar code generator is available at http://barcode.tec-it.com/
- a PDF417 generator is available at http://www.racoindustries.com/barcodegenerator/2d/pdf417.aspx

Optical and Intelligent Character Recognition

Optical character recognition (OCR) is a means to convert printed or bit-image representations of documents into editable form for a computer.

The earliest technology used matrix matching by comparing the shape of a scanned alphanumeric character with a database of letter shapes. Provided the shapes were in the database and a single font was used throughout the document, recognition could usually be guaranteed. Multiple font documents, however, could not reliably be converted.

Feature extraction followed and involved analysing how a letter was formed rather than its complete shape. The effectiveness of this approach was improved by 'noise elimination' whereby the software concentrated on the reliable fragments of a character and ignored extraneous marks or blemishes.

The later incarnations of OCR have true learning ability. Usually referred to as intelligent character recognition (ICR) products, they enable a user to enter via the keyboard the identity of characters or punctuation marks which the ICR software has failed to recognize. At subsequent encounters with the same symbol, the ICR software generates the appropriate ASCII code without the need for further human intervention. ICR products can be operated selectively in either standard or learning modes. Additional facilities may include spelling dictionaries, analysis of word position to increase the accuracy of the recognition and ability to retain the page layout including columns and graphics around the 'optically recognized' text.

Reliable recognition of hand-written documents cannot be guaranteed, although some success has been achieved with applications such as form-filling where the character set or vocabulary are limited and greater care is taken to ensure uniformity when entering the characters. Despite these difficulties, commercial deployment of recognition technology based on neural network modelling is used, for example to process cheques involving the recognition of dot-matrix printed and hand-written information.

Clearly defined text printed on paper can usually be reliably recognized provided the point size of the characters is not too small. Where an electronic raster image, such as a received fax, is subjected to OCR, the resolution at which the source document was scanned can be a major factor in determining the success or otherwise of the conversion. Increasingly, technology such as neural-network based recognition engines are being applied to improve the accuracy of converting bitmap images into editable text.

For normal size text (10 point or above), scanning resolutions down to 200dpi may be adequate. For smaller points sizes, however, low resolutions will not provide the necessary precision, hence scanning at 400dpi will be more reliable.

OCR technology can be used to facilitate speedier indexing of documents. Such indexing may involve applying OCR to the complete text, or to particular areas of the document where indexing information will be found. Forms or summary pages of reports are typical examples of the latter case. Data input by capturing information using specialized form-work software can operate at 100,000 keystrokes per hour for example.

This compares with the average data entry operator speed of just over 11,000 keystrokes per hour.

Even with the best endeavours an OCR system is very unlikely to operate at 100 per cent recognition across what will usually be variable font sizes and quality of original. This may not be important if the aim is to extract indexing words from the free text of a report, or correspondence. The fact that most words for the index will have been recognized accurately will usually still allow the document to be retrieved even if a certain number are not correctly translated.

Where maximum recognition accuracy is vital, the complete OCR system should be optimized for the types of document that are to handled. For example, if OCR is to be undertaken on form work, then it can be beneficial to employ form removal software first. This removes the form structure leaving a smaller data file whose textual information can therefore be more rapidly dealt with by the OCR software. The information is stored and overlaid on a single copy of the form structure at display time, for example.

OCR has now moved beyond desktop PC and network server applications to where it is now possible to undertake OCR online over the Internet, sometimes free of charge.

Machine Vision

Machine Vision is a broad concept (http://en.wikipedia.org/wiki/Machine_vision) rather than a specific technology. It has been described as being 'concerned with the engineering of integrated mechanical-optical-electronic-software systems for examining natural object and materials, human artefacts and manufacturing processes, in order to detect defects and improve quality, operating efficiency and the safety of both products and processes. It is also used to monitor and control machines used in manufacturing.' (Graves and Batchelor 2003).

While the technology may not be directly applicable to mainstream document and records management, the output from the visioning will be important records relating to productive activity. As such they should be managed and controlled according to sound data management and records retention principles.

Touch Screens

Touch screens offer immediacy with which actions can be initiated. This, coupled with developments in the technology (http://en.wikipedia.org/wiki/Touchscreen), have contributed to the attractiveness of products such as tablet computers and advanced mobile phones which have incorporated these advances. There are three basic systems that respond to touch:

- resistive
- capacitive
- surface acoustic wave.

The resistive system consists of a normal glass panel that is covered with two conductive layers which meet to record the touch, hence they can be operated with a stylus as well as a finger.

In the capacitive system, a layer that stores electrical charge is placed on the glass panel of the device and is distorted when touched. Capacitive screens require physical contact with human skin and usually cannot respond if gloves or other insulating material intervenes. This restricts their usability.

In the surface acoustic wave system transducers generate over the screen an ultrasonic wave which is disturbed by touch. Screens using this technology are more easily damaged by contaminants.

Speech Recognition

Traditional speech recognition converts the spoken word to text. As such it has three main uses:

- command and control, such as navigation of graphical user interfaces
- data entry, such as physicians and nurses entering data into forms while examining patients
- dictation, such as for creation of free-form or structured documents.

Speech recognition systems generally have three components:

- vocabulary or dictionary (which is often customizable to include specialist and additional words)
- language model (to identify spoken words from the context)
- speaker model (which is trained to the individual speaker).

Early systems used discrete-word input where users pause between words. Today, the move is towards continuous-speech recognition (that it, chunks of meaning) rather than individual words. All systems have large vocabularies and complex language components for free-form dictation. For structured report generation the language module will be simpler.

Extraneous noises can distort communication, and different dialects can confuse the speech recognition device. Some applications have a recognition accuracy approaching 100 per cent, but such a success rate is generally only achieved where the vocabulary employed is limited so that the recognition circuitry can be tuned accordingly. This approach is exemplified by interactive voice response systems as used to access call centres over the telephone.

There is also the reverse application where the recorded text is converted into synthesized speech. This can be used to read faxes and emails through a voice messaging service or words displayed by an e-reader device. The technology is also a valuable facility for visually impaired users.

An interesting variation on traditional voice dictation to tape is the use of open network dictation. Here dictation is stored on a network where it can be managed as part of a normal workflow, then retrieved and transcribed by typists no matter where they happen to be.

Since April 2005 Semantic Interpretation for Speech Recognition (SISR) has been a World Wide Web Consortium recommendation (http://en.wikipedia.org/wiki/Semantic_Interpretation_for_Speech_Recognition) and has given a spur to research in such areas as extracting or processing the contents and semantics of data in speech (Deng et al., 2010). For example, if an order for goods is placed over the phone expressed in whatever way the customer chooses, it should be possible for the key semantic details such as product name, delivery address and quantity to be automatically and correctly extracted and used to initiate the process to satisfy the request.

In addition to dealing with the semantics of language there is research into identifying individual speakers in a meeting, that is, who spoke when (Friedland and Van Leeuwen 2010). Progress on this is complicated by the difficulty of dealing with overlapping speech, such as two or more speakers speaking at the same time.

Speech recognition will become an integral part of commercial office software with the wider availability of systems based on continuous-speech input, and the benefits that will come from semantic technology to reduce influence of extraneous noise and create more flexible, speaker-independent models. Incorporating the full benefits from research in semantic computing will take somewhat longer.

Magnetic Stripe

The ubiquitous magnetic stripe includes very fine iron-based particles that are magnetized to store the required information which is read when the item on which the strip is placed is passed through a reader. If the stripe is to perform reliably and consistently conformance to established standards is vital. Thus for financial applications there is a standard for identification cards used for international exchange (ISO 7813 2006).

Magnetic Ink Character Recognition

MICR technology uses magnetically charged ink to print numbers and special characters on the bottom of cheques or other financial documents. These are designed to be read by high speed automatic readers but have the advantage over other auto-identification techniques of being human-readable. The print specification is the subject of an international standard (ISO 1004 1995).

Optical Cards

Optical memory is similar in concept to that used for recording music on CDs. It uses write once read many (WORM) media and is generally of a credit card physical format. It offers a storage capacity of up to around 6 MB of data which gives the ability to hold graphical images. The technology is covered by international standards (ISO 11693 2005, ISO 11694 2005). Optical security media can be combined with other machine-readable technologies such as bar codes, optical character recognition, contact chips, RFID tags and magnetic stripes.

Touch Memory

This information storage device is communicated with by touching it using a reading tool. It is available in different guises with the basic design being a data storage or computer chip enclosed in a small metal container, typically the size of a small coin. Data can be read from or written to the device which can be attached to movable or static objects.

A portable reader enables individuals to gain access to a facility or device to which the device is attached. It can be designed for a variety of applications including data logging, access security and e-cash for storing small amounts of money.

Smart Cards

Smart card is a generic title for credit card size devices incorporating programmable computer circuitry and having defined physical characteristics (ISO 7816 2011). There are two broad categories of circuitry (http://www.smart-card.com/2010/07/20/smart-card-wiki/), memory cards having non-volatile memory storage components, and microprocessor cards with volatile memory and microprocessor components. Originally requiring physical contact with a reading device, more recent designs operate without such contact and are used, for example, to make small e-cash payments. As compared with magnetic stripe, for example, smart cards offer improved security, this being further enhanced by embedded holograms.

Radio Frequency Identification

Radio frequency identification (RFID) technology is a well established AIDC method. It comprises a transponder in the form of a small tag to hold the data. This is attached to or embedded in an object, for example a physical paper file or oil rig valve. A separate reader unit with associated antenna activates the transponder to read the data it holds. Low frequency, medium frequency and high-frequency systems exist. Read and read-write versions are available. Versions are available to write data back to the tags which may be 'passive' (lack internal power), 'active' (battery powered) or 'semi-passive' (battery for memory storage).

It is proving to be a strong competitor to bar coding as it offers greater flexibility and functionality in such areas as records management for case file tracking, access security and records inventory. With this technology it is possible to read the contents of a file cabinet without opening the cabinet's doors, if each file has its own tag. Also, detectors fitted in doorways can track the movements of a tagged file throughout a building.

To cater for particular needs, it is possible to combine AIDC technologies such as RF and touch memory on a card or passive RF, magnetic stripe and optionally bar codes and digital imaging on a single card.

The proliferation of wireless communications devices is crowding the existing radio spectrum. Hence discussions in Europe may lead to RFID and similar devices having exclusive access to parts of the ultra-high frequency (UHF) bands.

4.5.3 E-COMMERCE TRANSACTIONS

These types of transactions are ones that are undertaken between organizations in the course of conducting business. Many involve the use of Electronic Data Interchange (EDI) which, along with email is the major messaging service.

Developed in the late 1970s, EDI provides savings for business transactions by transmitting orders, invoices and payments electronically. Third parties provide the necessary network services. The service is 'hub' driven in that dominant companies choose a network supplier and other members of the industry (suppliers and dealers) have to comply and use the same EDI services and rules (or protocols) for transmitting and receiving data. Unlike email messages which are free format, EDI message formats are defined and standardized. The major EDI standard is EANCOM, a GS1 EDI standard (http://www.gs1.org/ecom/eancom) based on UN/EDIFACT (United Nations Electronic Data Interchange for Administration, Commerce and Transport), which comprises a set of internationally-agreed standards, directories and guidelines for the electronic interchange of data. Standards are also formulated by individual industry groups (for example, SWIFT for banking and ODETTE for the automotive industry).

While EDI undoubtedly reduces the cost of commercial transactions as compared with paper-based system, an EDI system is costly to set up and operate. These costs can be prohibitive for small and medium-sized companies which are increasingly moving towards web-based approaches in the form of extranets. These are company-specific intranets which are extended via the Internet to a company's customers or suppliers.

The introduction of XML as a web standard is significant as it provides an alternative way to express messages for e-commerce which may be attractive to newcomers. However there are still arguments to be made for using EDI rather than XML as exemplified in Figure 4.10 (EDIDEV 2011).

Issues	XML	XML reality	Traditional EDI	EDI reality	Think about it!
Ecommerce Standard	• New technology • Internet based, easy to implement	• Many standards of multiple complex frameworks • Not as simple to implement	• Old, passé electronic standard	• Time tested and successfully works • Straight forward to implement	Why change it; it ain't broke?
Cost	• Cheap to implement and cheaper to deploy via the Internet	• Tools and developers still cost money • Consumers still pay for Internet connection • Bandwidth usage can be costly	• Traditionally expensive	• Cost of tools are getting cheaper e.g. EDIdEv Framework EDI • Can be implemented over the Internet • Less bandwidth	Why segregate when you can integrate?
Data Representation	• Intuitive, easy to read	• Verbose • Time consuming to implement • Storage requirements increase	• Cryptic	• Once understood, quick to implement • Storage requirements are minimal • Information can still be transported on floppy disk	Does the consumer really care? Does your developer really understand?
Companies pushing the technology	• New economy companies	• Consulting companies • High business risk	• Established companies (Fortune 500) and governments	• Status quo • Established global user base • Low business risk	Make a business decision not necessarily a technical one

Figure 4.10 EDI and XML compared

Source: Reproduced with permission of EDIdEv http://www.edidev.com/

4.6 File Naming Conventions

Every record saved should be given a concise and meaningful electronic filename. Naming records consistently and according to agreed conventions:

- avoids conflicts with applications accessing the files
- facilitates their subsequent retrieval.

The choice and format of the file name is governed by various factors including the intended use of the file, the operating system and the particular software and version used on the system. For example, file names need to conform to specific conventions if the file is to be displayed as a web page.

File names usually have a suffix which follows a full stop at the end of the name. This extension indicates the format for the file's contents and is applied by the file's creating program. No changes should be made to this extension other than through such options as 'save as' initiated by the software that created it.

Good practice that should be followed is provided as guidance in Figure 4.11 and is described further below; it relates primarily to documents. There may need to be exceptions, and any that are made need to be documented as part of the organization's document and records managements procedures.

Point	Topic
1	Keep file names short, but meaningful
2	Avoid special characters
3	Avoid gaps (white spaces) in file name
4	Use two-digit numbers, i.e. 01-99, unless it is a year
5	If using a date in the file name place years first YYYYMMDD
6	The version number of a record should be indicated in its file name
7	Put surnames before initials or forenames
8	Complete the 'Properties' box

Figure 4.11 File naming guidance

1. Keep file names short, but meaningful, avoiding common or unhelpful words at the start of file names such as 'draft' otherwise all such records will appear together in the file directory, making it more difficult to retrieve the one required. Ensure the file name is descriptive in its own right and does not also rely on the containing folder name. This is to ensure that if a file is moved to another directory it retains its fully meaningful title.
2. Avoid special characters such as \ / > < * ? " ; : [ ] & $ as these are frequently used for specific tasks in an electronic environment and could cause errors. Avoid using an additional full stop as this already exists in the file name preceding the file extension. It may not create a problem, but best to omit it.

3. Avoid white spaces as these gaps are not accepted by programming software and may cause problems when saved to web pages. 'Dashes', 'Underscores' or 'Capitalization' of each word are options, for example a document file to be named 'File name 1', could saved as File_name_1.doc, or File-name-1.doc or FileName1.doc.
4. When including a number in a file name always give it as a two-digit number, unless it is a year. This maintains the numeric order when file names include numbers.
5. If a date is included in the file name it should always be presented with the year first as per the international standard (ISO 8601 2000). This ensures that the chronological order of the records is maintained when the file names are listed in the file directory.
6. The version number of a record should be indicated in its file name by the inclusion of 'V' followed by a two digit number and, where applicable, 'Draft' or 'Final'. This guidance may not be appropriate where document and records management functionality (for example, from an EDRMS) is available to manage version control and 'declaration' of records. This is because such systems often have their own method of naming file versions and their drafts.
7. If personal names are included, placing surnames first will ensure correct alphabetical sorting where several surnames exist in a similarly structure file name.
8. Complete the properties box presented by the creation software. This metadata is searchable and will usually be migrated to any EDRM or similar system.

4.7 Conclusion

The capture stage in the life cycle is key to ensuring that the required material is best prepared for onward management. Information can be created by user action, or be acquired or received from external sources. It can be readily integrated with existing digital information by scanning the physical media such as paper or microfilm on which it resides. It may be held in coded form in bar codes or other automatic identification devices that facilitate rapid information capture. The individual captured electronic files need names that meet agreed guidelines, aid subsequent retrieval and avoid conflicting with applications that access the files. Once all these considerations are dealt the next process would seem to be – store the files away. This is where many of the problems arise as insufficient attention is given to key information management decisions prior to storage. Hence, for example, information is duplicated, made difficult if not impossible to retrieve or is disposed of without any consideration of its value. These key information decisions and processes are the subject of the following chapter.

5 *Manage Information*

'Everybody gets so much information all day long that they lose their common sense'. Gertrude Stein (1874–1946)

This chapter deals with the processes for managing information in the life cycle including an overview of the different types of storage media.

It concerns those processes that put the captured information into working order for subsequent utilization by:

- reviewing, editing and approving the information
- classifying the information to aid subsequent storage, retrieval, and disposal
- determining and implementing retention decisions regarding captured information
- storing and archiving the information
- providing retrieval aids and systems to enable exploitation of the information.

All of these will be present in some form or another within an organization even though they may not be recognized as discrete processes or managed with any degree of rigour. They can be divided into two broad groups:

- Records management processes for the formal administration and control of information identified as requiring protection as regards its access, retention and disposal. According to the international standard for records management a 'record' is defined as 'Information created, received and maintained as evidence and information by an organization or person, in pursuance of legal obligations or in the transaction of business' (ISO 15489–1 2001).
- Remaining processes – often referred to as 'document management' – relating principally to the drafting, review and approval of documents through their various versions, and their subsequent storage and disposal. A 'document' is defined as 'Recorded information, stored on a physical medium, which can be interpreted in an application context and treated as a unit' (ISO 15489–1 2001).

This division is shown in Figure 5.1 with an overlap where a decision is made as to whether the captured information is to be declared as a 'record' for onward control.

On this basis it is possible to have a 'document management system' without a 'records management system', but the reverse is not feasible. Where the organization has no formal records management processes in place the captured information will be stored directly without any concept of a 'declaration' decision being made.

With records management the main emphasis is on the organization and safeguarding of recorded information throughout its life cycle; there are thus strong administrative overtones in the application of this discipline.

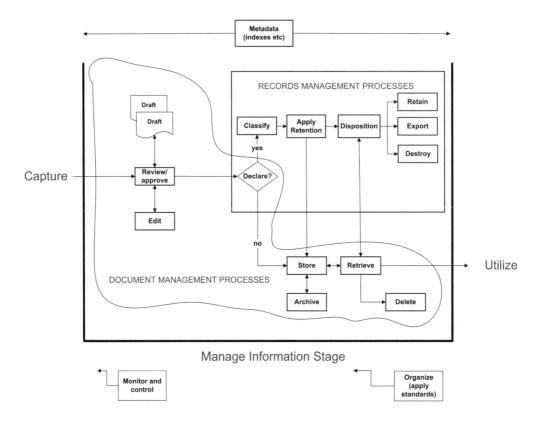

Figure 5.1   Manage information stage

Document management is more dynamic and transactional in nature, and is more readily comprehended by users. A comparison of the two is presented in Figure 5.2.

Some may question the need for records management, but consider the position of an organization where:

- accounting records are destroyed in a fire and details of major creditors are lost
- 'as-built' engineering drawings cannot be found quickly enough to deal with emergency maintenance on a chemical plant
- papers vital for the defence in a court action are not to be found in the defending organization's record files
- records that relate to one another are held on different media such as paper, microfilm and computer hard disk and cannot be integrated effectively to provide the complete picture
- reports are produced to no standard format and referencing system, thereby hindering their storage and retrieval
- forms are created without due thought as to their intended use and value, thereby proliferating rather than saving paperwork
- personal computers are filling up with unorganized word-processed documents and spreadsheets with no thought as to their value for retention.

	RECORDS MANAGEMENT	DOCUMENT MANAGEMENT
Principal focus of attention	Administrative control	Operational use
	Physical storage	Work flow
	File classification	Indexing
	Retention	Revision and version control
	Statutory and legal requirements	Operational needs
	Storage media	Information content
	Integrated series	Individual items

Figure 5.2   A comparison of records and document management

Records management and document management are not alternative ways to manage information. They are complementary approaches which must be applied in a coherent fashion. It is important to ensure that all the management elements are addressed so that an organization can capitalize on its available information. Nowadays a range of systems is available to support document and records management requirements.

The following processes as depicted in Figure 5.1 will now be considered in more detail:

- collaborative work including review, editing and approval
- version control
- declaration (relating to organizational value)
- classification of the captured information including business analysis to develop a file plan, dealing with case files, managing legacy records, information security and access control, digital rights management and paper records
- retention and disposition
- storage and storage media.

The chapter ends with discussion on legal admissibility.

5.1 Collaborative Work – Review, Editing and Approval

Created, acquired or revised information will need to pass through some approval or authorization procedure before it is processed or distributed further. These processes are interlinked as they are concerned with effecting controlled additions or changes to captured or created information (especially 'documents' as widely understood).

In any business there are types of document which require some form of formal review, approval or authorization, examples being:

- insurance claims
- engineering drawings
- invoices

- purchase requisitions
- quality plans
- standards and specifications.

Even everyday correspondence will be reviewed and edited by its respective authors.

Depending on the business application, the process of approval and authorization may involve one or more persons undertaking relatively simple or complex review cycles. In a typical office environment word-processing software incorporates ways to track changes to documents and to identify those who have added comments or amendments to 'drafts' as they are circulated, usually via email. This method can involve several people editing the source document and this leads to confusion and the introduction of errors.

Presenting the document in a format, such as HTML or PDF, for online access has the advantage that it can be made more readily available to a wider audience for review. Word-processing software usually incorporates means to generate an HTML format while various, often open-source, programs are available to create PDF formats of the documents. PDF has the advantage that it retains the look of the original.

However, the HTML and common PDF formats do not provide the encompassing control environment necessary to manage multiple inputs, changes and comments in a consistent and coherent manner. Clearly the degree of complexity and the degree of standardization of the process will be a determining factor in the choice of possible solution. Thus complex, standard review cycles may well merit the deployment of robust workflow software including those based on the use of a PDF variant. This functionality is to be found in many commercial document or records management products.

There are two main approaches to the implementation of workflow systems. The ad-hoc workflow tools use email, forms and messages as the system infrastructure where information and work is sent out to people whether they need it or not.

The higher-end workflow systems are concerned with the proactive management of the flow of work between co-operating individuals and groups of people based on defined procedures and tasks. These systems are usually referred to as engine-based, where the workflow engine handles the management of the actual process and calls other applications and facilities as and when required. They provide significant advantages where close integration is needed and where more sophisticated models of work matching are appropriate. Interchange of workflows between different systems is hampered by the different designs offered by vendors. The Workflow Management Coalition (WfMC) http://www.wfmc.org/ has endorsed an XML Process Definition Language (XPDL) to address this problem.

According to Stark and Lachal (1995), there are five conditions which need to be satisfied before one can be confident of gaining benefit from implementing workflow technology:

- processes should have explicit component tasks
- rules should be applied to determine the logic of transition between tasks
- digital information resources should be provided to support the processing of tasks
- tasks should be communicable to workers
- the process should be controllable.

The coming of the Web and the increasing use being made by business of the Internet has added another dimension as many of the new workflow products are entirely web-based. While offering rapid and less-expensive deployment than non web-based services, other issues emerge. These include security and the need for improved document management to ensure the underlying document base is up-to-date, approved and has appropriate access controls.

In summary, there is a range of interaction from ad-hoc to structured collaboration which can involve various levels of technology, as shown in Figure 5.3.

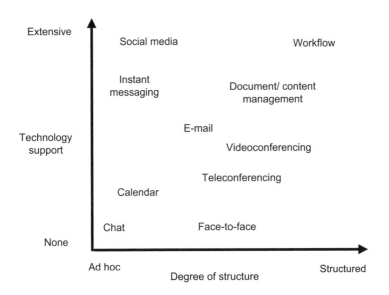

Figure 5.3   Ways of collaborating

As noted by Charlesworth et al. (2003), successful collaboration combines and integrates a number of technologies and tools, but success will depend largely on whether or not the culture of the organization is open to communication and information exchanges. Furthermore, data and content – unstructured information – needs to be integrated to provide the store of recorded knowledge on which collaboration can thrive.

5.1.1 VERSION CONTROL

In the era of photocopiers, faxes and printers, paper copies of existing documents abound. Similar proliferation arises in the electronic world with emails being 'cc'd' and attachments being included. In the case of paper, the copies may be made for convenience as so far technology has not been able to replicate fully the accessibility and manoeuvrability offered by the physical medium. Other than this, copies may be provided for review by recipients, 'for information' or possibly for no other good reason.

It is therefore important for guidance to be provided on controlling the production, use and disposal of copies. Such guidance should include ways of identifying which is the 'master' record that must be secured and managed according to formal records management policy. For example, copies of a contract may be circulated in paper or electronic form, but, depending on local practice, the master record may be the original signed paper copy. To help differentiate 'copy' from 'master', printers and other output devices can mark or overlay the copy with phrases like 'uncontrolled copy' or 'valid until date ... '.

Some types of document are subject to revision and may be re-issued as new revisions or versions (the meanings behind the terms 'revision' and 'version' can differ between or even within organizations). Key documents such as operational procedures, design drawings and standards will be subject to change during their lifetime. Failure to keep track of these changes will mean at the very least time and effort is expended unnecessarily in tracing the latest editions or updating material which has already been so processed. In the case of contract critical or safety critical documents, it could place business agreements and lives at risk or expose the organization to risk from litigation.

Hence when information is to be revised and multiple revisions of the same document may be generated over time, additional procedures need to be in place. Version numbering of some form or another is often included in the file name and in the document itself.

Where there is no automated assistance it is more difficult to maintain consistency in applying such control. Microsoft provides means to manage versions in its Word program, but generally its use does not seem to be recommended due to the increase in document size that it generates. By saving a document as 'read only' some measure of protection can be provided, as one has to save a changed document using a different file name.

Where it is required to manage and control these change processes and ensure users know what is current and what is superseded, it is essential that the system provides the required functionality. Such requirements arose early in engineering and R&D-based industries, but systems addressing this need are now commonplace and available for any type of business. Modern document management systems and similar technology now incorporate robust version controls that not only provide the coding for the file names, but also ensure that 'check-out' and 'check-in' procedures protect the integrity of the document and keep users informed of the document's status at any point in time. Thus a user accessing the system will be informed if a document is checked out, and by whom. If they wish to access the document they can do so but cannot check it out themselves to amend it further.

5.2 Declaring Organizational Value

The decision made at this point determines the extent of control to be exercised over the information that has (as appropriate) been reviewed and approved for storage. If it is considered that the information is of sufficient value to be managed as a formal record, the records management processes come into play. Certain records are considered 'vital' as without them an organization would encounter major operational or legal problems. If the information does not merit such 'declaration', it is filed away, either to an electronic or physical store. This is not to say that there are no management procedures in place for such information. There must be adequate monitoring and control of all recorded information whether or not considered 'masters', 'records', 'copies' or 'drafts', for example.

It should be noted that physical objects such as test samples or models represent records of a different kind which embody information of importance. Such information could, for example, be captured as a photograph or video recording.

This question of value needs further consideration, as it is core to appraising recorded information for retention and disposition which is considered in more detail later. Appraisal needs to be based on agreed criteria. In UK government circles, for example, it is based on the Grigg principles which divide paper files into two categories, policy files and case files, and recommend at what periods they should be reviewed for possible disposal. The system is not suited to dealing with digital information and there is a move towards 'macro-appraisal' which is defined as 'assessing the value of records at a government, departmental or unit level rather than at an individual document or file level' (Mercer 2004). The key aspect is that it encourages government-wide or organization-wide analysis of functions and associated activities as a guide to identifying records of value for business and archival purposes.

5.3 Classification for Records Control

It is human nature to order or otherwise structure information to make it more manageable and accessible. A classification exemplifies this and is 'a systematic distribution or arrangement in a class or classes' (OED 2001). In many organizations insufficient thought is given to this aspect of records design. There is often no consistency across the organization or even within individual departments. The arrangement of records may be left to individual staff, and with each staff change, the files are reorganized to suit the new incumbent. Consequently there is a lack of continuity in the records, and access to earlier information is severely impaired if not rendered impossible. Paper records and those held electronically both suffer in these respects.

Three ways commonly encountered to organize records are subject/thematic, organizational structure and functional. The relative merits of these are summarized in Figure 5.4 based on Todd (2003).

The focus on business functions as a way to organize records is to be found in the international standard on records management (ISO 15489–1 2001) which is based on the development of a business classification scheme (BCS) around business functions – often referred to as a 'functional hierarchy'.

With the availability of appropriate software support, the benefit of this approach is that it provides the opportunity automatically to apply records management processes to recorded information that has been linked to the appropriate part of the business function-related classification. In this way records can effectively be 'sentenced on creation'.

Recall that business functions are not to be confused with an organization's management structure. For example, a 'Finance Department' is an organizational structure which in part will undertake a business finance function. However, the Department will also internally be dealing with records relating to, for example, staff seeking promotion, problems with the accounting system, theft of personal possessions and local air conditioning failure. These records have nothing to do with a 'finance business function' and would need to be associated with other business functions relating to 'personnel', 'IT' and 'property management', for example.

Scheme	Description	Advantages	Drawbacks
Functional	Records are structured to align with business functions	• Functions change less frequently than organizational structures • Keeps like documents together regardless of 'ownership' • Staff can move within the organization and see the same standards in place • Base for determining security protection and access rights • Helps assignment of responsibility for managing of groups of records	• A strict functional approach will not support case files well • Records managers like functional structures (management is easier); users do not understand and dislike them (because they are hard to use)
Subject/ thematic	Records arranged by subject or themes	• Enables a more common approach across information systems: EDRM, websites, Intranets, etc. • More easily recognized and understood by users	• Interpretation and understanding may vary considerably between user groups
Organizational	Records arranged in line with management/ organizational structure	• Familiar structure to end users • Often originates from the paper environment	• Subject to frequent change. • Maintaining continuity over time is difficult
Hybrid	Functional design with subject focus	• Provides compromise between a strict purist approach and operational flexibility • Enables case material to be integrated, for example: functional at a broad level (with disposal rules mostly operating at that level), with cases or subject-based sub-classes	• Requires careful management

Figure 5.4   Comparison of records classification schemes

Source: Reproduced with permission of The National Archives. Crown copyright information taken from BCS Toolkit is re-used under the terms of the Open Government Licence (OGL)

Guidance on the design of such systems was published by The National Archives (Todd 2003). Commercial software is available to facilitate the design and maintenance of a BCS or file plan, the latter being the BCS together with the folders and records it contains.

The remaining discussions on analysis and design will concentrate on a functional design based on the international standard.

5.3.1 ANALYSIS OF BUSINESS ACTIVITY

An overview of the process to produce the required records classification is shown in Figure 5.5.

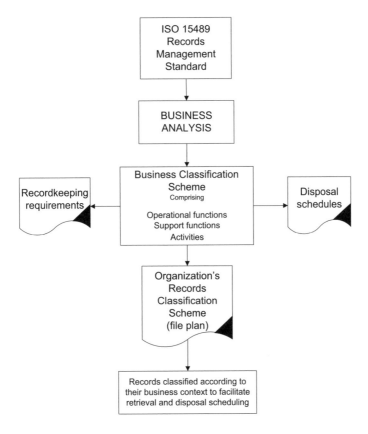

Figure 5.5   BCS to file plan

Creating a classification of a business's functions and activities requires the use of a variety of analytical techniques including business process modelling. It may be that the organization has already undertaken studies which will inform this analysis. Staff will have little enthusiasm for answering the same type of questions already posed by another 'consultant'! Quality or process improvement initiatives as described earlier can provide useful information including answers to such questions as:

- what are the organization's strategy and objectives?
- for whom does the person work?
- what information does the person need to undertake their tasks?
- from whom do they receive this information?
- to whom do they send information and for what purpose?
- what types of information are handled and where is it stored?
- what workflow processes are in place?

Some of the information gathered from such studies will be too detailed or of marginal importance so it is important to select only that which is relevant.

In addition to reusing available survey material it will be necessary to gather information in other ways to fill gaps in knowledge, expand on the existing detail and possibly validate that which is already known.

As an example, Figure 5.6 shows the range of information-gathering methods used and the principal players involved to produce a BCS (adapted from a project for a UK government organization).

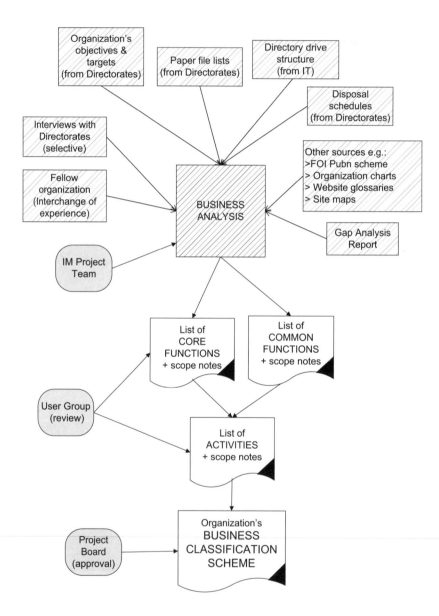

Figure 5.6   BCS production process

The organization's objectives and targets provided details of its business direction and thereby an indication of the types of activities that would need to be undertaken to achieve them.

Examination of existing ways of arranging paper and electronic files showed how individual users or the organization liked to classify and name their records.

Each of the organization's Directorates maintained retention and disposal schedules for their own set of records. Differences in the schedules and the review processes for determining disposition of the records were noted for later resolution.

Other documented sources consulted included:

- organization's Freedom of Information publication scheme
- organization charts
- structure and site maps of the organization's intranet and internet web sites.

The organization also consulted its equivalent in another country to exchange knowledge on records organization using a functional design.

In addition the findings from a gap analysis report were informative. The report was produced at the outset of the broader information management project and identified failings in such management in the organization. It also established the programme of work of which the development of a BCS was one element.

To complement the documentary evidence, interviews were conducted within selected Directorates. The meetings covered the following topics, although these were tailored or added to as appropriate:

- roles and responsibilities
- organizational structure
- staff/people (skills, IT)
- main functions (how does work arise, drivers; ad-hoc/planned)
- key information flows (to/from; media)
- policies and procedures (life cycle, retention; responsibilities)
- regulatory and legislative requirements (Data Protection, Freedom of Information; responsibilities)
- filing arrangements (electronic, paper, master, responsibilities)
- IT used (office, spreadsheets, database, emails, scanning, special systems)
- Internet use
- intranet use
- information management problems.

The work was undertaken under the control of an Information Management Team and the outputs were reviewed by a User Group composed of representatives from the Directorates. A Project Board was responsible for the final review and approval of the BCS.

5.3.2 DESIGN OF THE BCS

The design needs to take into account the intended use of the BCS as functional hierarchies are useful in a variety of contexts, for example in studies to determine information requirements and develop systems to satisfy this need. Here the focus is on their use in supporting records organization whether in a paper, electronic or hybrid environment.

In designing a BCS one needs to keep in mind that this will eventually be visible in some form or another to users as a file plan to which they will be required to conform when saving documents. Each person has their own views on ways to structure their files, none more so than senior management who are usually more resistant to change than their staff.

Although various mechanisms can be constructed to hide the complexity of the file plan or to present just those parts which are relevant to the user, the choice and naming of functions and the supporting descriptions should be readily comprehensible so as to ease adoption and ongoing use. It is therefore important to involve those who create the records in formulating the terms and their explanations.

The initial aim, following the analysis, is to produce a Business Classification Scheme comprising two main levels:

- business functions (top level)
- activities (second level sub-functions) which support the functions.

Terms at the business function level are fixed as they reflect the unchanging functions that the organization performs. Each function is associated with selections from second level activities chosen to reflect the topics being classified. Activity terms are similarly intended to be unchanging; however, additions and amendments can be considered, but this needs to be properly authorized and controlled corporately.

A third level is provided:

- transactions.

This provides greater granularity for the classification of records and is usually the point at which records series appear. Here, there is generally greater flexibility exercised as regards choice of terms used.

The BCS, together with the folders and records it contains, comprises what in the paper environment is called a 'file plan'. An example of these three levels for part of a personnel function is shown in Figure 5.7 (ISO 15489–2 2001):

A further example showing the position of records series is provided in Figure 5.8 adapted from Shepherd and Yeo (2003).

Much time and effort can be spent trying to design the 'ultimate' classification scheme. In practice some compromises always have to be made, particularly as regards granularity and the levels of hierarchy. The more levels that are introduced, the more difficult it can be to decide where to locate a record, or to find it when subsequently sought.

It is recommended to keep the number of levels as small as possible, preferably three or four; that is, to one level below the transaction level.

Function	Activity	Transaction
1. Managing Human Resources		
	1.1 Determining Allowances	
	1.2 Establishing Conditions of Employment	
		1.2.1 Appointments
		1.2.2 Apprenticeships
		1.2.3 Childcare
		1.2.4 Flexible work arrangements

Figure 5.7   Extract from a personnel classification

Source: Permission to reproduce extracts from ISO 15489-2 2001. ISO/TE 15489-2:2001 is granted by BSI. British Standards can be obtained in PDF or hard copy formats from the BSI online shop: www.bsigroup.com/Shop or by contacting BSI Customer Services for hardcopies only: Tel: +44 (0)20 8996 9001, Email: cservices@bsigroup.com

ID	FUNCTION	SUB-FUNCTION	SERIES
99	Managing human resources		
99.1		Ensuring optimum staff numbers and skills	
99.1.1			Assessing staffing needs of business units
99.1.2			Recruiting staff for vacant posts
99.1.3			etc
99.2		Administering employee relations	
99.2.1			etc
99.2.1			etc

Figure 5.8   Placement of records series

Source: Adapted with permission of Facet Publishing from Fig 3.4 on page 80 of Shepherd, E. and Yeo, G. 2003. *Managing Records – A Handbook of Principles and Practice*. London: Facet Publishing

5.3.3 SUPPORT AND OPERATIONAL FUNCTIONS

The difference between support and operational functions has been explained earlier. The former are common functions that most organizations need, the latter are the unique, core functions that identify each organization to the outside world and are the reasons for its existence.

A major proportion of a BCS and hence file plan will relate to support functions. To avoid starting from scratch there is merit in drawing on the experiences of others who have already produced a classification incorporating such functions. Such collaboration tends to be more readily achieved between government bodies than between those in the private sector.

For example, the States Records Authority of the New South Wales Government in Australia were pioneers in developing a set of descriptions for common functions, comprising top level functions, second level activities and third level subject descriptors, called Keyword AAA (NSW 2011a). It is the *de facto* standard in Australian government bodies and has been adopted by a number of UK organizations. The scheme is copyright but is available for internal use on payment of a one-off licence fee. Clearly the names of the functions and the choice of activities and descriptors may not suit the licensee so the scheme can be adapted to suit. An example of a file plan's support functions based on this approach is shown in Figure 5.9.

SUPPORT FUNCTION	DESCRIPTION
Goods and Equipment	Acquiring and maintaining goods and equipment
Information Resources	Acquiring and managing data, information and knowledge
Information Technology	Provision and support of computers and communications
Property Management	Managing and maintaining buildings and premises
Government Relations	Dealing with ministers and Parliamentary Questions
Media and Public Relations	Dealing with press and public
Professional Relations	Membership and involvement in professional bodies
Financial Resources	Manage money and budgets
Human Resources	Managing staff from recruitment to severance
Staff Development	Developing the skills and abilities of staff
Improvements and Change	Effecting improvements via projects and programmes
Strategic Management	Managing and directing strategy, direction and compliance

Figure 5.9   Support functions from file plan

No standard list of operational functions exists as the choice will depend on each organization's business. Where it can be arranged, it may be fruitful to discuss design and content with those working in similar fields. Often industry sectors such as oil and gas exploration, motor vehicle manufacture and pharmaceuticals will each have developed glossaries or more sophisticated ontologies that will be informative. A directory of metadata vocabularies is maintained by the Joint Information Systems Committee (JISC 2011).

As an example of collaboration, records managers in UK local government worked to produce the Local Government Classification Scheme (LGCS 2007). It was developed to ease the burden of developing classification schemes to support business activities undertaken in the local government environment. Records are classified according to a three-level hierarchy – function, activity, transaction. Organization-specific terms can be added at the third level.

An extract from the classification relating to the Legal Services function is provided in Figure 5.10 and shows how records series and types of records can be mapped to the scheme. Scope notes are included to aid understanding. These can be enhanced to suit individual organizations.

Class	Series	Records	Scope Notes
Legal services			Management of legal activities on behalf of the council as a corporate body.
. Advice			Information on advice provided.
. . Advice to the public			Community legal services.
. . Provision of legal advice			Providing advice to clients and services which are legally privileged relating to all aspects of the legal system.
. . Witness support			Witness support schemes.
. Bylaws			Local bylaws.
. . Enactment			The process of making local laws.
. . Enforcement			The process of administering and enforcing bylaws.
. Land and highways			Information on land and highways.
. . Acquisition		Road adoptions	Documentation relating to the process of acquiring land in relation to roads.
. . Disposal			Disposal of land associated with the highway.
. Land registration			Land registration.
. . Land charges		Searches	Searches and title investigations.
. . Land charges		Registers	Legal documentation relating to land charges.
. Litigation			Process dealing with civil and criminal litigation, debt recovery, commercial litigation.
. . Civil	Case files		Civil litigation.
. . Commercial	Case files		Commercial litigation.
. . Criminal	Case files		Criminal litigation.
. . Debt recovery	Case files		Debt recovery.
. . Precedent cases			Judgments relied on to fight current cases - setting standards to work within.
. Management of legal activities			Management of legal activities.
. . Archive deposits		Agreements	Legal documentation relating to archive depositors.
. . Agreements		Agreements	Agreements including non-contractual agreements between public bodies.
. . Conveyancing	Deeds	Conveyance	Commercial and other leases, Title investigations, Disposal of Freehold and Leasehold properties, Right to Buy applications etc.
. . Conveyancing	Deeds	Easements	Private right of way, right to light (an easement benefits one piece of land by exercising rights over another piece of land owned by another) procedures are in place to ensure the efficient and lawful use of easements.

Figure 5.10 Extract from the Local Government Classification Scheme

Source: Reproduced with permission of the Information and Records Management Society

A similar approach was pursued in Australia for the development of Keywords For Councils (NSW 2011b 2011).

5.3.4 CASE FILES

The LGCS example above showed case files placed in the classification. The adoption of a function-based approach poses problems for classifying case files. A case file is a container which brings together all the elements of a transaction or group of transactions which in some respect have the same subject; for example, a person's insurance claim or a patient's medical details. By their very nature such files will include records which relate to a number of functions (for example, finance and health) which in a true function-based system would be filed in different locations.

There are two main ways of resolving this dilemma for electronic records:

- create a virtual case file
- place the case file within the relevant function (as done for the LGCS).

With the first option the records which make up a case are filed with the relevant function/activity and are therefore scattered across the classification. They are given a common identifier so that all the material can be retrieved as a single case file. Depending on the functionality offered by the records system, this arrangement can mean that individual case records will be subject to the retention schedules that apply to the area where they are placed. Hence over time the case file will become increasingly incomplete.

The second option is the hybrid approach. This is where a functional arrangement is provided for all records except for case files which are maintained as single units under the appropriate functions and activities so that their contents can be subjected to the same retention schedule. Here all records in the case files are retained until the files themselves are disposed of. It may be feasible to apply retention schedules to individual records in a case file, but again the availability of this facility will depend on the capability of the software.

5.3.5 LEGACY RECORDS AND MIGRATION POLICY

The introduction of a new file plan is often part of wider project to introduce a commercial document or records management system that is capable of supporting the classification scheme. The successful adoption and on-going use of the file plan requires pre-planning and close involvement with all those affected. This is especially so if the scheme has a radically different design to that with which users are familiar. One key aspect that needs to be addressed concerns existing unstructured records, whether paper or electronic, and the extent to which they should be reorganized or migrated to the new regime. Structured records as in databases and spreadsheets are dealt with in Chapter 7.

Unstructured data is exemplified by that in text documents and emails, but can also be taken to include photographs, video and other graphic media. Such information is commonly held on networked drives which hold shared and personal data and are traditionally arranged in some form of hierarchical structure. The degree to which there is central, departmental or personal control over these structures will depend on local policies and procedures. Even where guidelines exist, the absence of any technical means to enforce them usually means that they are rarely followed over an extended period as organizations and personnel change.

Undoubtedly there will be information relevant to business needs on these networks and it will need to be migrated from the shared drives to the new system. Even where the network folders have titles or topics that can be equated to data fields or locations in the target system, considerable redundancy in the information will be found within and across the folders arising from such factors as duplication of information and proliferation of document drafts. Hence there is likely to be no benefit in automating the migration of such data. Exceptions can arise, of course, and decisions will need to be made on a case-by-case basis; in fact 'case' files may well be that exception as they do comprise a coherent set of information about an entity. Selection criteria need to be agreed to enable appropriate records to be available for users on 'go-live' day.

The process that is often adopted is to:

- agree with the users those records that must be currently available and migrate them to the new classification just before 'go live'
- provide a mapping for all existing types of record from where they are currently held to locations in the new scheme
- make the existing directories and network drives read-only for 'go live' so that users cannot save to them, but can copy and migrate files as and when needed using drag-and-drop facilities
- after an agreed time archive the drives then later wipe them clear of all data; the decision is informed by the frequency with which the old drives are accessed and the retention criteria that apply.

The details of the mapping and migration process will be greatly influenced by the functionality offered by the new information system and its capability to manage the records in the desired fashion. It is therefore not possible to be prescriptive as regards these processes.

Knowledge of the types of electronic files and of the existing folder structures is necessary before the mapping can be undertaken. Trawling through endless levels of directory hierarchies is time consuming and needs to involve the users to identify those files and folders that are important to the individual or the business. It is recommended to extract these hierarchies into spreadsheet form as this can then be developed into a migration template for later population. An example based on a migration project is provided in Figure 5.11 and shows existing network drives, folders and files on the left and the target location in the functional scheme on the right. Columns are provided to indicate ownership and add descriptions where appropriate.

One aspect that needs to be considered relates to directories or networked drives that are associated with and managed by separate management structures such as different departments and teams. Each of these parts of the organization may well be holding similar information to which only their staff have access. In a function-based classification this similar information needs to be associated with the same part of the file plan and hence these departmental files need to be migrated to the same location. This is exemplified in Figure 5.12 where budget planning files 'owned' by different departments (ECSD, ENT and GAS) are placed under the same third level transaction.

DRIVE	CURRENT FOLDER 1	CURRENT FOLDER 2	CURRENT FOLDER 3	Description	OWNER	Function	Activity	Transaction	New Folder 4	New Folder 5
U:	John Smith	Technical Specifications			JS	Access Management	Production	Copying	Copying – RC	Orders
U:	Susan James	Budgets	spreadsheets		SJ	Financial Management	Budgeting	Budget Planning	Budget Planning – RC	
U:	Susan James	Equipment	disposals		SJ	Goods	Disposal	Equipment	Equipment – RC	
U:	Susan James	Stock	stock takes		SJ	Goods	Inventory	Stock Control	Stock Control – RC	
U:	Susan James	Registry	Correspondence		SJ	Information Management	Control	File and Folder Management	File and Folder Management – RC	
I:	Purchasing	Faxes		Fax headers for suppliers	SJ	Information Management	Control	Post Management	Post Management – RC	
U:	Susan James	Film library	film lists		SJ	Intellectual Control	Control	Film Library	Film Library – RC	Film Lists
S:	Record Copying	Repro		Census orders	SJ	Intellectual Control	Projects	Census Project	Census Project – RC	Orders
U:	Susan James	Health and Safety	reports		SJ	Occupational Health and Safety	Accidents	Accident Reporting	Accident Reporting – RC	
I:	RCD minutes	Health and Safety		Minutes and papers	SJ	Occupational health and Safety	Committees	Occupational Health and safety Committee	Occupational Health and safety Committee – RC	
U:	Susan James	Line Manager	leave record		SJ	Personnel	Attendance Management	Leave	Leave – RC	
S:	Record Copying	Repro	Attendance	Spreadsheets of dept attendance	SJ	Personnel	Attendance Management	Timekeeping	Timekeeping – RC	
U:	Susan James	Line Manager	staff interviews		SJ	Personnel	Performance Management	Staff Appraisal	Staff Appraisal – RC	
I:	Fire Marshal List			Fire Marshal List	GH	Property Management	Security	Fire Control	Fire Control – RC	
S:	Record Copying	Repro	Training	Staff training	AB	Staff Development	Training	Induction	Induction – RC	
U:	John Smith	Business Plans	Reports		JS	Strategic Management	Planning	Corporate and Business Plans	Corporate and Business Plans – RC	
I:	Strategic Management			Risk register	SJ	Strategic Management	Risk Management	Risk Registers	Corporate Risk Register – RC	
U:	Susan James	Administration	RMIS barcode templates		SJ	Technology and Communications	Computer Operations	Ordering Systems	RMIS – RC	Forms

Figure 5.11 Migration template with example entries

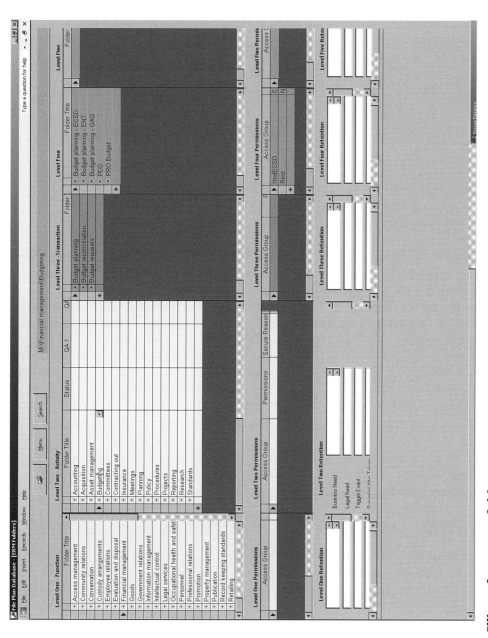

Figure 5.12 Filing of common folders

Source: Reproduced with permission of The National Archives. The data is Crown copyright. Microsoft Access is copyright Microsoft Corporation

5.3.6 INFORMATION SECURITY AND ACCESS CONTROL

'As a result of increasing interconnectivity, information systems and networks are now exposed to a growing number and a wider variety of threats and vulnerabilities' (OECD 2002). These concerns have made information security a major issue for organizations as most information resources are fully reliant on information technology and interconnections.

Information security is the protection of information from a wide range of threats in order to ensure business continuity, minimize business risk and maximize return on investments and business opportunities (ISO 27002 2005). More specifically Smedinghoff (2008) states that the main objectives of information security and the laws that address it are to:

- ensure the confidentiality of information
- control access to systems, networks, and information
- properly authenticate information, and persons and devices seeking access to it
- ensure the integrity of systems, networks and information
- ensure the availability of systems, networks and information.

Confidentiality is ensured through a combination of controlling access and authenticating the person attempting access. Both the last two criteria need to be satisfied to gain access to the information. (Access control is considered in more detail at the end of this section).

Integrity, in the context of information (data), is concerned with accuracy and completeness and ensuring that only authorized changes are made. Ensuring data integrity is a key role for a Data Manager.

Availability relates to the ability to access and use information. A usable record is one that can be located, retrieved, presented and interpreted in relation to a business activity or transaction.

Information security requirements should be defined as part of an Information Management Policy Framework (see Section 9.3.1) and should cover controls for:

- physical security – facilities, equipment and storage media
- technical security – access controls, identification, authentication, auditing etc.
- administrative security – contingency planning, personnel security etc.

Access Control

It is important that data entered into the system is not able to be accessed, altered, added to or deleted by those without the necessary approval. The ability to assign such privileges to different categories of users is important. Thus some users may only need to retrieve information for viewing. Others may have the right to amend and add, but not delete information. These rights can be applied very specifically, for example to specified document types or even individual documents. Such software features are particularly important when the system is to manage revision and version control of documents.

The example in the previous section indicates that each department may still want to control access to its files and prevent others from so doing. This may be appropriate because one department or team within it is dealing with confidential personnel data or with a contentious matter concerning another part of the organization and does not wish the latter to have access. Access control applied to a departmental folder is shown in Figure 5.12 for ECSD allowing full control by the Head of Department group for ESCD but to no one else (the Rest).

This situation raises the broader policy question that has to be answered; is the organization's access strategy to be 'open' (i.e. anyone can read anything unless controls are put in place to prevent access) or 'closed' (i.e. no one can access any information unless they have been given permission)?

Whichever way is preferred – open or closed – one will still need to know to what extent the chosen system can meet the requirement with its access controls, whether they relate to document and container (folder) levels or users.

Access control in a computer system can be managed using roles or groups and group members, for example. A group may be a department or team, or some *ad-hoc* grouping created for a specific purpose such as a user group. A person may be assigned to any number of groups; it is possible for a group to consist of just one member. Specific rights of access (read, amend etc) to an electronic folder are assigned to the groups linked to that folder. Arguably it is easier to manage access based on groups than on roles as organizations generally do not keep a tight rein on what roles are and who are assigned them. Even individual staff might not be clear what their roles are. Basing access on defined groups of people is likely to be easier to manage in this regard.

Active Directory is a Microsoft directory structure used on computers and servers to store information and data about networks and domains. It is an important component for controlling and administering user access to networked resources such as electronic files and folders.

Digital Rights Management (DRM)

DRM is technology that allows rights owners to establish and enforce conditions for the use of their intellectual property. As noted by Craig and Graham (2003) 'Recent technological advances have posed serious challenges to the traditional methods of rights management'. This is due to the widespread use of the Internet, the growth of electronic and mobile commerce and the development of common technology standards for text, audio or video which have made it easier for material to be copied by millions as soon as it is released.

Intending users of protected material do not generally welcome restrictions being put in place and there are tensions between them and the rights owners who understandably wish to see recompense for their endeavours. Organizations wishing to use externally generated information therefore need to be aware of an owner's rights. Owners, on the other hand, are beginning to see opportunities as organizations become established to facilitate publication and provide means to protect their rights.

5.3.7 PAPER RECORDS

Where paper records still need to be created and managed, similar issues to those found with electronic records will be encountered, and similar solutions can be applied. For example, the paper files are 'closed' the day before 'go live' and the new classification scheme applied to any new ones created. In this way hybrid files can be subject to the same classification.

There are two other options:

- reclassify the legacy records
- migrate existing paper records to the new scheme.

Reclassification should only be considered if the legacy records are still actively sought and the existing filing structure is of such poor quality that retrieval is difficult. Then reclassification may be worth the effort. Otherwise the existing and new arrangements will continue in parallel and be referred to as required.

Where legacy paper records are needed post 'go live', rather than migrating them as paper to the new scheme (which in the electronic world seems perverse) they can be converted to digital form by scanning and filed in the classification's electronic folders.

5.4 Retention and Disposition

There is a natural tendency for individuals, and organizations, not to destroy information as 'it might come in useful sometime'. On the other hand, when forced to think of destroying records, for example because of lack of storage space, destruction is often undertaken without assessing the operational or legal importance of the material, or the legal implications. Alternatively, records may be 'dumped' with a commercial records storage firm without proper consideration of retention periods or referencing and indexing requirements to facilitate their subsequent identification.

It is therefore necessary that all records, irrespective of the medium on which they are stored, should have a retention period allocated which properly satisfies criteria such as those based on operational, legal, research or historical requirements.

The retention period for records may be arrived at by considering the purpose behind the information contained in the records and the key retention criteria, as outlined in Figure 5.13.

The application of retention schedules can be informed by using the concept of record types which involves the categorization of records into mutually exclusive groups so that a different management policy (for example, retention scheduling, security category) can be applied to each record type. Record types tend to be categorized by the type of content rather than by the generic format, which is more akin to a document type. It is recommended (ISO 15489–1 2001), however, to have the records classified according to the hierarchical arrangements of a function-based scheme. This is because many of the records having the same functional classification will have identical retention periods. In this instance retention schedules are effectively applied to classes of records; that is, records which form part of an integrated series. This is far less onerous than undertaking a review of each paper file or electronic folder.

PURPOSE AND CRITERIA	RETENTION REASON	COMMENT
Purpose	To provide evidence	Records generated for statutory, regulatory or legal reasons. Prescribed or implied retention periods may apply
	To provide instructions	Records conveying instruction (e.g. policies and procedures) Implies long retention periods
	To provide information	Records conveying fact or opinion Retention period will vary depending on the nature of the information
Criteria	Legal	Records covered by statutory or legal provision
	Operational	Records required to undertake the day-to-day business of the organization
	Research	Records having actual or potential future value for research or development reasons or which are of historical significance

Figure 5.13 Retention guidelines

Although having default values for retention eases management of the collection, there will need to be exceptions, examples being:

- requests for information under the Data Protection Act (DPA) and the Freedom Of Information Act (which are specific to the United Kingdom). For example, once a request is received under the Data Protection Act, it becomes a criminal offence to destroy records subject to that request until the request has been processed and sufficient time has been allowed for the relevant procedure to be exhausted. This could include a tribunal hearing and an approach to the High Court
- policy and precedent records required for permanent preservation and transfer to The National Archives
- personnel issues
- legal and regulatory imperatives
- business needs (such as precedence cases).

Retention values should be applied to both active and inactive records and are typically assigned in months or years, or by way of codes if it is not possible to know the precise span of the retention period.

An example of retention periods assigned to records in the LGCS mentioned earlier is shown in Figure 5.14.

Class	Series	Records	Retention Period	Rationale
Legal services				
. Advice				
. . Advice to the public				
. . Provision of legal advice			Destroy - 6 years after last action, major precedent - offer to archivist for review	Limitations Act 1980. RGLA 4.2
. . Witness support				
. Bylaws				
. . Enactment			Permanent - offer to archivist	RGLA 9.22
. . Enforcement			Destroy - 2 years after matter is concluded	RGLA 9.23
. Land and highways				
. . Acquisition		Road adoptions		
. . Disposal				
. Land registration				
. . Land charges		Searches		
. . Land charges		Registers		
. Litigation				
. . Civil	Case files		Destroy - 7 years after last action, major litigation offer to archivist for review	RGLA 4.1
. . Commercial	Case files		Destroy - 7 years after last action, major litigation offer to archivist for review	RGLA 4.1
. . Criminal	Case files		Destroy - 7 years after last action, major litigation offer to archivist for review	RGLA 4.1
. . Debt recovery	Case files		Destroy - 7 years after last action, major litigation offer to archivist for review	RGLA 4.1
. . Precedent cases				

Figure 5.14 Example of retention periods assigned

Source: Reproduced with permission of the Information and Records Management Society

RGLA in the rationale column refers to the Retention Guidelines for Local Authorities produced by the Information and Records Management Society (IRMS 2005). The Limitations Act 1980 outlines the time limit within which a creditor can chase a debtor for outstanding debts. Under the Act the time limits are six years in simple contracts and twelve years for actions on a speciality, for example contracts under seal (Hamer 2011). This enables organizations to set the appropriate retention periods.

The following is the minimum data that should be recorded concerning retention decisions:

* identification of the record (for example, using the title and/or classification)
* total retention period according to the convention used
* reason for retention as per the guidelines.

Destruction of records must be authorized by a suitably responsible person. This authorization and the disposal must be recorded in a manner which accords to a documented procedure. In this way the likelihood is kept to a minimum of there being a challenge in a court of law on the basis that the disposal was not part of a normal business process. The complete destruction of paper records can easily be confirmed. For electronic records the use of the 'delete' button on a computer does not prevent subsequent retrieval and use of a document. To be sure that the records no longer exist in retrievable form, the storage medium must, for example, be reformatted with the process repeated if necessary and then physically destroyed.

Retention schedules should be regularly reviewed, typically annually, or when events occur which affect the management of records, for example the creation of new departments, company mergers or acquisitions. The retention schedule can also be used to note the security classification for the records, thereby providing a single point of reference when considering both duration of storage and access control issues.

National governments can exercise the necessary authority to manage their records and archives; for example, in the UK The National Archives has this mandate. However, in the private sector it is largely up to each organization to address this issue in the way they believe is appropriate. The British Archives Council (http://www.businessarchivescouncil.org.uk/) can supply advice and information on the administration and management of both archives and modern records. The National Archives were instrumental in establishing a website providing best practice guidance: http://www.managingbusinessarchives.co.uk/. A guide to document retention published by the Institute of Chartered Secretaries (Hamer 2011) is a further useful source.

Records which are not to be retained may be required by an external authority such as a local or national archive. The National Archives in the UK have an automated system for receiving electronic records as most government records are now created electronically as a result of the widespread introduction of computerized records management systems.

Retention policies and procedures should also embrace websites. Adoption of such a practice can have benefits beyond those relating to records management considerations (AIIM 2006). For example, it can:

- improve the quality of the website by removing out-of-date or inaccurate information
- reduce storage costs
- optimize website performance by, for example, archiving less-used material
- minimize the potential costs of e-discovery as redundant or superseded material is no longer there to slow down the costs of finding the required information.

5.5 Storage

Storage is in many respects the prime information life cycle activity. It is the means of ensuring that existing information is recorded in sufficiently permanent and accessible form to satisfy the requirements for retention and subsequent retrieval, and in such a way that the legal acceptability of the records and documents is not compromised.

When formulating a storage strategy for electronic records factors such as data volumes, speeds and frequency of access, data transfer rates, storage capacity and life expectancy of the storage media need to be assessed.

It is important to point out that some of the storage technologies, particularly some of the smaller removable ones aimed at the consumer rather than the business market, do not fully conform to *de jure* standards even if such standards exist at all. Also when investing in storage technology, be aware that the particular format or drive system chosen may be obsolete in just a few years and render the stored data inaccessible should the media or the drive fail. It is therefore important to have a storage management and data migration policy to protect one's information.

An overview of the various types of computer storage is provided in Figure 5.15 (Wikipedia 2007).

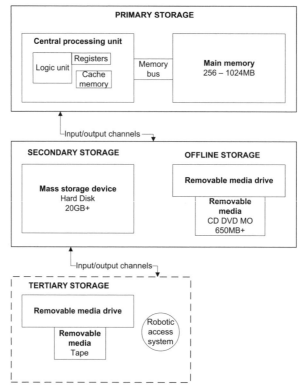

Figure 5.15 Types of computer storage

The following descriptions of storage media exclude consideration of primary storage.

5.5.1 MAGNETIC STORAGE

Digital information is stored by using read/write heads to orientate magnetic material on the storage device so that it corresponds to the information's data bits. The read/write heads read the data by sensing magnetic polarities.

Hard Drives

Hard disk drives, now with capacities well into the terabyte range, are the main storage devices for digital information as they offer fast and immediate response. Developments in drive media continue to increase areal densities – the amount of data bits in a given area. Hence it is unlikely that the newer technologies such as optical storage will overtake the performance and capacity of fixed magnetic devices in the immediate future.

Hard disks are an integral online component of a computer system and enable digital information to be accessed at will. Some disk drives accommodate removable hard disks and these are used for a variety of purposes including:

- providing additional storage when existing disks are full
- transferring data between systems

- enabling original data or copies to be stored offline for secure storage.

As regards the last point, hard disks are not suitable choices for archiving records as the design of the technology used – the drives, disks and associated software – is usually specific to those who produced the units. Hence design changes could mean that the information will be irretrievable due to lack of suitable hardware or software.

RAID

Several drives can be arranged to operate as if they are a single unit in order to improve fault tolerance and performance and offer greater storage capacity. This technology is called RAID (Redundant Array of Independent – once called inexpensive – Disks) and works by replicating the data across the various disks. Thus if one disk fails the system can still operate as normal as far as the user is concerned. RAID is available in levels (typically 0 to 10), each level being configured differently from the others so users can select the system that best meets their needs. Originally designed for corporate computing environments, RAID systems are now available for small business or home installations.

Direct-attached Storage (DAS)

Direct-attached storage refers to a storage system connected directly to a workstation or server, the latter being a device which manages shared access to a centralized resource or service in a network. Hence the data stored is only available through that device and cannot otherwise be shared with others.

Network-attached Storage (NAS)

Network-attached storage can be shared over a network irrespective of the operating systems environment. It has software to enable the data file locations to be seen and used by devices attached to the network. NAS can be readily expanded with additional storage and if required can form a component of a Storage Area Network.

Storage Area Network (SAN)

A SAN is a dedicated network to make storage devices, such as RAID, tape libraries and optical jukeboxes, accessible to servers over a high-speed network so that the devices appear as locally attached to the operating system. As the network can be spread over a wide geographical area SAN is particularly suited to the requirements of large organizations operating internationally.

Magnetic Tape

Magnetic tape has long been the main medium for data back-up and archival storage. It is available as small cartridges for individual use or as high-capacity tape libraries for storing, retrieving, reading from and writing to multiple units. Data can only be found by sequential searching of the linear tape, hence access times to reach the required information can be measured in several seconds or even minutes. Hence the medium is not an appropriate choice for online rapid data retrieval. Furthermore, tape is very sensitive to storage conditions, and life expectancy cited by manufacturers assumes an ideal storage environment.

Diskettes

As regards removable magnetic storage media, the 3.5in 'floppy' with a capacity of 1.44MB has long fallen out of favour. Although they may be needed when older equipment still uses this medium, 'floppies' have largely been replaced by small solid state storage devices with USB connection.

5.5.2 OPTICAL STORAGE

Optical storage media are direct-access removable disks on which the information is written and read by laser light. Although they do not yet have the speed of access and retrieval of magnetic media devices, they do not suffer corruption from stray magnetic fields, are less vulnerable to extremes of temperature and, although only proved by laboratory tests rather than real life, have a claimed life extending to 30 years or more.

The principal formats are:

- Compact Disc (CD)
- Digital Versatile Disc (DVD)
- Blu-ray Disc (BD)
- Magneto-optical (MO)

Note that the spellings 'disk' and 'disc' can be encountered, the latter is usually associated with specific optical media formats, the former is commonly applied as the generic term for the format.

Compact Disc (CD)

The first compact disc incarnation was the Compact Disc Digital Audio (CD-DA) format introduced to replace long play (LP) audio recordings. The subsequent success of CD-ROM technology for computer-processable data is due largely to it being based on widely agreed and adopted standards, a fact that has not applied generally to other optical disk formats.

While its main application has been for educational and professional publishing often involving multimedia, the inclusion of CD-ROM drives as standard equipment in PCs meant that the 120mm CD-ROM disc with its 650MB capacity became widely used instead of 3.5inch floppies for software program and documentation distribution. An international standard (ISO 9660 1998) specifies the volume and file structure of CD-ROM discs for the information interchange between information processing systems. A further standard (ISO 10149 1995) specifies the characteristics of CD-ROM discs for information interchange between information processing systems and for information storage.

Data can be recorded to the CD-R and CD-RW formats, but only the latter allows further data to be written again to the same disc. Both formats are suitable for data archiving or back-up but are limited in these respects by their storage capacity given the range of multi-media that users now wish to store. Hence DVD formats have gained favour.

Digital Versatile Disc (DVD)

The DVD format has the same overall dimensions of a CD, but considerably larger storage capacities. Originally focused on the market for pre-recorded film, DVD stood for 'Digital Video Disc'. However the development of the technology positioned it in the same market segment as CD-ROM, hence the change in name. As with CD technology the main DVD formats are available in write-once (R) and rewritable (RW) formats. Depending on the format, the discs can be single or double sided for recording and are available in two diameters, 120mm and 80mm.

There are two main competing camps promoting their particular DVD flavours; The DVD Forum is an industry association (http://www.dvdforum.org/forum.shtml) and the DVD+R Alliance a voluntary group of manufacturers (http://www.dvdservices.org/). More recently, the Blu-ray Disc Association (http://www.blu-raydisc.com/en/index.aspx) was formed to further the development and use of the Blu-ray format. The formats of concern to each of these bodies are considered further below.

DVD Forum

The DVD Forum is an international association of hardware manufacturers and users of DVDs for exchanging and disseminating ideas and information about the DVD Format and its technical capabilities, improvements and innovations. It promotes the following formats:

DVD-R

This has a capacity of 4.7GB for a single layer and 8.5GB for a dual layer. Originally designed for professional authoring, it is now available to the general consumer. As with CD-R, users can write only once to this disc. It is the subject of international standards (ISO 20563 2001, ISO 23912 2005).

DVD-RAM

This is a rewritable format disc which was originally housed in cartridges and hence was only compatible with devices such as camcorders and set-top boxes. Later the media became available as individual discs offering capacities up to 9.4GB depending on the disc size and whether in single or double-sided form. Applicable standards are ISO 17592 2004 and ISO 17594 2004.

DVD-RW

This format is similar to DVD-RAM except that its technology features a sequential read-write access more like a phonograph than a hard disk. Its read-write capacity is 4.7GB per side (ISO 17342 2004).

DVD Audio

This audio format is expected to replace the standard audio CD.

DVD-Video

This provides very high studio-quality video in standard and wide screen aspect ratios, high quality multi-channel surround sound, up to 8 languages or simultaneous audio tracks, up to 32 subtitle tracks and fully interactive menu features, allowing viewers instantly to see and hear any part of the disc.

DVD-ROM

This is the DVD-counterpart of CD-ROM and its basic technology is similar to DVD-video. It provides up to 4.7GB of data, making it suitable for wide distribution of large amounts of data. Every DVD-ROM drive is physically able to play DVD-Video discs. DVD+R and DVD+RW share many of the technical characteristics of DVD-ROM, meaning almost all DVD-ROM equipped PCs and notebooks can read DVD+R and DVD+RW discs.

DVD+RW Alliance

The DVD Forum's proposal for recordable DVDs did not match the vision of some companies which decided to develop the DVD+R and DVD+RW formats outside the Forum. As a consequence, the DVD+RW Alliance was established as a voluntary group of manufacturers including Dell, Hewlett-Packard Company, MCC/Verbatim, Philips Electronics, Ricoh Company Ltd., Sony Corporation, Thomson multimedia and Yamaha Corporation. The aim was to develop and promote a universally compatible, rewritable DVD format to enable true convergence between personal computing and consumer electronics products. It promotes the following formats:

DVD+RW

This rewritable optical disc technology stores 4.7GB of data, equal to about 6 CDs, and up to 8 hours of video per disc side, depending on the quality setting (ISO 17341 2006). DVD+RW was developed to be fully compatible with existing DVD-Video players and DVD-ROM drives in computers.

DVD+R

This recordable optical disc technology stores 4.7GB of data on a DVD+R disc, (ISO 17344 2006). It provides storage of up to 8 hours of video per disc side, depending on the quality setting. A DVD+R disc cannot be rewritten, making it suitable for the distribution of data and video or for archival purposes.

DVD+R DL

This double layer technology increases the capacity of a single sided disc to 8.5GB, equal to a pre-recorded double layer DVD (ISO 25434 2007). It provides 4 hours of high quality video, or up to 16 hours of VHS quality video.

Blu-ray (BD)

With the coming of high definition television the Blu-ray format emerged, initially to store high definition video. The development and promotion of the format is undertaken by the Blu-ray Disc Association (http://www.blu-raydisc.com/en/index.aspx).

A Blu-ray Disc has the same physical characteristics as DVD and CD and the disc specification covers the following formats (http://www.blu-ray.com/faq/#bluray_speed):

- BD-ROM – read-only format for distribution of, for example, HD movies, games and software
- BD-R – recordable format for HD video recording and PC data storage
- BD-RE – rewritable format for HD video recording and PC data storage.

Discs are available with a single layer which can hold 25GB or two layers which doubles the capacity. There is also support for multi-layer discs, which should allow the storage capacity to be increased by 25GB per layer in the future simply by adding more layers to the discs.

There are plans for a BD/DVD hybrid format, which combines Blu-ray and DVD on the disc so that it can be played in both Blu-ray and DVD players.

Magneto-optical disks

Magneto-optical (MO) is a hybrid technology that involves storing the information on a magnetic substrate, but reading the stored data using a laser. The most widely used disks are 130mm in diameter, provide capacities from 650MB to 9.2GB and are held in plastic cartridges for loading on the drive unit. MO storage has not been widely adopted due principally to advances in DVD technology.

A development of MO called Ultra Density Optical (UDO) uses phase change technology combined with a blue violet laser. The latter has a shorter wavelength and hence increases storage capacity to 30 or 60GB per disk.

5.5.3 SOLID-STATE STORAGE (SSD)

Solid-state storage has no moving parts and uses integrated circuits instead of magnetic or optical media to store the data. It can retain the data without electrical power.

It is available in various forms; for example, as substitutes for magnetic hard drives in portable computers, as portable flash memory devices using the Universal Serial Bus (USB) connection and in proprietary formats such as CompactFash cards, Memory Stick and Secure Digital SD cards. While using the same flash memory technology, these latter formats evolved for use in digital cameras and similar devices, while solid-state storage devices (SSD) were developed for use within computer systems.

While storage capacity lags behind that for magnetic or optical devices, SSDs offer greater convenience in portable format for such requirements as transferring data between computers.

5.5.4 LIFE EXPECTANCY

When statements are made about the life expectancy of data on a storage media, there are three major questions that need to be considered when assessing the validity or otherwise of the claims:

- is the life span based on actual experience?
- has the technology (for example, drive units) associated with the media also been assessed?
- what standards apply to the storage media or drives?

Microfilm has the advantage of having been in use for a sufficient number of years to prove its ability to retain information in a readable and accessible form. Optical media generally have their life expectancy estimated based on the results of accelerated testing, much of this having only been undertaken by the manufacturers.

In overall terms, erasable media have a shorter claimed life expectancy than write-once media, with the former ranging from around 10 to 40 years, while the latter is estimated to reach 100 years.

Failure to live out the claimed life span can be due to a number of factors, some of which do not have such a harmful effect in the case of microfilm. Thus dust particles have been shown to be a more important factor than was at first realized. They adversely affect not simply the integrity of the data on the disk, but also the workings of the various systems and sub-systems; hence the developments by vendors to prevent the formation and entry of dust by improving component design and construction and to extract it where it might arise by controlling air flow and introducing filters.

These problems highlight the second major issue noted above, namely that one cannot simply focus on the life expectancy of the disk media. Images on a microfilm are readable by the human eye, given relatively unsophisticated mechanical aids. Simple observation can confirm the continued existence of the stored images in a readable form. With optical media, however, the information stored on a disk needs technology to render the same outcome. Highly engineered disk drives are required operating in conjunction with sophisticated sub-systems and software. The life expectancy of this associated technology is in most cases going to be less than that of the storage media, particularly if the amount of data that comes to be handled by the system accelerates usage of the system beyond its rated capacity.

When looking to replace ageing technology the third issue comes to light, that is the lack of standardization. The media themselves, the physical formats and the logical file structures are present in a variety of incarnations not all subject to all-embracing standards. While manufacturers might like to retain their existing customer bases by providing backward compatibility should the customer upgrade to the latest systems on offer, such compatibility cannot be assured. Market forces coupled with the irresistible advance of technology tend to stay in advance of standardization. Without proper planning, therefore, the unwary customer can find that their archived optically stored information cannot be read on the equipment they have just acquired.

The 'proper planning' referred to must include giving due attention to records management considerations as described earlier. Thus if the retention schedules devised for business records show that certain records need to be kept for 'the life of the company', for example, then the records management strategy must deal with such factors as media choice and conversion. This means choosing the storage media that provide the proper balance between such factors as the need for, and frequency of, access to the records, and their retention periods. The strategy may well adopt a dual media approach with some records being placed on microfilm for longer term retention, but having them on optical media for ready access.

To take account of the estimated life expectancy of any optical media that the business uses at present, and the changes in technology over time, the strategy should include plans and time-scales for transferring the existing optically stored information onto new (not necessarily different) media. This is no more than data processing departments have done for many years with data stored on magnetic tape.

Currently there are three international standards relating to the life expectancy of optical media (ISO 18921 2008, ISO 18926 2006, ISO 18927 2008) and one relating to archival lifetime (ISO 10995 2011). Further standards provide guidance on storage practices for optical media (ISO 18925 2008), care and handling of magnetic tape (ISO 18933 2006) and storage environment for multiple media archives (ISO 18934 2006).

In general, the integrity of data will be more readily ensured where the media is write-only since there will have been no possibility of the data being overwritten or otherwise altered.

5.6 Legal Admissibility

Having the originals of documents would seem to be the surest way of guaranteeing the legal acceptability of such records and the information they contain. For many people the word 'original' implies a paper-based document. However, with the advent of computers and associated software such as that used for word-processing and electronic trading, the 'original' is usually created in electronic form and may, in fact, never be printed out. The use of such technologies can therefore lead to a blurring of the distinction between originals and their surrogates.

While micrographic images have an established history of being presented in court the same does not apply to electronic imaging and optical storage, for example. Electronic imaging has the additional handicap, however, of being a newer technology and there is still a lack of industry and user experience based on stable and well-understood equipment. Furthermore, electronic images are readily amended given the appropriate software, and the changes are likely to be 'seamless'.

The issues of admissibility continue to be addressed on two main fronts. Thus governments have laws and regulations relevant to the use of records as evidence, as exemplified by the 'Federal Rules of Evidence', 'Uniform Rules of Evidence' and 'Uniform Photographic Copies of Business and Public Records As Evidence Act' in the USA and the 'Police and Criminal Evidence Act' and 'Electronic Communications Act' in the UK. This last Act, for example, admits electronic signatures in legal proceedings provided they have been certified.

Alongside the regulatory approach, there are standards and guidelines relevant to legal admissibility. Thus BS 10008 (2008) specifies the requirements for the implementation and operation of electronic information management systems, and for the electronic transfer of information from one computer system to another, addressing issues relating to the authenticity and integrity of the electronic information. Codes of practice relating to the implementation of BS 10008 are available (BIP 0008 2008)) together with a compliance workbook (BIP 0009 2008).

Although in the end it is up to the Court to decide what is, or is not admissible, gaining legal acceptance for a particular record is more likely to be the norm if suitable care and attention have been taken over the operational procedures that have lead to its creation, and the management policies that have been applied to monitor, control, audit and document such procedures.

In essence to maximize the chances of legal acceptability:

- ensure the digital records such as images provide the best evidence available
- ensure the records have been created and used in the normal course of business activities
- have a comprehensive and documented records management strategy with accompanying policies, procedures and retention schedules that are in operation, are being monitored and controlled and are auditable

The related topic of e-Discovery is considered in Section 6.8.6.

5.7 Conclusion

Effective and efficient management of information that the organization captures provides the best assurance that up-to-date and relevant information is organized and available to those with the authority and rights to access it. Collaborative work is aided by functionality such as strict version control and content integrity offered by many content and records management systems. Structuring the records, including case files, according to the organization's business functions provides continuity during times when the management structure is reorganized. It also eases the assignment of retention schedules and decisions over retention, disposal or transfer. The introduction of new systems may require paper-based filing to be replaced or legacy computer systems to be retired and data migrated. The information management processes need to cover such eventualities. Finally, the storage media and devices chosen to receive the files should be appropriate for the intended future use of the captured information taking into account life expectancy and legal admissibility.

Resources spent on capture and management are of little consequence unless the information is readily retrievable for subsequent use. These aspects are covered in the next chapter.

6 *Information Retrieval and Use*

'The number of books will grow continually, and one can predict that a time will come when it will be almost as difficult to learn anything from books as from the direct study of the whole universe'. Denis Diderot (1713–1784)

Diderot was acknowledging the plethora of information and the challenges of acquiring relevant information. Since the eighteenth century not only has the number of books increased greatly, but so have the types of media on which information can be recorded, copied and reproduced and by which it can be communicated and made available. Hence there is a major challenge to find the needed information before it can be used – in Diderot's case to further learning.

In this chapter the focus is on the means of searching and retrieving information and, once found, how the information might be used, as depicted in Figure 6.1.

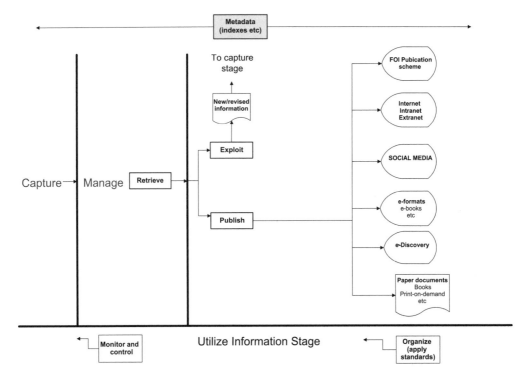

Figure 6.1   Utilize information stage

Before one can utilize information it first has to be found. Once retrieved, the information is available for exploitation, which in this context means using the information intellectually. The output of this activity will need to be captured into the system, thereby emphasizing the dynamic nature of the information life cycle. Alternatively, once retrieved the information may be published in different formats and through different media.

6.1 Seeking Information

At the time of Diderot the route to finding the required information may have involved such stages as:

* realizing an information need, possibly arising from the lack of information in immediately available personal sources
* determining where best to go for that information – the necessary referral to an archive or records collection, for example, may have come from a knowledgeable acquaintance
* identifying the documents that may contain the required information; hence references to them are needed
* provision of the relevant documents so that finally the required information can be extracted from them.

These stages are summarized in Figure 6.2.

INFORMATION STAGES	TYPE OF SOLUTION
Information need?	Sources to-hand
Where located?	Referral service
What document etc.?	Reference service
Where obtained?	Record provision service
What does it contain?	Information retrieval

Figure 6.2   Information seeking stages

While all these stages remain relevant in the twenty-first century, the one that has been revolutionized is that relating to information retrieval (IR). Whereas computer-based indexing and retrieval was once the sole domain of academics and libraries, few of us now go a day without exercising some mode of information seeking which involves computing or communication technology and the use of search aids. Furthermore, we are often able to avoid having to consider where information is located, in what form it exists and where can we get it. This is because modern search engines, such as those used on the web, are indifferent in these regards, being able to deal with and deliver recorded information from whatever source that has been made available in a form that is amenable to automated indexing.

With the ability to create information in, or to convert existing information into, machine-readable and searchable form there is the potential for recorded knowledge to be readily available to organizations. An overview of the types of information sources that can constitute such knowledge is provided in Figure 6.3.

This portrayal appeared in the first edition of this book and despite advances in technology and proliferation in communication channels, recorded information is still 'packaged' in such a fashion to suit users' needs, irrespective of whether the content is held electronically or on paper.

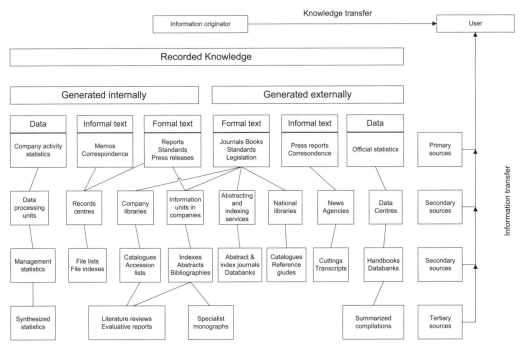

Figure 6.3   Sources of recorded knowledge

6.1.1 RETRIEVAL FROM STRUCTURED AND UNSTRUCTURED INFORMATION

'Information' possesses some unique characteristics, for example:

- its usefulness, relevance or value can vary with time
- it can be used simultaneously by more than one person
- it can exist independently of physical form i.e. in one's brain (as knowledge)
- it can be open to different interpretations and degrees of acceptability depending on such factors as social and cultural background, gender and one's state of motivation

For example, a service report from a maintenance engineer is unlikely to be of interest to those in the legal department. However, if it transpires that as a result of the service, equipment has severely malfunctioned, then the company lawyers may well become involved in litigation and have need to see that report along with other documents such as time sheets and appointment records.

A procurement department will typically organize purchase orders by order numbers which provide the main means for departmental reference and access. Those responsible for paying the suppliers' invoices, however, are more likely to organize their files by the suppliers' names and addresses than by order number. Hence different retrieval aids are required to get at related, if not essentially the same, information.

It should be clear from just these two examples that knowledge of the types of query that information seekers may pose is vital in the design of an IR system. More than that, the IR system may need to cater for the ad-hoc query that departs from the planned and expected approach; for example, finding by means of e-Discovery that elusive piece of correspondence needed to defend a lawsuit.

In the examples just provided, the service report is likely to have been a word-processed document, while the purchase order information may have been generated from a database management system (DBMS) holding procurement data and providing means to query the information. Hence the report is an example of unstructured information, while the purchase order information is structured in the form of database tables.

Searching the database for order information to find if a specific supplier is on the system will typically involve either:

- posing queries to the database using a Structured Query Language (SQL); or more likely
- using a menu on the screen through which the name of the supplier is entered.

Assuming the supplier exists on the database, the result of the query will be that the details of that supplier are displayed. If the supplier is not on the database a nil return will result.

As regards the service report example there may be a need to undertake some further research to determine if the type of failure resulting from the service has occurred in other equipment. As there is no database recording this information in structured form, the search query will therefore be less well defined or structured than that undertaken to find the supplier, and may have to be used across a diverse information collection. Hence it is quite possible that after the search is performed not all examples of the type of failure will be found, nor will all that is found relate to that failure type.

In broad terms the basic distinguishing features of DBMS and IR systems are shown in Figure 6.4.

For DBMS systems there usually has to be an exact match between the query posed and the information stored to have a successful conclusion. DBMS have therefore mainly been used where such predictable conditions prevail, typically in transaction processing-type systems. The design of such databases is centred on the concepts of data and process modelling, and of structuring the data into related entities (customer, order, invoice, for example). Various designs of DBMS software – principally hierarchical, network and relational – exist to provide the necessary linkages between the entities, the choice of design being largely dependent upon the nature, frequency and predictability of the search queries.

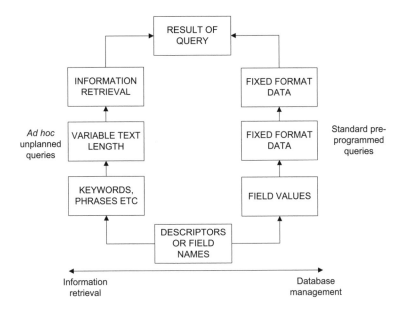

Figure 6.4   Contrasting DBMS and IR systems

Information retrieval systems, on the other hand, are aimed principally at unstructured information. They involve the use of more natural language than the somewhat artificial query languages such as SQL often found in DBMS. Furthermore, they do not rely on an exact match to achieve useful results. As an example, when seeking information on accidents at railway level crossing, details may be found of personal injuries from crossing railways. Although this information is not precisely what was sought it may prove to be sufficiently relevant and therefore useful.

This chapter is principally concerned with information retrieval rather than database management systems.

6.1.2 ASSESSING RETRIEVAL PERFORMANCE

With the supplier query on the database there can be no uncertainty as to the accuracy and precision of the result; the enquiry has resulted in retrieving 100 per cent of what is sought (details of the one supplier) and 100 per cent of the required item (in this case just one supplier). These measurements, termed recall and precision, are important measure of retrieval performance.

For the service failure query not everything that is relevant is retrieved, hence recall is less than 100 per cent. Also some irrelevant items are retrieved so that precision is also less than 100 per cent.

Put in terms in which retrieval performance is usually quoted:

Recall =
Number of relevant item retrieved divided by the Number of relevant items in the database

Precision =
Number of relevant items retrieved divided by the Number of items retrieved

In general, for searching unstructured information, recall and precision are inversely proportional so that as recall increases, precision decreases.

Much research has been undertaken and is ongoing into evaluating the performance of information retrieval systems. One such is the Text REtrieval Conference (TREC) http://trec.nist.gov/, co-sponsored by the National Institute of Standards and Technology (NIST) and U.S. Department of Defense. This was started in 1992 to support research within the information retrieval community by providing the infrastructure necessary for large-scale evaluation of text retrieval methodologies.

6.2 Transaction and Non-Transaction Documents

The 'formal text' information noted in Figure 6.3 can be divided into two broad categories of document:

- transaction documents
- non-transaction documents.

While there is often a need to retrieve information across both categories of document, there are important distinctions between them as regards indexing needs and the requirements for retrieval.

6.2.1 TRANSACTION DOCUMENTS

Transaction documents, for example purchase orders, invoices, credit notes, deeds, cheques, insurance policies and certified as-built engineering construction drawings, provide a record of a business event, such as the placing of an order. Such documents are intimately associated with transaction processing applications. Transaction processing systems represent the longest-established type of computer-based information system.

Transaction documents provide evidence of the business event having occurred. As part of an integrated series of records, they show the consequences that followed. They contain prescribed types of information usually arranged in a structured format.

Because of their evidentiary nature and their inherent association with business events, it may be important that transaction documents are retained. Retention may be as originals (in paper or electronic form depending on the initial method of creation), or as facsimiles such as images or photocopies, provided there are no problems over legal acceptability. The emphasis with transaction documents is therefore more on retrieval of the document, at least in the first instance, than retrieval of the information within it.

Since they contain structured data, transaction documents do not usually pose major indexing problems. Thus an index for purchase orders might be adequately based on the order number and name of supplier. A more comprehensive index may be required, however, if an order tracking system is required. In this case the date of the order, the required date of delivery and the name of the requesting department might have to be recorded, for example. For an engineering drawing register, the drawing number, revision number, date and drawing location may be perfectly sufficient for retrieval.

With the increased use of e-commerce and the adoption of XML mark-up language, transaction documents have become more dynamic objects and their data content more accessible for further processing. Even so, technology is available to:

- capture documents via scanners, faxes, email or directly from line-of-business systems such as procurement
- extract data from the captured documents to update other systems
- store index data via OCR and if necessary store it with the original document.

6.2.2 NON-TRANSACTION DOCUMENTS

This second category of document is more problematical as regards indexing because it relates to administrative and reference-type material. Such material is generally less structured and less uniform in make-up than transaction documents. Furthermore, it often originates from outside the organization hence control cannot usually be exercised over content and structure.

Documents in this category include policies and procedures, standards and specifications, operating and maintenance manuals, minutes of meetings, research reports, consultancy reports, trade literature, press cuttings, journal articles and books.

While transaction documents are an integral part of day-to-day business processes usually dealt with by staff dedicated to such tasks, non-transactional documents have a broader and more diffuse set of users. Concerns here focus on such issues as management and control, business strategy, research and development, project management, design and production, sales and marketing, and public and press relations. These are the functions peopled by 'knowledge workers'. They are more interested in the information content of documents.

The emphasis here, then, is on subject-based information-retrieval rather than document-retrieval. Such a requirement is far more demanding of the indexing system since there may be little or no prior knowledge as to the type of query that a user will pose. Furthermore, there is frequently a need to integrate information across a range of possible sources, be they collections of documents or databases containing structured information, or sources internal or external to the organization.

6.3 Document- as Opposed to Information-Storage

The preceding section was concerned with retrieval rather than storage. This distinction is important because the retrieval process, involving as it does the indexing of information, is essentially an intellectual process. Storage is a separate physical activity.

In the design of the overall computer-based information storage and retrieval system the decision has to be made as to whether complete documents, document surrogates (such as abstracts), pure data independent of any documents or any combination of these, are to be stored. This possible range of information types is exemplified in Figure 6.5.

INFORMATION STORED	EXAMPLE OF DATABASE	INFORMATION RETRIEVED
FULL DOCUMENT with text, tables, figures etc	Court cases	Case rulings
DOCUMENT SURROGATE e.g. abstract	Article summaries on crime	Relevant references
DATA	Crime statistics	Required facts

Figure 6.5   Types of information stored

Despite this range of options, there is usually certain basic and mostly structured retrieval data to be found in an index to documents, for example:

- document type
- originating organization
- reference number of document
- security classification
- publication date
- file reference/classification code
- title
- author(s) names
- summary/abstract of document
- keywords (for example, from controlled vocabulary)
- names of recipients
- retention date (from records retention schedules)
- destruction date
- name of person authorizing destruction.

Categorization of documents into mutually exclusive document types can aid the designing of document templates, and hence capture of metadata, at the creation stage. It also aids subsequent retrieval by allowing users to search by document type. Examples of widely recognized categories include correspondence, forms and reports. More specific categories can be devised to suit the needs of individual organizations.

The last three items listed above arise from records management considerations (see Chapter 5). Much of above information may appear on a standard data page in the document. This data, or selected parts of it, might be captured electronically by having links between the document's word processing template and the indexing engine of the document management system, or by digitally scanning pre-defined areas of the page where the document is paper-based.

Note that with the implementation of document imaging, additional decisions would need to be made as regards paper documents:

- should the paper be scanned and converted to a digital image?
- if so, should the original paper be kept along with the image, or should only the image be retained?
- should the image be subjected to OCR?

- should the OCR versions be retained along with its associated image?
- should the image be converted to a portable document format such as Adobe Acrobat PDF?

Deciding which of these options to adopt, either singly or in combination, depends on a number of factors. These include the needs of users for access to the document rather than the data it holds and any constraints imposed by available technology such as storage capacity and response times over a network. Image files are large compared with text files and can be slow to access over a network. The totality of documents and the information they contain must be indexed in a suitably coherent and consistent fashion irrespective of the storage media strategy that is adopted.

6.4 The Nature of an Information Retrieval System

An IR system[1] is more than is implied by the word 'retrieval'. According to Chowdhury (2010) its main functions are to:

- identify the information sources relevant to the enquirers' interests
- analyze the contents of the source-documents in the broadest sense
- represent the contents of analyzed sources in a way that matches the users' queries
- analyze the users' queries and represent them in a form suitable for matching the IR database
- match the search statement with the stored database
- retrieve and present the sought information.

A simplified representation of this is provided in Figure 6.6.

The 'index' is at the core of an IR system, but it has many manifestations as will be described later. For now, according to the OED (2001) an index is 'A list of things in (usu. alphabetical) order; esp. a list, usu. at the end of a book, giving the names, topics, etc., mentioned in the book and the places where they occur'.

The concept of a book index is applied in many IR and database systems for text retrieval. It involves the creation of an inverted file which contains all the index terms extracted automatically from the electronic document store with pointers to where each of the indexed items resides in the store.

In order to avoid indexing unwanted words such as 'and' and 'the' a stop word list is used to ensure these are ignored during the automated extraction stage. What is placed in the stop list needs careful thought. For example a packaging company that makes cans will not want the word 'can' in the stop list otherwise searches for a packaging-type 'can' will retrieve nothing.

Before delving further into indexing, other ways to organize information to aid retrieval need to be described, namely cataloguing and classification.

---

1   Section 6.4: Adapted with permission of Facet Publishing from text on pages 6 and 7 of Chowdhury, G.G. 2010. *Introduction to Modern Information Retrieval*. London: Facet Publishing.

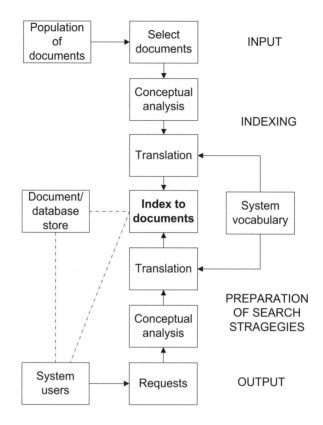

Figure 6.6   Main components of an IR system

6.5 Cataloguing

If you don't find it in the index, look very carefully through the entire catalogue.
Sears, Roebuck, and Co., *Consumer's Guide*, 1897

A catalogue is 'A list, register, or complete enumeration; now spec. one systematically or methodically arranged, often with brief particulars or descriptions aiding identification etc.' (OED 2001).

It has long been the practice for libraries to organize their stock to facilitate access, by enabling users to find works by:

- author
- title
- subject.

Rules for cataloguing draw on the work of the International Federation of Library Associations and Institutions (http://www.ifla.org/) and their International Standard Bibliographic Description (ISBD). In the English-speaking world the Anglo-American Cataloguing Rules, Second Edition, (AACR2 2005) are commonly used and enable additional descriptive entries to be made over and above the three noted above. The rules, designed originally for manual cataloguing, provide for three levels, each successive level enabling greater amounts of detail to be added.

With the coming of Online Public Access Catalogues (OPAC) and the increasing use of the web for accessing information resources, the limitations of existing cataloguing rules to deal with the greater variety of electronic and web-based information became clear. To address these shortcomings AACR2 was succeeded by the Resource Description and Access (RDA) (http://www.rda-jsc.org/index.html), which was released in June 2010 and was the result of collaboration between national libraries.

RDA is based on conceptual models (entities, relationships and attributes) and provides a comprehensive set of guidelines and instructions covering all types of content and media.

6.5.1 METADATA

Aside from 'author, title, subject' there is a range of other attributes that are attached to an information resource to help find or manage it in some way. Various interest groups have created metadata standard,s the principal ones being:

- e-GMS (2004) is the UK Government Metadata Standard and defines how metadata should be applied to government resources. eGMS is published in XML but is available in other formats.
- ISAD(G) (1999) provides general guidance for the preparation of archival descriptions.
- EAD (2002) Encoded Archival Description is an XML standard for encoding archival finding aids, maintained by the Library of Congress in partnership with the Society of American Archivists.
- Dublin Core (2010). The Dublin Core Metadata Initiative, or 'DCMI', is an open organization engaged in the development of interoperable metadata standards for electronic resources.
- MARC (1999) are USA standards for the representation and communication of bibliographic and related information in machine-readable form.

In addition there is the international standard (ISO 11179 2004) which specifies in six parts the kind and quality of metadata necessary to describe data and describes the management and administration of that metadata in a metadata registry.

Of relevance to records management are the Modular Requirements for Records Systems (MoReq10 2010). This is more prescriptive than previous such specifications, especially over the metadata elements that each compliant records system must keep so as to facilitate interchange of records between different systems.

Catalogues are essentially lists of holdings or resources and are not primarily designed to find required information by subject, although terms in the titles are available for searching. For subject access more reliance is placed on classification and indexing.

6.6 Classification

Classification involves the conceptual and often physical grouping together of items within a hierarchical (tree-like) subject-based structure. One has in effect to determine to which conceptual 'pigeon hole' a piece of information is assigned. A file plan derived from a Business Classification, and a web directory services as provided by the Internet-based portal company Yahoo! are examples. The structure helps users navigate to information of interest.

Many types of document fall naturally into conceptual groupings which are to a degree self-indexing. Thus invoices and purchase orders will usually be referenced by their respective invoice and order numbers, and can therefore be arranged accordingly. If the queries posed on such collections are only based on these numbers, then a self-indexing arrangement is sufficient. However, that is rarely the case as information such as the supplier's name may be sought. In such cases additional indexes need to be created, since for all but the smallest collection of documents, searching through the complete collection for these names is not a realistic option.

Widely accepted universal enumerative classification schemes are available, such as the Dewey Decimal Classification (Dewey 2011) in the library field. However, their principles can be difficult to apply consistently. This problem will be appreciated by anyone who has tried to decide into which single drawer file a piece of correspondence that deals with a variety of topics should be placed.

Such classification schemes assign codes to subjects, and these codes are usually employed to determine the filing order for the information, particularly in paper-based systems. More than one classification code can be applied to a document to reflect different subject viewpoints. In filing terms this is similar to copying one paper document onto the several different files with which it is concerned, or providing cross-references to the item from the related files.

The widely adopted universal classifications such as Dewey and UDC are designed principally for organizing physical general library collections. Bespoke classifications have been devised for special interest groups, examples being the Association for Computing Machinery Classification Scheme (ACM 1998) and the National Library of Medicine (NLM 2011).

To provide more flexibility in assigning classifications than is provided by enumerative schemes, analytico-synthetic and faceted classifications were developed. An example of the former is the Universal Decimal Classification (UDC 2005) and of the latter the Colon Classification (Ranganathan 2006). Faceted classifications provide the ability to assign multiple classifications to a resource. The theory behind them has influenced the development of later IR systems.

6.7 Indexing – the Key to Retrieval

The subject classification approach described above will normally direct one to the part of a collection most likely to include the information that is sought, rather than pinpoint the required information precisely. Indexes, however, will indicate specific and likely relevant items of information within that collection. Indexes exist in many forms and may be produced manually, or with the aid of computers, or by a combination of the two.

6.7.1 MANUAL INDEXING

In order to index an information resource manually it is necessary for the indexer to perform subject analysis which Chowdhury (2010) defines as 'the presence, identification and expression of subject matter in document texts, databases, controlled and natural languages, information requests and search strategies'.

Guidelines exist to aid the indexer in BS 6529 (1984) which outlines two steps:

- identification of concepts which are essential elements in a description of the subject
- translation of the concepts into indexing terms contained in or added to an appropriate indexing language (system vocabulary), which may incorporate a thesaurus.

The standard does not prescribe whether the chosen index terms are to be used in pre- or post-coordinate fashion. In pre-coordination the combining of index terms is undertaken by the indexer rather than the searcher. Entries in a book index exemplify this, for example an index entry for a Venetian blind might be 'Blinds – Venetian'. In a post-coordinate system the individual words are combined by the user at search time using Boolean logic; that is, the search would be for 'Venetian' AND 'blind'. These terms are then compared with those in the index file to find a match and effect the retrieval.

An advantage of post-coordinate indexing is that single words may be combined, which increases recall. However, precision is reduced as some of the material retrieved may contain the search term but in the wrong context. Thus the search for 'Venetian' AND 'blind' may recall articles about 'blind Venetians' as well as the window blind. Pre-coordinate indexing in contrast will tend to increase precision, but decrease recall.

An issue with manual indexing is that no two persons will necessarily arrive at the same set of concepts, nor may they use any existing indexing language in the same way. Hence the indexing terms that are the product of the process may differ.

6.7.2 AUTOMATIC INDEXING

Automatic indexing involves the analysis of text by means of computer algorithms. Its advantages as compared with manual indexing were said by Salton (1989) to include:

- greater level of indexing consistency
- index entries are produced at lower cost
- indexing time is reduced.

Initially starting with the identification and counting of individual words, the process was refined by various means to assist with subsequent search and retrieval by, for example:

- detecting phrases rather than just single words
- applying weights to terms; for example, if they appeared in the title or if they appeared more than three times in the document
- applying a stop word list to avoid recording connecting words such as 'and', 'a' and 'the'
- clustering involving the bringing together of similar documents; a form of classification
- citation indexing in bibliographic databases which provides an index of citations in and between publications.

The main advances came when instead of merely searching for a string of characters such as 'C A R' about which the computer had no idea of the underlying concept, it became possible to comprehend the meaning behind it. Thus the search for 'C A R' might also retrieve information about vehicles, other makes of car and transport which might be very relevant for the enquirer. The ability to achieve this is due to such techniques as semantic analysis, which is language specific, and pattern matching which is language independent.

Indexing the web involves the use of spiders or crawlers which progressively fetch web pages, extract the text and URLs (Uniform Resource Locators). The decision on which pages to index depends on criteria that are generally only known to those holding the intellectual rights for the search engine. The additional facilities provided to aid subsequent search and retrieval mirror those noted above and include page ranking which is similar in concept to citation indexing in that the most important pages are considered to be those having the most links to them.

Applying tags is an important means to help structure and process information. Prime examples are HTML, XML and XHTML. XML has created great interest for the interchange of information and as an alternative way of storing structured information for retrieval. However, XML files become progressively larger and require more processing as the requirement to be more specific in indexing increases, which can limit their use.

The Semantic Web aims to provide a common framework that allows web data to be shared and reused across application, enterprise, and community boundaries. While currently links on the web are between web pages, the aim of the Semantic Web is to establish relationships between any two resources; there is no notion of 'current' page. Another major difference is that the relationship, that is, the link itself is named, whereas the link used by a human on the traditional web is not and their role is deduced by the human reader. The definition of these relations is provided by the Resource Definition Framework (RDF), which is one of the fundamental building blocks of the Semantic Web (W3C 2004). From these definitions a kind of data model can be envisaged using an RDF schema and vocabularies developed, for example, using the Web Ontology Language OWL (Antoniou and van Harmelen 2009, W3C 2009).

An interesting initiative from OASIS is the Unstructured Information Management Architecture Standard (UIMA 2009) which defines platform-independent data representations and interfaces for software components or services called analytics, which analyze unstructured information and assign semantics to regions of that unstructured information. It aims to enable interoperability of analytics across all formats – text, audio, video, and so on.

6.7.3 THE SYSTEM VOCABULARY

In creating an index whether manually or with computer-assistance, there are two basic approaches. Thus index terms may be 'natural language' terms such as those appearing in the original text of the title, abstract or body of the information resource. Alternatively, the terms are determined by the indexer, possibly drawing on a pre-determined, 'controlled language' vocabulary such as a subject classification, a list of subject headings or a thesaurus.

A thesaurus is a vocabulary of controlled indexing language, formally organized so that a priori relationships between concepts are made explicit. Guidance on thesaurus construction is provided in an international standard ISO 2788 (1986) which is to be replaced by ISO 25964, under development at the time of writing.

In devising such a controlled language, it needs to be matched to the subject content of the particular information collection that is to be indexed, to the type and detail of the questions that will be posed and to the relative experience of the users of the retrieval system. While there may be existing controlled languages that are suitable as the basis for devising a new scheme, considerable intellectual effort and time may still have to be expended to create the desired thesaurus. It is therefore important to ensure that such effort is commensurate with the associated benefits. To avoid this expense commercial information retrieval software may come with the ability to create a thesaurus based on the entire universe of information that is accessed. Furthermore, the thesaurus is dynamic and is automatically updated as new terms emerge or change their meanings in some way.

The use of controlled languages is well-established and pre-dates the computer era. However, use of natural language only became a realistic option with the advent of the computer and machine-readable text as generated by word processors or optical character recognition software operating on digitally-scanned documents. In general terms, natural language indexing saves effort at the input (indexing) stage, but places an increased burden on the searcher. Controlled languages incur higher indexing costs, but facilitate searching. There are proponents for both approaches, and in fact it is possible to combine them in various ways to enhance performance for specific applications. The controlled vocabulary, if used at all, could be applied at the input or output stages or in both cases as shown in Figure 6.6.

At the extreme of controlled vocabularies one can include expert systems. These are computer programs encapsulating the knowledge of experts on a particular subject so that the knowledge is available to others. An expert system is composed of three elements:

- a knowledge base containing facts and rules
- an inference engine which manipulates the knowledge base
- a user interface to these first two elements.

The knowledge base contains a semantic map (akin to a thesaurus, but with more explicit relationships) and rules based on an 'IF.THEN' logic. Its success is based on the quality of the data and rules obtained from the human expert. Expert systems can work reasonably well in relatively closed systems such as for medical diagnosis, equipment repair and training. However, if even a simple problem is posed just slightly beyond their experience, they will usually provide a wrong answer, without any recognition that they are beyond their range of competence. Also, such programs can not readily share their knowledge, as each represents its bit of the world in idiosyncratic and incompatible ways.

Taking a wider view of the extent to which language can be expressed, Uschold and Gruninger (2004) outlined a continuum from applying simple terms to describe an information resource through data dictionaries and database schema to formal taxonomies and higher order semantic logic; see Figure 6.7.

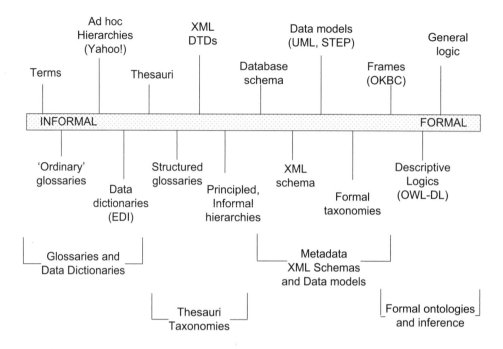

Figure 6.7   Kinds of ontologies

Source: Reproduced with permission of Michael F Uschold

The amount of meaning capable of being specified and the degree of formality involved increases as one moves along the continuum and in so doing it reduces semantic ambiguity.

6.7.4 INFORMATION RETRIEVAL FACILITIES

A variety of aids and techniques are available to assist with searching and retrieval of unstructured information. Some have already been mentioned, but for completeness a summary is provided in Figure 6.8.

An example of the use of such aids is provided by Elsevier's ScienceDirect full-text scientific database (http://www.info.sciverse.com/Home) which offers subscription-based access to peer-reviewed journal articles and book chapters. Citations and abstracts and a limited amount of full-text content are free to a Guest User. The search facilities available include:

- subject groupings (2 level classification)
- personal names
- years (single or span)
- title of article or book
- journal title
- volume number and pages
- images
- Boolean searching

- wild cards
- word fragments
- proximity searching
- singular and plurals
- saving searches.

On retrieving the results the user is offered the options:

- view previews (typically an abstract)
- download PDF versions
- export the citations contained in retrieved items
- email the item
- find related items.

Facility	Explanation	Comments
Approved ('go') word list	Only indexes words that match a list of approved terms	Facility may be provided by a thesaurus
Boolean operators (connectors)	Link search terms using the operators 'AND', 'OR' and 'NOT' e.g. find 'A' AND 'B' but not 'C'	May be possible to combine operators into a more complex search statement by the use of brackets. Important to know the order of preference recommended by the system
Concept tree	A user-definable hierarchical arrangement of subject terms to build up subject profiles reflecting the areas of interest to the enquirer	Essentially a micro-thesaurus. Profiles may incorporate operators connecting terms to sub-terms, and weights to allow the retrieved information to be ranked in order of their relevance to the enquiry
Date searching	Enables dates stored in different formats to be searched	Dates are located regardless of the form in which they are expressed in the query or in the document. Ambiguity is resolved by reference to the regional settings
Fixed field searching	Searches can be limited to a specified field (such as an author field) or a set of fields (e.g. those containing subject term, i.e. title, keywords and abstract fields)	Used with structured databases; provides high degree of precision
Homograph control	Prevents irrelevant information being retrieved due to the search words having the same spelling but different meanings	Scope notes used to differentiate. Usually found in thesaurus-based retrieval systems. Improves the precision of searching

Figure 6.8   Retrieval aids

Facility	Explanation	Comments
Hyperlink	A predefined linkage between one object and another. The link is displayed either as text or as an icon	Browsers are used to navigate the Internet through a vast lattice of hyperlinks using HTML
Hypertext	A linkage between related text, e.g. by selecting a word in a sentence, information about that word is retrieved if it exists, or the next occurrence of the word is found	A navigation aid rather than a retrieval mechanism
Links and Roles	Used to prevent false co-ordination of search terms or incorrect relationships; e.g. an article on lead coating of copper pipes would not be relevant if one just entered the words as search terms but was seeking copper coating of lead pipes	The terms are grouped or provided with role indicators at indexing time. Usually found in thesaurus-based retrieval systems. Improves the precision of searching
Phrase searching	Phrases e.g. 'information retrieval' rather than the individual words are retrieved	Improves precision of searching
Proximity Searching	This enables the user to specify the relative positions of search terms, e.g. the words must be next to each other, within a certain number of words of one another, in the same sentence or in the same paragraph, or preceding one another by a specified number of words	Improves the precision of searching
Range searching	Enables searching for information within a ranges of dates or numbers	For example, find documents dated between 01/01/1995 to 31/12/1998 or containing a value between £3M and £9M
Refining searches	Refining or expanding the previous search because the initially retrieved items may prove to be too great, or too few in number	Most retrieval systems provide an indication of the number of items that have been found in response to the search query
Related items	Finding others resources related to those retrieved. The way relationship is determined will be system-specific. For example keywords are extracted from the retrieved document and used to conduct another search, and/ or terms are weighted based on frequency of occurrence	Widens the search to find other possibly relevant items. Likely to increase recall, but reduce precision

Figure 6.8 *Continued*

Facility	Explanation	Comments
Relevance ranking	The answers received to a query are ranked according to some measure of relevance to the enquirer	Ranking may be based simply on the frequency of occurrence of a search term in the text or e.g. on a pre-stored subject interest profile coupled with statistical and linguistic analysis of the text – see 'Weighting'
Saved searches	Completed searches are saved for future use, e.g. following an updating of the database	Can be used to store a user's interest profiles which are run regularly against the database. User can be notified of, or sent the retrieved information (an example of 'push technology')
Singular and plurals	Searching for singular version will pick up plurals, e.g. enter 'city' will also find 'cities'	Improves recall
Sound-alike	Ability to search for words or phrases which sound similar	Improves the precision of searching
Stop word list	Avoids indexing common words such as 'and', 'the', 'a'	List should be user-amendable.
Summarizers	Automatic creation of reasonably accurate and intelligent abstract from the content of a document or set of documents	Abstracts can be fed into full text retrieval software as a query-by-example
Synonym control	Prevents scattering of synonyms across the database, typically by having preferred and non-preferred terms.	Usually found in thesaurus-based retrieval systems. Improves recall of information
Weighting	Applying values to index terms or search terms to indicate their relative importance in documents or search programs	May be found in thesaurus-based retrieval systems. Improves the precision of searching
Wild card searching	Where the precise spelling or format of the character string is not known, a 'wild card' character can be inserted into the search string	Depending on the type of wild card chosen, it may represent a single unknown character or any number of unknown characters
Word fragment searching	Searching for a particular string of characters irrespective of what other characters either follow that string or precede it, e.g. CORR* will find all information indexed by words beginning with CORR such as CORRosion, CORRoding and CORRode, while *CORR will retrieve deCORRode	A truncation facility helps find relevant information, particularly where a thesaurus has not been used. The required string may also be located in the body of the word, so that both forms of truncation are used. Improves recall of information

Figure 6.8 *Concluded*

6.8 Information Utilization

Information and knowledge are of no value unless they are used to help achieve particular ends. This is the key activity in the life cycle model since it justifies the existence of the whole system. Recorded information can be exploited in some way or published (see Figure 6.1).

Exploitation involves consulting source information (for example, by reading recorded information or talking to those with the required knowledge), adding to it, copying or deleting it, or otherwise integrating it in some way to render it more useful and applicable to solving current problems. The output of the exploitation then needs to pass through the life cycle again.

Publication is the action of making the information known by some means to an audience, which may be the general public or one that is specifically targeted such as customers, suppliers or internal users. The act of publication does not materially alter the content to a point where it constitutes new or formally revised information. It may, however, be reformatted in some way to render it suitable for the output medium.

Even though the information content has not changed, it may be justifiable to capture this format of the recorded information and subject it to document or records management procedures. It is up to individual organizations to decide the criteria on which such a decision is made. Control of what is published can be exercised through an EDRM or Content Management System that provides functionality such as version control and means to log the publication step such as replication to a website.

6.8.1 UK LEGISLATION IMPACTING ACCESS TO AND USE OF INFORMATION

Access to information from public authorities and protection of personal data are the subject of two important pieces of UK legislation:

* Freedom of Information Act 2000 (FOIA) and
* Data Protection Act 1998 (DPA).

The Information Commissioner's Office (ICO) (http://www.ico.gov.uk/) is the body that oversees these Acts, and also the:

* Environmental Information Regulations, 2004 SI 2004/3391 (EIR) and
* Privacy and Electronic Communications Regulations (PECR).

Aside from the FOIA, all the other legislation arose from the UK government's obligations as a member of the European Union.

The FOIA and EIR apply to the vast majority of UK public authorities (of which there are over 100,000). Key exceptions include the security and intelligence organizations and the Queen and the Royal Family. FOIA also applies to companies that are wholly owned by public authorities and it may be extended to include other organizations in the UK which may carry out work of a public nature. The EIR applies to most public authorities that are covered by the Freedom of Information Act, but according to the ICO they can also apply to any organization or person carrying out a public administration function, and any organization or person that is under the control of a public authority and has environmental responsibilities.

The PECR concerns contacts with potential or existing customers by means of electronic marketing. New regulations concerning how to use cookies and similar technologies for storing information on a user's equipment such as their computer or mobile device came into force on 26 May 2011.

The Freedom of Information Act

UK public authorities have a legal obligation to provide information through an approved publication scheme and in response to requests. The Scheme has to:

* set out the types of information that must be routinely published
* explain the way in which the information must be provided
* state what charges can be made for providing information.

A code of practice is available for records managers (MOJ 2009), the use of which is explained in a separate guide (ICO 2007). Guidance is also available from the National Archives (TNA 2008)

Decisions on retention and disclosure are impacted by the Act and the code. It is important that records disposition outcomes and requests for information are fully logged and documented to help address appeals arising from non-disclosure. This may be undertaken using a system dedicated to the task, or may be a function offered in the information management system.

The UK Government is becoming more proactive in making information public via the Internet (Birkinshaw 2010). The following are examples at the time of writing:

* datasets from various departments http://data.gov.uk/
* information asset register for sources of unpublished information holdings http://www.bis.gov.uk/site/foi/information-asset-register.

The Data Protection Act

The DPA covers both the private and public sectors. The latter sector is under duties covering a broader range of personal data which were added by the FOIA.

Under section 41A of the DPA the Information Commissioner may serve data controllers with an assessment notice to enable the Information Commissioner to determine whether the data controller has complied or is complying with the data protection principles. A requirement can also be imposed on the data controller to submit to a compulsory audit. In other circumstances an organization can request an assessment to help ensure that it is following good practice.

A guide to the DPA covering definitions, principles and practical examples is available (ICO 2011). A code of practice for records managers relating to the DPA is available from The National Archives (Healy 2007).

6.8.2 GUIDANCE ON SHARING INFORMATION

The Information Commissioner's Office is the prime source of guidance relating to the aforementioned legislation especially where it concerns personal information. Beyond this, the UK Home Office provides guidance on information sharing aimed at community safety practitioners and their managers (Chainey 2010).

Bessant (2009) provides the following advice when contemplating the sharing of information:

- Consider:
    - the information to be shared
    - the means by which, or basis on which, information was acquired
    - the purpose and thus the benefits of the information sharing
    - the amount of information to be shared, no more and no less than necessary
    - the person or bodies with whom information will be shared, and what they will do with the information
    - the legal power which authorizes information sharing
    - whether any legal provision restricts or prevents information sharing
    - technical factors which may prevent safe, secure information sharing
    - risks (including risks of breaching the law) posed by sharing or failing to share information, and safeguards to counter the risks (such as a scheme under which information is marked as restricted or confidential).

6.8.3 PUBLICATION TO THE WEB

Publication to the web in the context of this book is the placing of existing documents or other information on already created websites. The aim should be for single-source publishing where existing office documents are converted into a standardized format that can be accessed through a standard web. The principal such formats are PDF/A, HTML and XML.

The format that offers the greatest flexibility for output production is XML (AIIM 2006) as this provides for:

- structured content which is consistent and reusable
- built-in metadata using semantic tags
- separation of content and format facilitated by document type definition (DTD)
- database orientation as DTDs aid storage of all content and its elements
- support for multiple media outputs using XML style sheets; XSL supports output to standard media such as paper, PDF, Web, HTML and wireless devices.

Publishing should also take into account the developments surrounding Web 2.0. This is not a step change in the underlying technology of the web but rather a number of developments which together facilitate participation, information sharing and interoperability. One such development is the Semantic Web referred to in Section 6.7.2.

6.8.4 SOCIAL MEDIA

'Social media' is a difficult concept to grasp as it is open to many different interpretations (Lake 2009). For example:

- 'A category of sites that is based on user participation and user-generated content.'
- 'Social media are works of user-created video, audio, text or multimedia that are published and shared in a social environment, such as a blog, wiki or video hosting site.'
- 'An umbrella term that defines the various activities that integrate technology, social interaction, and the construction of words and pictures.'
- 'Software tools that allow groups to generate content and engage in peer-to-peer conversations and exchange of content (examples are YouTube, Flickr, Facebook, MySpace etc).'
- 'Social Media is the collection of tools and online spaces available to help individuals and businesses to accelerate their information and communication needs.'

Baym (2010) refers more broadly to 'personal communications in the digital age'.

Organizations need to be cognizant of the impact of social media, the development of which can be traced through the following examples (not necessarily in order of their appearance on the scene):

- email – the first means of mass personal digital communication allowing the writer to interact with one or more recipients known to them
- mailing lists – some of the recipients will not be personally known to the writer
- usenet newsgroups – worldwide distributed Internet discussion system
- Internet forum – online discussion site using posted messages
- blogs – personal websites on which an individual or group of users record opinions, links to other sites and so on, on a regular basis
- wikis – websites or databases developed by a community of users, to which any user may add and edit content
- video and photo sharing sites
- social networking sites (SNS) – individuals upload and maintain their personal profiles and connect via multiple communication nodes; members can share their interests by joining groups and forums.

Blogs, Internet forums, and wikis are reasonably well-established forms of communication used by organizations, their staff or individuals to promote their expertise and exchange information. Social networking sites started out by attracting young people but soon grew to involve people of all ages, backgrounds and interests.

Wikipedia (2011a) lists over 200 social networking sites (the term is interpreted broadly), most of which focus on some kind of special interest, for example video games, the gay community, investing, art or nationality, and therefore limit their audience in these respects. For the wider community there are those sites that cover no particular subject and as such provide a blank canvas on which individuals can present themselves to the world.

Although businesses may target specialized social media where their products and services match the interests of the members, they have realized in recent times the importance of exploiting the generic social media sites of which Facebook and Twitter are well-known examples. These are places where individuals have been able to voice their pleasure or discontent on a variety of matters. This has occurred to such an extent that the organizations referred to have had to embrace the technology themselves not only to counter the brickbats but also to market themselves proactively.

The almost too-ready availability of personal details on the web has also captured the interest of those in the recruitment industry and companies seeking staff. LinkedIn, the online professional networking site, has proved to be a rich source of such information.

Exploiting Social Media

As McIvor (2011) said, speaking for the UK Institute of Directors 'Social media is proving to be an excellent additional channel through which people can market their business … My advice is don't jump on the bandwagon unless you can fully support it because while the media channel itself is relatively low cost, it can be incredibly time-consuming and resource intensive'.

Given the immediacy and ease with which information can be added to these sites, there can be little opportunity for an organization to introduce new, or apply existing vetting and approval procedures to what is posted.

Technologies and ways of exploiting social media have emerged under the banner Social Business which has been defined as 'the use of social technologies and processes to improve internal collaboration and external customer engagement' (AIIM 2011a). Key factors are seen as empowerment and trust. Users need to be trusted to do what is right with the new social tools and processes, while supporting them with the training and governance required for them to be accountable for that trust.

6.8.5 ELECTRONIC PUBLISHING

Aside from publishing to the web, the sale of books published in electronic form alongside their paper counterparts has increased notably as usable and affordable e-readers have emerged and publishers have embraced the format, by necessity if not choice. However, as with any new technology, many different 'standards' are to be found (Wikipedia 2011b) and one cannot guarantee that a book bought in one format for one reader will be readable on another.

The three main formats that are widely supported are:

- plain text
- PDF
- ePUB.

Plain text is based on the ASCII standard. It, together with the Adobe PDF format, is supported on all major readers. The main candidate for industry-wide standardization is the ePUB format (EPUB3 2011) from the International Digital Publishing Forum. It is a free and open standard based on XML and has been adopted by most of the publishing industry.

There are various hardware and software producers entering this market, one example being Mobipocket Reader software which is an e-Book reader for some personal organizers, phones and desktop operating systems. It is one of the formats used, for example, by ISO for publishing its standards.

Despite the rise of e-publishing it has been noted that there are some issues to resolve around digital rights management (DRM). Examples noted in Bott (2010) include:

- lending of eBook/eMagazine
- lending libraries (public and/or private)
- eBook exchanges
- portability of eBooks/eMagazines between devices
- colour versus monochrome (battery life, photo, maps, charts, and so on)
- transfer of eBooks/eMagazines (for example, by gifting or inheritance).

6.8.6 PAPER PUBLISHING

Despite the rise of electronic formats and new ways of accessing and navigating through the text, paper is likely to retain its advantages which are largely based on its non-reliance on electrical or battery power and it not being tethered to, or constrained by, any form of technology.

The publishing industry and its retail outlets have embraced the concept of publishing on demand (POD), a process which is mirrored in organizations when electronic documents are printed out for convenience when required.

Authors wishing to publish their own works can use a wide range of commercial services, some of which are available over the Internet. The types of facilities offered may include anything from book cover and jacket design through copy editing and proof reading to book distribution, e-book versions and marketing advice.

As examples of innovation:

- on the retail side, for example, booksellers are looking at in-shop printing from digital bank of out-of-print or current titles (EBM 2011)
- flipbacks (http://www.flipbackbooks.com/) opens top to bottom and has sideways-printed text. The aim is to produce a pocketable format that can compete in size with the smaller e-book readers.

6.8.7 E-DISCOVERY

e-Discovery is the process by which electronically stored information (ESI) is sought, located and secured with the intent of using it as evidence in a civil or criminal legal case. Interest in this activity has increased due to environmental disasters and failures of financial institutions in recent years and the requirement to find relevant documentation and data to prosecute the resulting cases.

The activities that surround e-Discovery have been modelled in the Electronic Discovery Reference Model (http://www.edrm.net/), with the acronym EDRM as depicted in Figure 6.9.

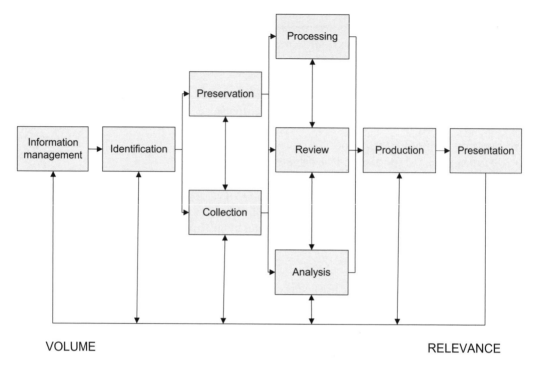

Figure 6.9   Electronic Discovery Reference Model

It involves the following stages:

Information Management

Obtaining electronic information in order to mitigate risk and expenses should e-Discovery become an issue, from initial creation of electronically stored information through its final disposition.

Identification

Locating potential sources of ESI and determining its scope, breadth and depth.

Preservation

Ensuring that ESI is protected against inappropriate alteration or destruction.

Collection

Gathering ESI for further use in the e-Discovery process (processing, review, and so on).

Processing

Reducing the volume of ESI and converting it, if necessary, to forms more suitable for review and analysis.

Review

Evaluating ESI for relevance and privilege.

Analysis

Evaluating ESI for content and context, including key patterns, topics, people and discussion.

Production

Delivering ESI to others in appropriate forms and using appropriate delivery mechanisms.

Presentation

Displaying ESI before audiences (at depositions, hearings, trials, and so on), especially in native and near-native forms, to elicit further information, validate existing facts or positions, or persuade an audience.

Although there is a legal slant to many of the processes, they align closely with the functional requirements of an EDRM in the sense of records management. Thus many of the suppliers to the records management and content management market have capability for e-Discovery. The rise of e-Discovery has therefore increased corporate interest in records management.

6.8.8 ASSESSING THE QUALITY OF INFORMATION

The wide variety of sources for structured or unstructured content available to the information seeker range from those that provide some form of quality control over their content, such as peer reviewed academic journals, to those that effectively are uncontrolled, as exemplified by many of the social media.

It is difficult to define criteria for information quality (Wikipedia 2011d) and much of what has been produced tends to be focused on structured information, namely data. One of the principal aims of the International Association for Information and Data Quality (http://iaidq.org/) is to build and maintain a body of knowledge and a certification program for information and data quality. It operates under a code of ethics and professional conduct covering:

- honesty and integrity
- respect, fairness, confidentiality and trust
- professional growth
- community and public service.

It conducts a certification programme involving an exam covering the aspects of quality relating to:

- strategy and governance – structures and processes for making decisions on an organization's data
- environment and culture – the background to enable employees to provide information quality to meet customer needs
- value and business impact – to assure the quality of the data blueprint for the organization
- measurement and improvement – steps to conduct quality improvement projects such as gathering and analysing business requirements for data
- sustaining information quality – as exemplified by data conversion and migration projects.

These concerns would not be out of place in job descriptions for those managing corporate content.

The diverse nature of quality on the web poses problems for the information seeker. Tate (2010) proposed the five evaluation criteria of authority, accuracy, objectivity, currency and coverage and intended audience, all with their origins in the print world. Such evaluation criteria can equally be applied by those creating new information sources so that the resulting product proves to be acceptable to the consumer in these regards. Additionally Tate (2010) noted that web resources pose other challenges due to such factors as inconsistent or missing web page links, the dynamic nature of web content when it is database driven, retrieval of orphan pages by search engines and the susceptibility of web pages to alteration.

The problem of relying on web search engines to search unstructured information in the absence of a classification scheme was demonstrated by Fresko (2011) using Google, Bing, Altavista, Yahoo, Ask and AOL. It was found that the results of the searches can be inconsistent over time and between users, can rank results in unexpected ways and can lack precision and recall. (Repeating the searches noted in Section 3.2 using these search engines will further illustrate this problem).

6.9 Conclusion

Finding relevant, substantiated quality information is a major challenge. Often the requirement is not that demanding and an acceptance criterion of 'that will do' is sufficient for many purposes. In any event there still needs to be some way in which information is categorized, indexed or otherwise organized to provide search and retrieval facilities for the enquirer. Different types of facilities are needed for searching structured data than for narrative-type documents where there is no common structure imposed. Automatic indexing has become commonplace due to the large amount of information that exists and the continued growth of the digital universe. Intellectual effort, however, is needed more than ever to define system vocabularies of various types, for example to help index information resources and enable different subject domains to be accessed in an integrated fashion.

The proliferation of digital personal information across commercial organizations, governments and states as well as on social media provides legislative, regulatory and personal challenges for those wishing to exploit the data and those, on the other hand, wanting to restrict usage. Guidance on using and sharing information is prescriptive in areas where legislation is concerned, but is otherwise less definitive.

Despite the opportunities being grasped by budding authors and digital media producers there are aspects of copyright and rights management in the digital age that have still to be resolved.

The following chapter considers aspects of data management, including data and process analysis, that must be addressed if data is to be of acceptable quality and relevance to the business of the organization.

7 *Data Management*

'No data yet', he answered, 'It's a capital mistake to theorize before you have all the evidence. It biases the judgement'. A Study in Scarlet. *A. Conan Doyle*

Data, defined as 'quantities, characters, or symbols on which operations are performed by computers' (OED 2001), can be considered to be elemental information given that virtually all recorded information is available in some electronic form or another. Sound management of this primary element is therefore a prerequisite for creating, managing and utilizing information resources that are logically and physically well designed.

The scope of data management and the techniques of process analysis and data analysis for understanding how a business works and how information is defined are the major topics in this chapter. In addition, approaches for dealing with data that needs to be migrated from existing systems are considered.

Defining the scope of data management is as problematical as defining that for information or knowledge management, however. Various interest groups, as depicted earlier in Figure 3.6, each assert rights over parts of the landscape which overlap with those claimed by others. This cannot be avoided, and in fact it indicates areas where each speciality can make positive contributions when working collaboratively.

The Data Management Association (DAMA) exemplifies the interest groups. It sees data management as covering the following ten functions, with data governance being at the core (DAMA 2008):

- data governance – planning, supervision and control over data management and use
- data architecture management – as an integral part of the enterprise architecture
- data development – analysis, design, building, testing, deployment and maintenance
- database operations management – support for structured physical data assets
- data security management – ensuring privacy, confidentiality and appropriate access
- reference and master data management – managing golden versions and replicas
- data warehousing and business intelligence management – enabling access to decision support data for reporting and analysis
- document and content management – storing, protecting, indexing and enabling access to data found in unstructured sources (electronic files and physical records)
- metadata management – integrating, controlling and delivering metadata
- data quality management – defining, monitoring and improving data quality.

DAMA relates these functions to a set of seven environmental elements – goals and principles, activities, deliverables, roles and responsibilities, technology, practices and techniques and organization and culture – to produce a list of activities that need to be undertaken to fulfil data governance.

In this book much attention is given to unstructured content as it poses unique management problems. These problems are more readily addressed if aspects such as data flows, relationships, quality and standardization of data through process analysis and data analysis are considered, as discussed below.

7.1 Process Analysis

Analysing and modelling processes and information inputs and outputs can be used for a number of reasons and in a variety of situations, for example:

- to study processes and associated information as they currently exist, thereby providing a baseline for planned change or to identify opportunities for change
- to investigate the possible benefits of revised or new processes and the resource implications
- to provide the detail necessary for programming workflow or similar systems.

Specifically, models can help identify:

- sources and recipients of information
- functions and activities for developing business and records classification schemes as was noted in Chapter 5
- sets of data requiring quality improvement or standardization
- areas where process improvements could be made by eliminating, adding or otherwise changing workflows.

The analysis is usually undertaken functional area by functional area as each will have a reasonably coherent set of processes to examine. The analysis will reveal information flows between the functions and elsewhere, thereby building a business-wide view. Data models for each area may also be created at this time.

The three main types of process model – flow chart, data flow diagram (DFD) and activity diagram – are compared in Figure 7.1 based on Ambler (2004).

Flow charting was one of the earliest diagramming methods used by programmers and analysts and predates the introduction of structured approaches for developing information systems.

MODEL	DESCRIPTION
Activity diagram	A unified modelling language (UML) diagram used to model high-level business processes, including data flow, or to model the logic of complex logic within the system
Data flow diagram (DFD)	A diagram that shows the movement of data within a system between processes, entities and data stores
Flowchart	A diagram depicting the logic flow of a single process or method

Figure 7.1   Comparison of process models

Source: Reproduced with permission of Cambridge University Press

Data flow diagrams are commonly used in structured analysis and design and show the external entities (such as people and organizations) from where data originates, the data flows from one process to another and where the data is stored.

Activity diagrams are a more recent modelling technique arising from the object-oriented programming method. They are more suited to modelling a particular activity than a complex workflow and are not considered further here.

7.1.1 DATA FLOW DIAGRAMS (DFDS)

The DFD in Figure 7.2 shows the data flows for dealing with the enrolment of a student on a course. The example is based on one in Ambler (2004).

The various diagramming shapes will differ somewhat from one tool to another. Here they are made up of:

- numbered rectangles: denoting processes which take information inputs, process it in some way and send the result onwards
- open-ended rectangles: representing information stores; those coded 'D' store data, those coded 'M' hold manual, physical information or objects
- ovals: represent external entities which are sources of or destinations for information
- arrows: denoting information flows which can be electronic (single arrow heads) or physical resources (double arrow heads). Note that the tool used – an early CASE (computer-aided systems engineering) tool SSADM Professional – did not allow the payment to the cash drawer to be shown as a physical resource (hard cash), hence the single headed arrow.

Descriptions or notes can usually be associated with each process, store, entity or flow.

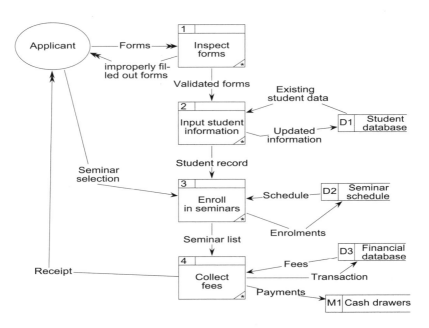

Figure 7.2   DFD for student enrolment

Source: Reproduced with permission of Cambridge University Press

The diagram represents one analyst's views of how to represent the application process. Another analyst may depict the processes and flows somewhat differently, but either view may provide a perfectly valid basis on which to seek improvements, 're-engineer' the processes or inform future design.

While there can be justifiable variations in the way processes are portrayed, the same cannot necessarily be true for data, as will be discussed later.

7.1.2 FLOW CHARTS

The process of enrolling a student is shown as a flow chart in Figure 7.3.
The drawing conventions are:

- rectangles: represent activities
- diamond shapes: denote decision points
- arrows: indicate control flows.

The main differences between the DFD and the flow chart are that the latter tends to be more detailed as it closely follows the logic of the business process and depicts decision points wherever they are needed.

Although a drawing tool was used to create the DFD and flow chart, they could equally have been produced by hand, which does have the advantage of immediacy.

7.2 Data Analysis

Data analysis is used to help identify and define the data needed to support business processes in the organization and to inform the design of software applications. Candidate data will have been identified during any process analysis or modelling that may have been conducted. However, more detailed examination of the data is required to render it suitable for use in software applications and to address data quality issues. Normalizing and modelling the types of data and their relationships is invaluable in this regard.

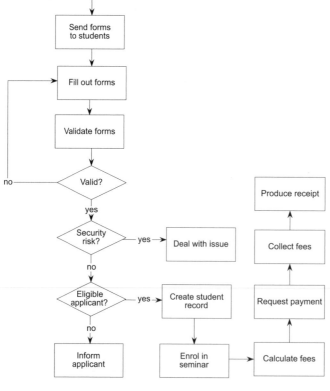

Figure 7.3   Flow chart of enrolment

Source: Reproduced with permission of Cambridge University Press

7.2.1 DATA NORMALIZATION

As will be described later the data model provides a vehicle for examining data, its attributes and its relationships, in more detail with the aim of:

- rendering the model more amenable to change such as the addition or elimination of entities and relationships
- reducing redundancy of data.

To help achieve this, a technique called 'data normalization' can be applied. Although this process is intuitive for experienced analysts, it is worth describing for the benefit of others who have an interest in ensuring their data is appropriate and well organized.

Its use is described in relation to a purchase order example, adapted from OU (1980) as shown in Figure 7.4.

Order Number	1023		
Supplier Number	500106		
Supplier Name	J. Smith and Sons, Chichester		
Supplier Address	14 High Street, Burgess Hill, RH16 2BA		
Order Date	25/07/10		
Delivery Date	31/08/10		
Part Number	Part Description	Quantity ordered	Price £
0463	Hook	150	15.00
1492	Line	1000	10.00
3164	Sinker	10	5.00
		Total	30.00

Order Number	1056		
Supplier Number	500106		
Supplier Name	John Smith		
Supplier Address	14 High Street, RH16 2BX		
Order Date	30/07/10		
Delivery Date	01/09/10		
Part Number	Part Description	Quantity ordered	Price £
1492	Line	400	3.50
0463	Hook	600	45.00
		Total	48.50

Figure 7.4   Sample purchase orders

Source: Adapted with permission of The Open University

The details about the purchase order (the entity being considered) can be written as follows to fully describe its make-up which is uniquely identified by the Order Number and is underlined:

Purchase Order (Order Number, Supplier Number, Supplier Name, Supplier Address, Order Date, Delivery Date, (Part Number, Part Description, Quantity Ordered, Line Item Price), Total Price).

However, some of the information (the attributes) is difficult to obtain. For example, to find the total quantity ordered of a particular part, one would have to go through every purchase order to find each occurrence of the part number. On examining the entity, the group (Part Number, Part Description, Quantity Ordered, Line Item Price) is seen to be a repeating group as several of these Purchase Items make up an order (see Figure 7.4). So if it is separated out as a new entity type, **Purchase Item**, it would be easier to access individual purchase items.

This produces the following two entities and represents the first step in normalization (indicated by the suffix '-1'), to remove repeating groups and rewrite them as new entities.

PurchaseOrder-1 (Order Number, Supplier Number, Supplier Name, Supplier Address, Order Date, Delivery Date, Total Price)

PurchaseItem-1 (Order Number, Part Number, Part Description, Quantity Ordered, Line Item Price).

The attribute Order Number is required in the **Purchase Item-1** entity to retain the original information that a purchase item is related to a particular purchase order. Order Number and Part Number are composite identifiers for the entity **Purchase Item-1**; that is, both identifiers are required to uniquely identify a purchase item.

Examining the **Purchase Item-1** entity shows that the attribute Part Description is not functionally dependent on the whole of the identifier for the entity as it relates only to the Part. Hence it should be separated out as another entity as a second step in normalization.

PurchaseOrder-2 (Order Number, Supplier Number, Supplier Name, Supplier Address, Order Date, Delivery Date, Total Price)

PurchaseItem-2 (Order Number, Part Number, Quantity Ordered, Line Item Price)

Part-2 (Part Number, Part Description).

This arrangement avoids repetition of part descriptions in every purchase item. It also enables details of parts and additions of new parts to be managed independently of whether they are part of an order.

Further examination of the purchase order entity **Purchase Order-2** shows that there is functional dependency between the non-identifying attributes Supplier Number, Supplier Name and Supplier Address. Hence further rationalization is possible by separating these out as the third step of normalization to arrive at the following entities:

PurchaseOrder-3 (<u>Order Number</u>, Supplier Number, Order Date, Delivery Date, Total Price)

PurchaseItem-3 (<u>Order Number</u>, <u>Part Number</u>, Quantity Ordered, Line Item Price)

Part-3 (<u>Part Number</u>, Part Description)

Supplier-3 (<u>Supplier Number</u>, Supplier Name, Supplier Address).

7.2.2 DATA MODELLING

At the beginning of the modelling process the analyst is faced with the real information world of the business from which they need to abstract the key information elements to gain some concept of what is relevant to the particular objective. This is recorded in the conceptual model showing the broad relationships between the data and possibly identifying some significant attributes to supplement the definition of entities.

A conceptual model is often created as the precursor to a logical data model (LDM) which:

- provides a graphical representation of an organization's business requirements
- contains the entities of importance to the organization and how they relate to one another
- contains definitions and examples.

The LDM thereby:

- helps common understanding and confirmation of business requirements
- gathers metadata (attributes that the entities possess) and facilitates its re-use and sharing
- facilitates business process improvement
- decreases development and maintenance time and cost.

Neither type of model takes any account of how the data might be organized physically in the production system, for example a relational database supporting an EDRM. This is important as the data needs to be modelled in a way that reflects the logic of the business requirements and can be discussed with the business. The logical model design (schema) must not be constrained by how the logical system will be implemented, but it does form the basis for the subsequent physical database design.

Hence a succession of models – conceptual, logical and physical – can be used throughout the process, as shown in Figure 7.5.

A range of modelling tools is available to assist with model construction, some being challenging to use and comprehend as far as their outputs are concerned. The use of concept mapping at the initial stage of data modelling can facilitate discussion with others and was mentioned in Section 2.8.2.

The content and construction of an LDM needs to be explained so that its use in managing and improving data can be better understood.

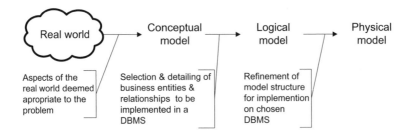

Figure 7.5   Types of data model

An LDM is made up of Entities, Attributes and Relationships as described below:

Entity

An entity is a person, place, thing, concept or event about which an organization collects data. For example, in a law firm dealing with litigation cases, entities will include:

- case
- claimant
- client
- court
- invoice.

Attribute

An attribute holds a piece of data particular to an entity. For example:

- case reference of a case
- name of claimant
- address of client
- type of court
- date of invoice.

Relationship

Relationships define how two entities are associated with each other. Relationships can be optional or mandatory and are usually one-to-many. For example:

- a 'case' must have at least one 'claimant'
- an 'invoice' must be composed of one or more 'invoice items'
- a 'purchase order' must have one or more 'purchase items'

Note relationships can be 'read' from either direction, for example:

- a 'postal code' must apply to one or more 'postal address'; conversely a 'postal address' must have only one 'postal code'

- a 'purchase item' must apply to only one 'purchase order'

One-to-one relationships may exist but are redesigned out as are many-to-many relationships. An example of the latter is: an 'organization' may be contacted by more than one 'contact mechanism' (land line, mobile, fax, web address etc) ; conversely a 'contact mechanism' may be used by more than organization'. This is resolved by introducing another entity, an intersection entity, 'organization contact mechanism' linked to the other two.

These one-to-one, one-to-many and many-to-many relationships are known as the cardinality of the relationship.

Figure 7.6 illustrates how the components of a logical model for the purchase order example discussed earlier can be expressed. It was produced using the Enterprise Architect tool (http://www.sparxsystems.com.au/).

In the diagram:

Entities

- Are shown as boxes and are always named in the singular at the top the box.
- These boxes are drawn in a form – a table indicating columns – that render them acceptable for populating a relational database.
- The modelling tool used (Enterprise Architect) requires the joining together of the words of a name, that is, with no gaps, as such format is required for future programming. To aid understanding the first letter of each word is capitalized.

Attributes

- Are named in the boxes. Each attribute has after its name an indication of the type of data, for example SupplierNumber is an integer, DeliveryDate is a date, TotalPrice is money and SupplierAddress holds characters with the allowed length noted in brackets. This enables a database to handle the data correctly.

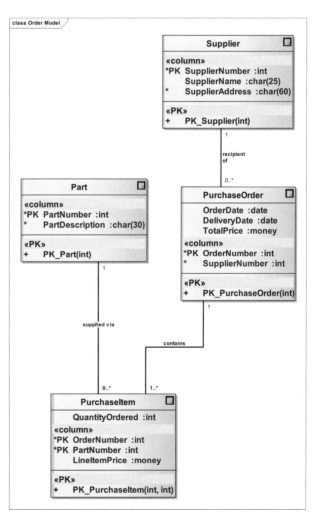

Figure 7.6   LDM of purchase order example

- Attributes may be either part of the unique identifier of an entity (also referred to as a primary key – PK), mandatory or optional.
- Some attributes comprise standard list of terms (standing data) which form 'pick lists' from which appropriate terms are selected. Thus there could be an additional entity 'PartType' linked to the entity 'Part' to classify them according to some agreed criteria, for example the type of material from which parts are made.

Relationships

- Are lines joining the entities with associated wording to clarify the relationship.
- The cardinality at each end of the relationship is indicated by the following convention:

1	= one and only one (mandatory)
0...*	= zero or more (optional at the zero at the end of a relationship indicates it may not apply)
1...*	= one or more (mandatory)
0...1	= zero or one (optional)

- For example, each PurchaseOrder can only have one Supplier, but a supplier may be the recipient of no PurchaseOrder, or one or more orders. Hence it is possible to maintain a list of suppliers and their addresses even though some of them have not received an order. Similarly a Part may be part of a PurchaseItem and it is possible to maintain a list of parts some of which have not been ordered. However, a PurchaseItem must relate to only one part.

7.2.3 THE RELATIONSHIP BETWEEN DATA ANALYSIS AND PROCESS ANALYSIS

Data analysis and process analysis should go hand-in-hand, but need not be undertaken simultaneously or in any particular order. If process analysis is undertaken first it may generate local data and process models for each functional area. The individual data models can then be combined to create an initial global data model.

If the analyst is sufficiently knowledgeable of the organization's business, a global data model may be constructed first and refined over time as information is obtained from the process analysis of the functional areas.

The way data and process analysis interact is shown in Figure 7.7 (OU 1980)

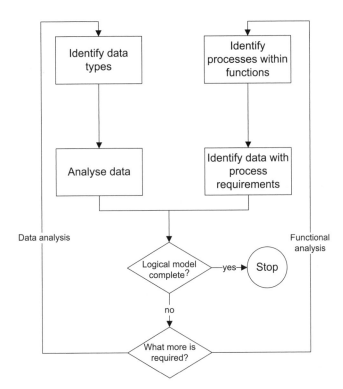

Figure 7.7   Interaction of data and process analysis

Source: Reproduced with permission of The Open University

7.3 Determining the Required Entity Attributes

So far the data analysis has focused principally on modelling the entities and ensuring they are normalized to provide the required flexibility for future changes.

In the real world users will want to ensure that they will be able to record, search and retrieve information using the terms with which they are familiar and in the context of business processes that may have been improved.

The business analyst should have gathered lists of terms, codes, classifications and so on that users currently employ. Within these there are likely to be instances of, for example, poor definition, lack of clarity, duplication and gaps in the listings.

Broadly there are two types of data held in a computerized information system:

- data that remains relatively unchanged and is pre-stored in the system to provide a user with a choice (such as a pick list). This is often referred to as standing data (or list of values); examples might be subject terms in a thesaurus, part numbers in an engineering firm, staff grades in a human resources system or (as in the earlier example), types of part.
- data that is generated automatically or is non-standardized so that the user has to enter the data as and when required; examples might include invoice total (summed automatically from the individual purchase items) and names of witnesses in lawsuit which have to be entered manually.

Well-chosen standing data enables the provision of consistent management information and provides the means to manage and oversee the progress of any activity.

Dealing with personal injury claims provides an example of how data requirements might be determined for a law firm entering this already crowded field.

7.3.1 PERSONAL INJURY DATA EXAMPLE

Claims are generally associated with injury to the body, but injury to the person could also include loss of personal possessions or claims for damages, so it is important first to determine the scope of the requirements.

Focusing on injuries to the person, specific claims from those injured might be:

- slipped at work
- bitten by dog at kennels
- lost hearing through noisy equipment in factory
- lung damage through exposure to asbestos
- injured eye when struck by Frisbee in playground
- electric shock from equipment at work.

Knowing that different types of injury warrant different levels of claim, the firm may wish to record a range of details about the claims so that it can monitor over time which ones delivered the best return for the effort expended.

Looking at the examples above one could have a list of these claims as worded and select from these when the same type occurred again. However, the likelihood of exactly the same claim arising again varies. For example 'slipping at work' is likely to be a frequent occurrence while a claim for 'injured eye when struck by Frisbee' may never arise again. Also, how would one best classify new injuries such as -'injured eye hit by cricket ball', or 'injured finger hit by Frisbee'? In relation to injuries already encountered, the former relates to the same body part, but the object involved is different while the latter involves the same object but a different body part.

This is where some analysis is needed. Examination of claims shows that it is possible to classify their components into meaningful and distinguishable groups. Thus there is cause of the injury, where it occurred and to what part of the body. Using these classes the elements of the claims can be broken up as shown in Figure 7.8.

There are gaps in the information and also the 'cause of injury' class needs further thought as it contains not just the cause but also the type of injury. So there needs to be a further division as shown in Figure 7.9 and the gaps to be filled in with any additional information obtained from the claim details.

So now one has four categories – cause of injury, location, injury type and body part – from which a lawyer could select the appropriate terms to classify claims to aid subsequent searching, retrieval and analysis.

Further consideration needs to be given to the types of terms noted so far. Of the categories, cause of injury contains extra information for some claims, for example noise arising from lathe and electric shock arising from a kettle. It may be helpful to record both the noise aspect and from where it arose – the lathe; similarly for the faulty kettle. This implies that the lawyer may wish to select more than one term from a class to describe a claim.

CAUSE OF INJURY	BODY PART	LOCATION
Slipped		Work
Bite by dog		Kennels
Lost hearing through noisy equipment	Ear	Factory
Lung damage through exposure to asbestos	Lung	
Injured eye when struck by Frisbee in playground	Eye	
Electric shock from kettle		

Figure 7.8   Initial analysis of personal injury claims

CAUSE OF INJURY	LOCATION	INJURY TYPE	BODY PART
Slipped	Work	Strain	Leg
Dog	Kennels	Bite	Hand
Noisy lathe	Factory	Lost hearing	Ear
Asbestos	Factory	Industrial disease	Lung
Frisbee	Playground	Swelling	Eye
Electric shock from kettle	Work	Burn	Whole body

Figure 7.9   Further analysis of personal injury claims

Also, how many claims will be received involving a Frisbee as compared with a dog? Dog bites are very common; injuries due to Frisbees are rare. And what about bites by other animals – cats, horses and so on?

The final listings presented to lawyers needs to take into account such factors as:

- ease of selection when entering new claims
- benefits from using the terms for subsequent search and analysis.

Hence it may be worth having a general term 'animal' for cause of injury to cover all animals but include 'dog' as a sub-category. As regards Frisbee, this could be referenced as a 'moving object'.

The requirements now include the need to select more than one term from a class and to handle sub-categories within a class. The ability to achieve this in reality will depend on the functionality on offer from the chosen or developed system. Assuming this is possible, Figure 7.10 shows a flow chart of a more fully populated list of standing data that could be presented to lawyers.

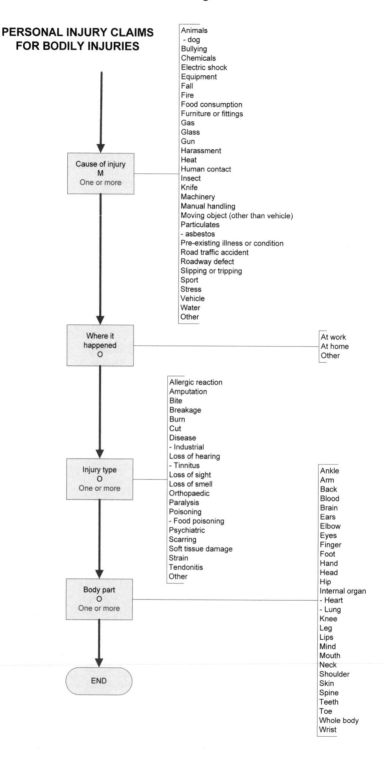

Figure 7.10 Flow chart for personal injury claims

The following should be noted:

- only the Cause of Injury menu is a mandatory entry (signified by 'M'); the remaining menus (location, type and part) are optional (signified by 'O').
- more than one selection can be made from each menu.
- some thought would still need to be given to some choices; for example, the location 'kennels' would be indexed under 'At Work' or 'Other' depending on who was injured – the kennel worker or a visitor. 'Lathe' would be indexed under 'Machinery'; 'Factory' under 'At Work'; 'Playground' under 'Other'; there is no entry to cater for 'Swelling' so perhaps an entry would be made under 'Injury Type'.
- the system should also provide fields where comments or additional information can be added. What is entered here should be reviewed over a period of time as there may be a need to update the standing data with terms that appear frequently and therefore justify being included in the pick lists.

Overall guidance would need to be given to users and the list kept under review as experience in its use is gained. This emphasizes the need for someone – a Data Manager – to be responsible for managing data content.

7.4 Dealing with Existing Systems

The introduction of new technology such as an EDRM may require the development of interfaces or integration with existing systems. If existing systems are to be replaced, detailed analysis of the data they hold is required if it is to be migrated to the new system. In this case the key tasks to be undertaken will include:

- identifying and analyzing existing data as regards quality, cleanliness and volume
- assessing the relevance of this data to the new system
- proposing approaches to migrate relevant data
- identifying any translation rules to convert, for example, format to that required
- documenting existing and required system interfaces.

The information gathered will also provide the basis for discussions with the supplier of the new system and also inform the development of a data migration plan in line with the roll-out of the new system.

The systems from which data is required may exist in a variety of forms, the principal ones being likely to be:

- databases
- spreadsheets
- unstructured data.

The migration of unstructured data was dealt with in Section 5.3.5. Here the focus is on the first two.

7.4.1 DATABASES

The databases could be desktop applications or networked software capable of handling many users and large data volumes. The first step is to examine and document the data and structures in the existing system, noting any quality deficiencies that might need to be dealt with. It is helpful to start with if there is some system documentation such as a data model, list of database tables or training manuals. It is not unusual to find that such information is lacking, or out of date.

Database tables are particularly useful as they are the physical representation of entities in a logical model and enable the data to be reviewed across and within the various tables to determine data characteristics (for example, type, size, frequency and distribution of values, cardinality and uniqueness), data redundancy (for example, duplication) and data dependency between attributes, and to detect and analyze data content quality problems.

An example of a database table format to assess quality issues, identify action required and future possible migration is shown in Figure 7.11. This relates to the purchase order example discussed earlier (see Figures 7.4 and 7.6) and assumes that the purchase order is produced from one database table.

The columns in the table are:

- User label – the screen label as seen by a user of the current database
- Field name – the name given to the field in the database
- Type – the type of data held
- Size – the maximum length for data entered
- Description – narrative entered to describe the field
- Comments – additional comments about the field and any proposed action
- Cleansing – what is needed to address poor quality
- Migrate? – indicates if the data is needed in the new system; YC indicates yes, after cleansing.

In the example it is noted that the following quality issues need to be addressed:

- the data needs to be normalized (as per Section 7.2.1)
- totals are not being calculated automatically but are being entered manually (in reality this is not likely to happen!)
- address details are inconsistent or incorrect and need to be revised accordingly
- supplier names similarly need cleansing.

The following are other aspects that would need to be examined:

- empty fields (which should contain values)
- duplicate values being entered
- content of free text fields to see if it is appropriate for intended purpose
- illegal or reserved characters in the fields
- conformance to data types (for example, numbers in text fields, dates in number fields, and so on)
- standing data – is it complete and appropriate?

- orphaned records
- widowed records.

An orphaned record is when a record in the many-side (child or related) table relationship has no corresponding record in the one-side (parent or primary) table. An example of this may be a Product in a Products table that does not have a Supplier in the Suppliers table, therefore the Product is an orphan record.

A widowed record is when the record in the one side of a one-to-many or one-to-one table does not have a corresponding record in the other table. You may have a Supplier who has no Products in the Products table.

User Label	Field name	Type	Size	Description	Comments	Cleansing	Migrate?
PO No	OrderNumber	int	4	Purchase order number	Calculated automatically by the system	None required	Y
Supplier	SupplierNumber	int	6	Supplier reference number	Needs to be normalized out	None required	Y
Supplier Name	SupplierName	char	25	Name of supplier	Some entries contain town; also inconsistent naming	Remove extraneous data e.g. Address details and make names consistent	YC
Supplier address	SupplierAddress	char	60	Supplier's address	Inconsistent and incorrect entries	Remove inconsistencies	YC
Order date	OrderDate	date		Date on order		None required	Y
Delivery date	DeliveryDate	date		Requested delivery date		None required	Y
Part No	PartNumber	int	4	Part number identifying the product		None required	Y
Part Desc	PartDescription	char	30	Description of part		None required	Y
Quantity	QuantityOrdered	int	3	Amount ordered		None required	Y
Price	LineItemPrice	money		Total cost of the line item	Should be calculated from a unit price for part	None required	N
Total	TotalPrice	money		Total cost of items ordered	Should be calculated from sum of purchase items	None required	N

Figure 7.11 Analysis of purchase order table

7.4.2 SPREADSHEETS

Much of the required information will be contained in spreadsheets. These formats are commonly used for inventories, financial calculations and work monitoring, for example. Hence they often replace the use of traditional database software if the application is relatively simple. While they may be simpler to set up than a database, they do not automatically impose the same rigour over design, content and use. Hence it is not uncommon for spreadsheet data to be deficient in some aspects of quality.

Although column headings in a spreadsheet might indicate its use as a source of well-structured data, the following problems may be encountered:

- text is spread across more than one row
- mandatory entries are not enforced
- the use of pick lists (standing data) may be limited
- data types are not properly controlled; for example, numbers in what should be text fields
- multi-line contact details that include such information as address, telephone numbers and email addresses are contained in a single cell and need to be normalized to assist migration
- the content duplicates information held in other existing systems.

A spreadsheet can, however, be usefully employed as a transit mechanism for data between a database that requires quality issues to be addressed and the target database.

7.4.3 DATA MAPPING

The data to be migrated, whether from a database or spreadsheet, needs to be mapped across to the new system. This is made easier if data models are available. The comparison between the source and target data models may indicate metadata items in the source that are required but are not available in the target and hence need to be created there. The mapping also needs to include any standing data.

The table in Figure 7.11 can be extended to the right to provide space for recording the details of the target database such as:

- table name
- field name
- size of field
- whether the entries are mandatory or optional
- if null entries are permitted; that is, fields could be left blank
- field length.

This can only be completed once the precise nature of the source data is known following any cleansing and remedial work.

The ongoing work to develop the target database will involve such tasks as data extraction, transformation and loading, the discussions on which are beyond the scope of this book. However, if the data analysis outlined so far is undertaken the outcome will facilitate knowledgeable discussion with the developers.

7.5 Conclusion

Structured information in the form of computer-stored data is too often viewed as something to be managed separately from documents. In taking this stance an organization cannot manage its information resources in a coherent and consistent manner. Furthermore, the expertise and experience of those working in such areas as records centres, libraries and IT departments are likely to be difficult to coordinate and exploit. Business processes often involve creating, accessing and communicating a range of information types. Process analysis and data analysis must be applied in a coordinated manner. In this way types of data and their relationship to processes can be identified and used to inform the development of logical data models. Such models help to obtain an understanding of business requirements and enable the gathering of metadata (for example, index information) relating to entities of interest, whether they be documents, customers, organization and so on. The rigour that such analysis imposes is invaluable as it can help resolve misunderstandings and differences in opinions over such matters as the meaning of terms. Detailed analysis of data is also necessary when planning migration between systems so that data quality problems can be identified and remedial action taken.

All these activities should, where relevant, form part of a formal project, the management of which is covered in the final two chapters.

3 *Projects*

8 *Undertaking a Project*

'How does a project get to be a year behind schedule? One day at a time'. Fred Brooks

Aspects of general project management and the various approaches that can be adopted to progress its activities are dealt with in this chapter. Those specific to undertaking information management-type projects are covered in Chapter 9.

The word 'project' is open to a number of interpretations. The OED (2001) defines a project as: 'An individual or collaborative enterprise undertaken usually for industrial or scientific research, or having a social purpose'. PRINCE2, a widely adopted project management method (http://www.prince2.com/what-is-prince2.asp) defines a project as 'A temporary organization that is created for the purpose of delivering one or more business products according to a specified Business Case'.

In general, projects have the following attributes (BS 6079 1996):

- they are non-repetitive
- they may have significant unique features likely to be novel to the management
- they carry risk and uncertainty
- they are approved in return for delivery of specified results within specified time-scales, quality and safety and health parameters
- they are usually undertaken by a team which has a temporary existence and whose make-up and numbers may vary with time
- they may be subject to change as the work progresses
- events inside and outside the organization may affect the outcome if the project is of long duration.

Of these the key attributes that should be present if the undertaking is worthy of being called a project are:

- specific objectives and conditions
- defined responsibilities for those involved
- a budget
- a plan
- starting and fixed end or target dates.

During this period there needs to be control and management of two components:

- the project in its own right using appropriate methods and documentation that are essentially common to all types of project
- the matters that relate to the objectives – the deliverables – which are unique to the project.

A project brings about change and delivers an outcome that, hopefully, is one that was intended and desired. The intention will in some way have been expressed as objectives and more detailed requirements. The process of software development needs to follow an appropriate method, as does the overall project management.

8.1 Software Development Methods

To get from objectives to outcome, requirements need to be determined and the system designed. The designed system then needs to be put in place and tested, and if all is well it is installed as a live system at which point it is usually formally accepted and passes into the post-project maintenance and support phase.

This linear process is called 'Waterfall' (Figure 8.1) and, just as water cannot flow backwards in a waterfall, so there is no going back from one stage of the project process to a prior one. What happens at each stage is dependent on an agreed and fixed outcome from the preceding stage.

Those involved in defining requirements often change their mind as time progresses and as they see less than desirable outcomes from the design or testing phases. In such circumstances there needs to be some mechanism by which changes that are justified can be accommodated. Iterations therefore need to be built into the whole process. This concern, together with others relating, for example, to the emphasis placed on documentation over software led to the emergence of Agile software development (http://agilemanifesto.org/), the elements of which are shown in Figure 8.2.

A comparison of the two methods is provided in Figure 8.3 (Haughey 2009) and can help decide which one is appropriate for a particular project and organization.

As regards a document and records management project, the choice will depend to a large extent on how well the standard functionality offered by commercial systems meets requirements. Where there is a good match, there will be little need for bespoke (that is, specially written) software and the Waterfall method may suit. If the requirements deviate markedly from standard offerings, or the project involves extensive website development then Agile might be preferred. It is possible for elements of both approaches to be used where the requirements cover both standard and bespoke developments.

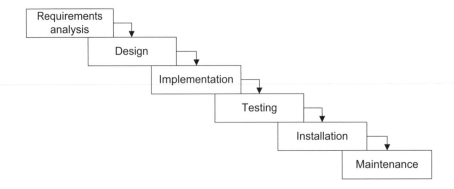

Figure 8.1   Waterfall stages

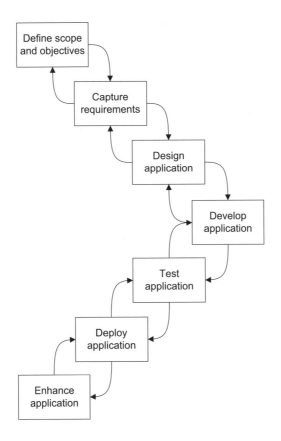

Figure 8.2   Agile software development

	ADVANTAGES	DISADVANTAGES
WATERFALL	Detailed documentation.	Slow start.
	Agreed and signed off requirements.	Fixed requirements difficult to change.
	Can be delivered using developers with a lower skill set.	No customer visibility of software until the development has been completed.
	Reduced number of defects through thorough design planning.	Lack of flexibility making it difficult to change direction.
	Defined start and end point for each phase, allowing progress to be easily measured.	Customers often unclear about their requirements initially.
AGILE	Quick start, incremental releases and regular customer reviews and feedback.	Can be misinterpreted as unplanned or undisciplined.
	Evolution of requirements over time.	Needs a high-quality, customer facing development team.
	Ability to respond to change quickly.	Needs a high-level of customer involvement.
	Less rework, achieved through continual testing and customer involvement.	Lack of long-term detailed plans.
	Real-time communication among the development team and customer.	Produces a lower level of documentation.

Figure 8.3   Comparison of Agile and Waterfall methods

8.2 Project Management

All projects will exhibit the following stages, irrespective of the type of deliverable (intangible software or physical artefact) or the software development:

- initiation
- design
- build
- termination.

Most organizations will have some method in place to manage and control these stages and to provide the supporting documentation based on a plan and agreed resources, both financial and human. If an organization requires guidance, this is available from BS 6079 (2010). It aims to cover all aspects of planning projects including management, planning, benefits and the project life cycle.

8.2.1 PROJECT MANAGEMENT METHODS

An example of a widely used method is PRINCE2 (http://www.best-management-practice.com/). Originally aimed at managing projects in IT environments in the UK public sector, its scope was expanded to cover any type of project. Like any project management method, it is open to criticism by some as being overly bureaucratic and complex. However, used sensibly it delivers benefit. The key features of PRINCE2 are:

- continued business justification
- learning from experience
- defined roles and responsibilities
- managed by stages
- managed by exception
- focuses on products and their quality
- tailored to suit the particular product environment.

It is based on a process model, having eight management processes reflecting the life cycle of a project and a further eight components applied to the processes.

PRINCE2 is focused on the delivery of products, be they documents, such as those covering system design or acceptance procedure, or, for example, software to provide specified functionality. A typical organizational framework is shown in Figure 8.4 in which the key players from the user, business and solution supplier communities can contribute effectively.

An indication of the roles and responsibilities of the organizational members is given in Figure 8.5. It is common sense to ensure that all those who need to contribute, or are affected in some way with the outcome of the project, have a way to communicate through a project management structure.

The Project Board, through its Executive Chairman, will typically report to a corporate Executive Committee, possibly with organizational-wide responsibility for information systems.

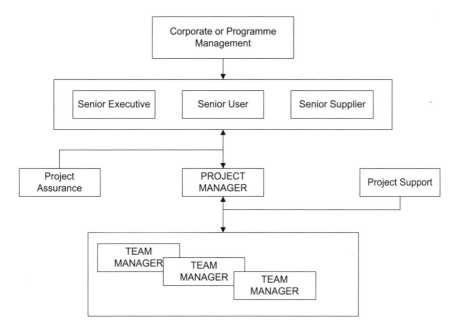

Figure 8.4   Project management structure

ROLE	KEY RESPONSIBILITIES
Project Board	Commitment of resources. Approves all major plans and authorizes major deviations from stage plans. Responsible for Project Assurance either directly or by delegation
Executive	Ultimately accountable for the project. 'Owns' the business case. Provides the link to Corporate or Programme management
User representative	Accountable for products supplied by the users e.g. ensures user requirements are clearly and completely defined; provides user resources; ensures project products and outcomes meet user requirements and expected user benefits. Responsible for Project Assurance from user perspective
Supplier representative	Accountable for products delivered by the solution supplier(s) – e.g. a commercial vendor for the required system. Represents interests of those designing, developing, facilitating, procuring, implementing and possibly operating and maintaining the supplied products. (Multiple suppliers may require additional representation on the Board)
Project Manager	Has day-to-day responsibility for managing the project throughout all its stages and within constraints laid down by the Board
Team Manger	An optional role where the Project Manager requires to delegate responsibility for planning the creation of certain products to a team of specialists

Figure 8.5   Roles and responsibilities

There are however no hard-and-fast rules for structuring reporting relationships. Each organization will differ in detail as to its approach. Suffice to say it is important that the business users and management for whom the system is intended should ultimately be in control. The IT function in the organization is there to provide a service and to advise on matters within their competence, such as corporate and industry standards for hardware, software and networking. Records management aspects, however, may still not be fully understood by many IT personnel and management. Hence, it is important that all those who will be involved in the project (users, business managers and IT representatives) gain a common and sufficiently detailed awareness of the disciplines as well as the technology so that informed debate and decision-making is possible.

8.2.2 INITIATING A PROJECT

Having identified the business area and business applications that are to be the focus of attention, the project needs to be formally initiated. This is effected by producing a Project Initiation Document (PID) for approval by the Project Board before any further work is undertaken. Typical contents for such a document are shown in Figure 8.6.

SECTION OF PID	EXAMPLE CONTENT
Background	Sets the background to the project, where the organization finds itself at present
Objectives	Succinct description of the project's objectives; what is needed to deliver the business case
Approach	How the project is to be undertaken in broad terms e.g. project methodology Waterfall or Agile
Major deliverables and key milestones	The main outputs of the project with expected dates of delivery
Scope	The boundaries of the project are clearly delineated
Exclusions	Aspects that are to be excluded from the project are stated. These might be parts of the organization, decommissioning of legacy systems or areas of functionality
Constraints	Any aspects that may prevent the project adhering to timescales, budget or scope need to be stated. Examples are availability of expertise or limitations in the IT infrastructure such as speed of the network
Interfaces	Any linkages needed to existing systems (whether human or machine) should be stated
Required effort	The resources (people and money) needed to complete the project should be summarized including an outline project plan
Expected benefits	The benefits that are expected to be delivered should be summarized. Full details will appear in the separate Business Case
Assumptions	Any assumptions made in preparing the plan should be included here. These might relate to the intended method of procurement for example
Organization's roles responsibilities	The main project and related roles and responsibilities should be detailed
Implementation strategy	The expected way in which the project deliverables will be put into service, for example a phased roll-out involving pilot installations or a model office
Risk and issue management	An initial risk and issue register should be included stating how they will be managed
Quality assurance and control strategy	The processes to be used to ensure that the deliverables are fit for purpose. Any quality assurance roles should be defined
Configuration management	Procedures to manage changes in the project deliverables or project management

Figure 8.6   Example content of a project initiation document

Eventually all the summary information provided in the PID will need to be expanded into separate documents covering, for example, requirements, configuration management, control and invitation to tender.

It is important to emphasize that the effort and resources needed to produce this documentation must be commensurate with the likely cost of the solution. For one client, a prospective supplier responded to an Invitation to Tender (ITT) congratulating them on the comprehensiveness of the document. However, they noted that if they complied with all the requests for information and the terms and conditions of the ITT, the cost to them would be several orders of magnitude greater than the profit they would make on selling the package. They therefore offered to let the client have the software to test themselves. The lesson from this is that if the required software package is of relatively low cost, then it may be more appropriate to 'beg or borrow' several competing products and evaluate them against one's requirements – which should still be clearly specified. The package that emerges best from the evaluation can then be tested more vigorously and selected or rejected on the basis of the test results.

8.2.3 BUSINESS CASE

Before a project can formally commence, it needs approval from the relevant authority, usually senior management. Their support (whether they represent the users, the executives or the IT fraternity, for example) will be essential – particularly if the project is resource-hungry, high-cost, extends over many months, and may hit problems later.

To enable them to come to a decision they need to see some form of justification, usually in terms of financial return. This justification is presented in the business case in which the types of question noted in Figure 8.7 should be addressed.

For projects undertaken in the private sector the form and content of the business case will follow the procedures and practices in each organization. Governments are generally much more prescriptive as regards what a business case must contain. In the UK, for example, the HM Treasury's 'Green Book' (http://www.hm-treasury.gov.uk/ data_greenbook_business.htm) requires that justification must be provided from five standpoints:

- strategic case
- economic case
- commercial case
- financial case
- management case.

A business case must not be based on justifying a single solution. Other options need to be presented and reasons for their rejection stated.

QUESTIONS TO BE ADDRESSED	TOPICS TO BE CONSIDERED (examples only)
What is recommended?	• A description of what is proposed • References to business needs that are being addressed
Why should we do it?	• Business rationale for the development (usually a qualitative focus) • Business benefits (typically as cost-benefits – a quantitative focus) • Consequences of not doing it • Alternatives considered and why rejected
How much will it cost?	• Total cost covering e.g. • Internal staff • External contractors • Software licences or services • Hardware/equipment • Installation • Running costs • Training • Support/maintenance
When will it be delivered?	• Deliverables by date • Money spent over time • Benefit delivered as money over time
How will it be achieved?	• Project management organization • Training or other purchased assistance • Technology to be used • Key risks and control measures • Key dependencies
How will we know when we have arrived?	• 'Before' and 'after' scenarios • Metrics used to measure business improvements

Figure 8.7 Elements of a business case

8.2.4 JUSTIFICATION AND BENEFITS

A key element of a business case is presentation of the benefits that are considered to result from the successful implementation of the project and the ongoing operation of its outputs. Generally it is preferable to have a mix of near-term and long-term objectives so that benefits can be delivered over a period of time.

Business benefits can be categorized according to whether they improve efficiency or effectiveness, for example. Efficiency is concerned with such matters as minimizing the time and effort of undertaking uncreative, routine but necessary procedures. Examples range from payroll administration to document filing. The benefits of increased efficiency usually manifest themselves as savings that can be quantified in monetary terms.

Effectiveness, in contrast, is concerned more with doing something extra or different with the same resources. The benefits of improved effectiveness arise from gaining more from existing resources, such as improved return on assets.

Whether a benefit is viewed as improving efficiency or effectiveness there will arise at some point the need to justify the investment to deliver the benefit.

The business justification may have relied on strategic or tactical objectives being achieved. The former are often associated with 'soft', 'qualitative' benefits which can be difficult to translate into monetary terms. Nevertheless it is more likely that a project proposal will be accepted if, under robust examination, the cost of achieving the benefits is shown to be outweighed by the cost savings.

Quantified, hard tangible benefits, preferably portrayed in cash terms, are ones that are most often sought after by decision makers. Even where valuation in monetary terms is not possible, as is the case with many soft, intangible benefits, important costs and benefits should be recorded and wherever possible quantified using, for example, techniques based on scoring, weighting and ranking.

Improvements that may be sought can therefore extend from the hard, tangible end of the benefit spectrum, through quasi-tangible benefits to the soft, intangible extreme. How 'benefits' are verbalized and how each is categorized as soft, hard, tangible, intangible, strategic or tactical, will differ from one person to another and from one organization to another. Some that have been applied to justify records and document management initiatives are provided in Chapter 9.

Just as the range of benefit types may be extensive, so are the associated approaches for justifying an investment. They may range from those that focus on the financial impact to those that are more an act of faith.

Financial evaluation normally involves undertaking the following:

- identifying net cash flow changes
- reducing these to a single index
- consideration of unquantifiable factors
- recognition of any uncertainties
- comparison of results for the competing projects.

The evaluation takes account of the time-related value of money. The particular method of measuring and presenting this will usually need to conform to the practice followed in one's own organization. Usually the process involves calculation of one or more of the following:

- net present value (NPV)
- discounted cash flow (DCF)
- internal rate of return (IRR).

The criteria used to judge the worthiness or otherwise of a project may include:

- speed of payback
- first year return
- overall percentage return on investment
- annual average rate of return on the original investment.

8.2.5 PERFORMANCE MEASUREMENT

Benefits in a business case are predicted. It is therefore important to monitor the progress towards achieving these and ensure they are realized (Bradley 2010).

Evaluation of a business change requires that some form of performance-based management process exists. Typically performance-based management will include the following steps (GSA 1998):

- Step 1: link projects to organizational goals and objectives
- Step 2: develop performance measures
- Step 3: establish a baseline to compare future performance
- Step 4: select projects with the greatest value
- Step 5: collect data
- Step 6: analyze the results
- Step 7: integrate into management processes
- Step 8: communicate the results.

The derivation of performance measures can be assisted by answering the following questions:

- what is the output of our activities?
- how will we know if we have met user/customer requirements?
- how will we know if we have met stakeholder requirements?
- how will the system be used?
- for what purpose will the system be used?
- what information will be produced, shared or exchanged?
- who will use the results?
- for what purpose will the results be used?
- why do the output and results matter?
- how do the results contribute to the critical success factors (CSFs)?

A variety of more formal techniques can be deployed and the choice will depend on local preferences and practice. An approach to managing stakeholder relationships was noted in Section 2.4. Two generalized techniques are the Goal Question Metric approach (GQM) and the Balanced Scorecard. The latter was discussed in Chapter 2.

GQM involves identifying each business goal, formulating questions that help determine what is required to meet each goal, then defining and collecting the data required to answer these questions. Although originally developed to improve aspects of software engineering, the principles can be applied more widely.

The output from GQM is a hierarchy of goals, questions and metrics. An example of a GQM is shown in Figure 8.8.

Of the other matters considered at the outset of a project those concerned with project objectives, scope, deliverables, resources and delivery dates are particularly important. Without an understanding of, and agreement on, what these are it will be difficult to direct and manage the project to a meaningful conclusion.

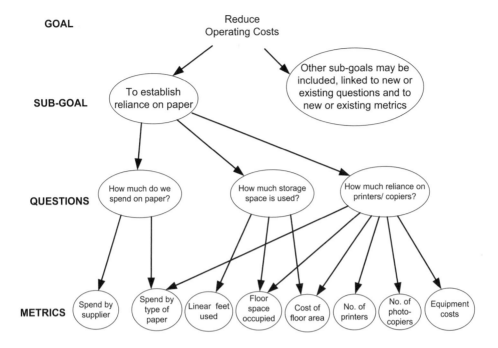

Figure 8.8   Goal Question Metric example

8.2.6 OBJECTIVES

Those who believe they will benefit from the outcome must be clear as to the project's objectives. Objectives differ from requirements. Thus the desired objective might be:

'To procure a records and case management system by 31st July that will enable social workers to handle increased case loads, and improve case management processes thereby reducing cost per case'.

Requirements, however, specify what needs to be delivered, for example:

'The system must enable current and completed case records to be migrated from the existing case management system'.

A useful pneumonic to help formulate or assess an objective is SMART – Specific, Measurable, Achievable, Realistic and Time-bound.
     In the foregoing objective, for example:

- the objective is specific
- it is measurable in terms of cost saving outcomes
- it is assumed that the objective is achievable and realistic.
- the objective is time-bound as it should be completed by 31st July.

8.2.7 SCOPE

The scope defines the boundaries within which the project operates. It may, for example:

- limit the deployment of the system to specific parts of the organization
- exclude specific functionality such as retention scheduling which will be the subject of a later project
- exclude the introduction of scanning (although a requirement is that the acquired system should have the capability to integrate with scanning technology)
- include the migration of live case files, but not those that are closed.

Adhering to the scope may be difficult. Users may often want additional features added as they become familiar with the possibilities on offer. They may also make assumptions about what is to be delivered if the project scope has not been clarified.

A clearly defined scope which includes assumptions, exclusions and inclusions enables the impact of any requested deviations to be more readily assessed and any additional effort to be costed.

8.2.8 DELIVERABLES

These are the artefacts, the things that are to be delivered at agreed stages in the project. They are the planned outputs of the project and as such must be focused upon at all times.

Deliverables may be divided into 'Management Products' and 'Technical Products'. The former relates principally to project management documentation that is common to most projects, while 'Technical Products' pertain to the matters that are unique to the project, for example the delivery of an EDRM or CMS.

These deliverables must align to existing objectives. If they do not then this may provide evidence of wasted work or scope creep, for example.

8.2.9 RESOURCES

Financial and human resources are required to undertake project activities. People resources will include users in taking time for interviews, reviewing project deliverables and testing prototype solutions, for example. Where users normally charge out their time, it is possible that they will require the effort they provide to the project to be included in the project's budget.

In addition there may be a requirement for equipment (for example, computers) and facilities (such as accommodation). These may or may not be included in the projects costs; such decisions should be defined in the project documentation.

Projects should not be initiated or pursued without an agreed budget which should be realistic in the eyes of the project management team. The budget can usefully be considered in terms of the costs relating to project management (staff, travel, and so on) and to the deliverables. This provides a focus on those costs that will not directly be delivering benefit to the users on project completion.

There may be costs arising on the completion of the project that have not been anticipated. For example, a new case management system is superseding one that has been in place for some time. The project may be required to decommission the system and deal with legacy paper records. The inclusion or exclusion of such activities must be included in the project scope.

8.2.10 SCHEDULED DELIVERY

For a timetable to be workable it has to be based on knowledge of what is to be delivered, the resources available and the dependencies between the various activities. The first step is to divide up the project into manageable pieces of work in the form of a work breakdown structure (WBS). While it will not happen in the first draft, once the team has finished its iterations and the WBS is complete it should meet the following criteria which are based on the ProjectConnections WBS Completion Checklist (ProjectConnections 2008):

- one (and only one) owner can be assigned to each of the lowest level activities
- clearly defined outputs (deliverables) are obvious for each activity
- quality can be monitored through completion criteria for each activity and/or its deliverable
- the work listed at one level 100 per cent defines the work needed to accomplish the activity at the level above it in the WBS
- the activities communicate the work to be accomplished to the person who is accountable
- the likelihood that an activity is omitted or workflow forgotten is minimized
- each activity is well defined and small enough so that estimates of work effort and duration are credible. Work effort or duration at lowest level should be less than five per cent of the total project, to ensure visibility into progress, at a small enough resolution to recognize quickly if the project is off track
- the project is broken down to the level at which you want to track progress.

8.2.11 ASSIGNING ACTIVITIES AND OWNERSHIP

Responsibility for each of the activities needs to be assigned, for example to a project team member or external supplier. Sometimes responsibility for a group of activities or products is assigned as a work package, the details of which should be documented and agreed with the person or body responsible for its delivery.

At this stage one has a list of the work in some logical order with responsibilities assigned. The next stage is to refine the logical relationships and identify the dependencies.

8.2.12 DEPENDENCIES

So far the WBS and activity assignments may have been recorded as a word-processed document or spreadsheet. Neither of these lend themselves easily to show dependency relationships that might exist between different tasks. Bar charts can be linked to help achieve this, but they are only suitable for small projects and lead to confusion and misinterpretation if the number of tasks goes beyond three figures. Drawing a process flow diagram of the project activities to be undertaken is a useful way to generate a WBS and show the dependencies and the inputs and outputs from the activities (see Section 7.1).

Aside from these widely applicable tools there is a range of commercial software dedicated to project planning, scheduling, resource assignment and tracking.

One type of dependency that must be identified relates to the critical path. This is defined as 'a sequence of stages determining the minimum time needed for the execution of an entire project (OED 2001)'. No activity on a critical path can commence until its predecessor has completed. If one of these activities is late, for example by one week, then the project end date will be extended by one week. 'Slack' indicates the activities that are not on the critical path and these can, with some thought, be delayed without impacting the start date of a subsequent activity.

8.2.13 REQUIREMENTS SPECIFICATION

A key deliverable from a project is a system that satisfies users' requirements. While the term 'users' is usually associated with those who will gain business benefits from its deployment, there are other types of user, each with their own set of requirements as exemplified in Figure 8.9. The titles given to user types may differ between organizations; however, the important point is to recognize that there is a spectrum of users with differing needs.

USER TYPE	EXAMPLE REQUIREMENTS
Business users	System should satisfy functional requirements
Technology architects	The technology should be compatible with the organization's IT standards (software, hardware and networking)
Technical support	Technology should be easy to support (e.g. upgrading to new product releases)
User support	System should be reliable and predictable (thereby placing minimum burden on First Line support) and well documented
System administrators	System should allow ready, but controlled addition of users. System should allow ready, but controlled changes in users' access rights
Trainers	System should be easy to learn and have sufficiently comprehensive training manuals and on-line help

Figure 8.9 Types of users

Given this perspective it is important that requirements are properly identified, amplified, documented and agreed before significant project resources are deployed and costs are incurred. By all means adopt the 'Agile' approach for systems development with its greater flexibility for embracing changes, but this should still be undertaken within a controlled project management environment that has accepted this approach within its configuration management plan.

The requirements specification, whether intended for use with in-house developers or as part of a tender document for a prospective external supplier, should cover the needs of the various types of user and include the following elements, in summary, where appropriate:

- business background for the development; scene-setting and aims and objectives
- functional specification; overview and detailed list of functions required (categorized as to how important they are, for example mandatory or desirable)
- timetable for proposed phasing of delivery of functions
- business models; current (physical) data and process models; logical data and process models
- volumetrics; quantities of documents – legacy and ongoing; numbers of expected users; access rates (helps to size the hardware and networks)
- current technology environment; software, hardware, networks
- existing information systems and applications affected by project
- required or planned technology environment; standards, technical architecture, user interfaces, service performance, service operational requirements, security and access controls, disaster recovery, system support
- design methodology, for example Waterfall or Agile
- quality plan
- required deliverables; hardware, software, networks, documentation, training, project management products, support services, legacy data loading.

Where possible, the requirements should be referenced to relevant *de facto* and *de jure* standards and codes of practice. This not only reduces the size of the requirements document, but also ensures that what is put in place as the eventual solution conforms to well-known and established practice.

8.2.14 THE PROCUREMENT PROCESS

The procurement process includes supplier selection, contract negotiations, order placement and payment. All organizations have some form of procurement policy and associated procedures.

There are special rules for procurement by public bodies in the European Union (EU). The EU procurement rules apply to public authorities, including government departments, local authorities, health authorities and some utility companies operating in the energy, water, transport and telecommunications sectors. They set out the following four options for the award of contracts whose value equals or exceeds specific thresholds, the values of which are subject to review and change (OJEC 2011a):

- open procedure
- restricted procedure
- negotiated procedure
- competitive dialogue procedure.

According to the open procedure all those interested may respond to an advertisement placed in the Official Journal of the European Community (OJEU) by tendering for the contract.

Under the restricted procedure a selection is made of those who respond to the advertisement and only they are invited to submit a tender for the contract. This effectively reduces the number of tenders that have to be evaluated.

For the negotiated procedure a purchaser may select one or more potential bidders with whom to negotiate the terms of the contract. An advertisement in the OJEU is usually required but, in certain circumstances described in the Regulations, this is not necessary.

The competitive dialogue procedure is the latest of the procedures to be introduced. Following an OJEU Contract Notice and a selection process, the intending purchaser enters into dialogue with potential bidders to develop one or more suitable solutions for its requirements and on which chosen bidders will be invited to tender. It is intended to be used where the level of complexity of the project makes it necessary for contracting authorities to discuss all aspects of the proposed contract with bidders before deciding on the preferred solution.

8.2.15 THE INVITATION TO TENDER

If it has been decided to seek assistance from outside one's company, all the foregoing is directed towards producing some form of documentation for distribution to a set of chosen prospective suppliers who are invited to tender. The form that this document takes and the procurement procedure that is followed will depend on the practice followed by the procuring organization.

For those organizations lacking any formal procurement procedures, and where the size of the envisaged contract in terms of complexity, resource allocation and cost is significant, then guidance on the structure and content of an Invitation to Tender (ITT) document will often be available from professional institutions. Thus the Institution of Mechanical Engineers and the Institution of Engineering and Technology offer a model form of general conditions of contract and guidance which, although slanted towards engineering projects, does address the needs of those procuring computer hardware and software (IMechE 2010).

Examples of the general conditions that one would expect to see in an ITT include:

- basis of tender and contract price
- warranty and performance
- contractor's (supplier's) obligations
- software and system acceptance
- title to the standard software (that is, the contractor's standard software as listed in an accompanying schedule)
- title to bespoke software (that is, that part of the software to be developed by the contractor)
- purchaser's general obligations
- installation of hardware
- confidentiality
- source code deposit (for example, via an Escrow agreement to protect the purchaser in the event of the supplier going bankrupt)
- training
- manuals and user documentation
- defects liability.

These general conditions, which would be part of any ITT, are amplified by a series of schedules specially formulated for the particular project and detailing requirements and obligations. Typical schedules might include those headed:

- instructions to tenderers (for example, detailing the format of response, specific questions to be answered by the tenderers and the basis on which the tenders will be evaluated)
- particulars and special conditions (amplifying and adding to those in the general conditions)
- requirements specification
- project management (covering project plan, resources, organization and change control and incorporating consideration of risk, safety and quality issues)
- testing (covering more detail on the approach, responsibilities and acceptance criteria)
- training (details of those to be trained and types of training)
- form of tender (including any payment schedule linked to defined deliverables)
- software licences and maintenance agreement
- hardware maintenance.

8.2.16 EVALUATION OF THE TENDERS

It is important that all the tenders received are evaluated according to a pre-defined, auditable documented process and a set of evaluation criteria acceptable to the purchasing organization and outlined, at least as to its key general approach, in the Invitation to Tender.

The evaluation procedure should:

- define the evaluation process itself
- identify the evaluators and their roles
- specify the evaluation criteria
- indicate the priorities and any weightings applied to the criteria
- state who will review and approve the results of the evaluation.

Typical categories of requirements to which weighting may be applied are:

- functional
- commercial
- infrastructure (technical aspects)
- operational
- support
- training.

Within these categories the specific requirements can be individually weighted. For example, those that are mandatory will be more highly rated than desirable requirements. The first cut evaluation could be focused on the degree to which mandatory requirements are met.

As with other aspects of the procurement process, the make-up of the evaluation approach may well be dictated by established practice within one's organization.

An important aspect is to ensure that there is separation of responsibilities as regards, for example, those who prepare the tender and those who evaluate the responses to it.

8.2.17 CONTRACT NEGOTIATION AND SUPPLIER OPTIONS

Given that the evaluation process has resulted in the identification of preferred suppliers, the next stage is detailed contract negotiation. If it is a close call between two or more suppliers, it is sensible not to discard all but the one that came out on top. This provides a safeguard should contract negotiations fail with one's first choice. The aim of the negotiating process is to arrive at an agreement satisfactory to both parties. If the purchaser causes the supplier to leave the completed negotiations dissatisfied in some way, then it is more likely that they will stick strictly to the terms of the contract and give no latitude should the purchaser default from their obligations under that contract. This is not to say that striking a hard bargain should be avoided, but both parties should be able to leave the negotiations feeling that they have achieved their objectives.

In parallel with the negotiation stage, and before contract signing, it may be required to produce a Supplier Options Paper for senior management. The paper should revisit the Project Initiation Document and any cost-benefit appraisal that was undertaken then, and present an appraisal of the current situation with recommendations of the way forward with the preferred supplier.

In estimating the time that a procurement phase may take, it is often the case that the negotiation stage is allocated too little time. This is a critical stage of the procurement cycle and should not be skipped over lightly. Decisions made then become binding on contract signing and may be regretted later.

8.2.18 UNDERTAKING THE PROJECT

The point at which a supplier is selected concentrates the mind wonderfully. Now the real work begins. Some of the types of activity that need to be undertaken in an information management project are dealt with in Chapter 9. Many of the activities will have started well before the procurement stage in order to prepare the organization for change.

8.2.19 GETTING AND KEEPING COMMITMENT

The new system is being introduced to achieve stated objectives. However, to achieve these objectives the staff involved have to be convinced not simply that these aims are achievable, but more importantly that their new or revised functions and tasks deliver benefits to them as individuals. To arrive at this point requires proper involvement of the staff during the project phases so that they do not encounter any surprises, and can contribute positively and appropriately to the specification, design and selection of the systems they will eventually utilize.

A key to success is the continuing commitment of both users and business managers supported by IT personnel. The project organization, if established along the lines outlined in PRINCE2 for example, helps ensure that all parties are involved at the key decision and product review points of relevance to them. Additionally, instilling awareness of technological developments in the staff and their management, coupled with specific training and visits to existing users of such systems at other sites, will help ensure a smooth transition from project to operational use.

An additional way of facilitating commitment is to establish Internal User Panels linked to the Project Assurance Team. Also, if the supplier has a User Group for its product, then user representatives should attend these meetings.

As the project achieves its various milestones, this success should be publicized to other parts of the organization which may in some way have an interest. This can be effected in various ways, for example by newsletters, 'open day' demonstrations, or via a corporate intranet where one exists.

All this education and awareness process should be set within the context of the broader business picture, so that participants can appreciate the significance and potential of new developments. Once fully committed, the staff 'at the sharp end' are often the main champions of the system and are best placed to wring further gains from it.

8.2.20 POST-PROJECT REVIEW

An oft-forgotten stage of a project is to prove that the implemented system has achieved its objectives. This involves a post-project review timed sufficiently long after the system's formal acceptance to allow its steady-state performance and functionality to be more accurately assessed.

This review will mean revisiting the original business case and justification (as may have been subsequently amended as part of the project's change control procedure) and undertaking a fresh cost-benefit analysis, this time based on real rather than projected operational experience. Naturally such an evaluation is not possible unless the same metrics have been applied both before and after the project timeframe.

If the project has been effectively and efficiently planned and managed, then there should be no surprises at this, the final project milestone.

8.3 Conclusion

Research reported by McManus and Wood-Harper (2008) indicates that only one in eight information technology projects could be considered truly successful. Failure related to projects that did not meet the original time, cost and quality requirements criteria. Sound and robust project management should help avoid such failures or at least provide means to manage agreed changes in such parameters. However, it is easy to become engrossed in the minutiae of project procedures and documentation. While essential project components such as a plan and business case must remain, the bureaucracy of management should be avoided.

This chapter was concerned with those elements of project management that are common to all projects. The next and final chapter continues the theme of project management, but with a focus on activities particularly relevant to the focus of this book.

9 Information Management – The Project Focus

'Don't do a project where you don't think you'll learn something on the way'.
Jim Coudal, Keynote Speech, SXSW 2006

General principles of project management (the 'management' products) were dealt with in the last chapter. Here some of the aspects specific to the undertaking of an information management initiative (the 'technical' products) are considered.

9.1 Strategic Planning

Since any project initiative concerned with management of recorded information is likely to have wide impact, it is important to ensure that the project is an integral part of the wider organizational strategy as discussed in Chapter 1. If the project is confined to a particular business function or department, it is still necessary to identify the information and business process interfaces with other parts of the organization and with those that reside outside the organization. This will facilitate the design of the interfaces, for example by encouraging suppliers to conform to information interchange standards, and will lay the foundation for any future expansion of the programme beyond its initial scope.

An important consideration is to what extent the development of the intended system is to be undertaken in-house as a software development project, rather than buying in a 'packaged' solution (that is, a turnkey system). These options represent the extremes of a spectrum of solution provision. In reality, few software developments make no use of existing software solutions or components, while turnkey systems rarely involve no configuration or tailoring of the 'package'.

By far the most common route is to opt for commercially established solutions. These will often involve the integration and configuration of a range of third party products (the provenance of which is often hidden from the user) around a core system from the chosen supplier. The benefits of this approach are, for example:

- support and maintenance should be more readily available due to the commitment the supplier has to its existing user base
- problems and wish-lists can be discussed with other users of the product outside one's organization
- the user is not locked into a single supplier (whether internal or external) who has delivered a solution unique to that user.

Although there has been much consolidation in the marketplace in recent years one can never be sure that the chosen supplier will be around in the same guise in the future. For example, with one client, all three short-listed suppliers including the vendor, whose system was implemented, were subsequently taken over by competitors. It is therefore important to assess the commercial and financial soundness of a prospective supplier. These criteria should also be applied to internal solution providers. It is not unknown for in-house IT departments to be re-organized, down-sized, outsourced or even disbanded.

9.2 Selecting the Business Area

Before substantive work is commenced, it is necessary to determine the scope of the project as regards the parts of the organization to be included. Candidate areas for change may become apparent from pro-active studies to achieve strategic or tactical benefits, for example:

- to support enterprise knowledge management initiatives
- to improve customer satisfaction
- to increase speed to market
- to eliminate unnecessary tasks
- to reduce costs.

On the other hand areas with the following business problems may merit attention:

- increased storage costs for documents
- difficulties in accessing and retrieving information from archives
- delays in dealing with customers' orders
- slow, bureaucratic document approval cycles
- need for simultaneous access to documents.

The more general techniques and methodologies outlined in Chapter 1, taken together with process and data analysis described in Chapter 7 and the records- and document-specific tasks outlined later, provide a range of approaches for reviewing and analyzing the business and thereby identifying the areas of greatest need. Candidate areas can also be identified by considering the types of processes that are undertaken as exemplified by those in Figure 9.1.

Application	Comments
Transaction or form processing	Based on handling single documents, e.g. as in bank cheque clearance and recording credit card counterfoils. The processing tasks and procedures are pre-defined, relatively simple and repetitive. Actions are not varied by the actual contents of the 'document' and usually consist of extracting data and transferring it to an alternative form for storage
Case transaction processing	Involves accessing the accumulated documents linked to a specific key, for example a file concerning a named defendant in a set of such files handled by a lawyer, or an individual's records held by an insurance company. The reasons for accessing the file will vary but may involve undertaking standard tasks, e.g. to review renewal premiums, or for ad hoc research purposes
Customer service enquiry	Oral or written requests are received from customers. Document retrieval provides the information for answering the query. The workflow element is minimal
Corporate publishing	Typically associated with desktop publishing it may involve the integration of digitally generated images and scanned-in photographs
Quality management	Adherence to quality system standards and adoption of quality management systems involve the documenting of policies, procedures and possibly detailed work instructions. Document management coupled with workflow can facilitate the creation and maintenance of quality documentation
Corporate administrative and management documents	Documents will include policies and procedures for the various business functions such as human resources and sales and marketing. The production and management of these documents will require the same kind of activities as those applied to quality management
Records management	Retention scheduling of corporate records is incorporated into the document management system along with controlled archiving using appropriate storage media (e.g. on-line, near-line and off-line)
Library services	Libraries are typically responsible for acquiring and managing externally published or sourced information. Commercially available systems have long existed for e.g. cataloguing, ordering, periodical (serials) management and loans management and for providing full text searching. Document management functionality is provided by some vendors, or as add-ons by third parties to help integrate this external information with other corporate information. Searching of the document collection is usually undertaken for research and reference purposes
Office documentation	General office documentation such as word-processed correspondence, spreadsheets or scanned-in images from paper have long been candidates for document management systems. Access is provided by searching on structured indexes or occasional full-text searching. Links to work group scheduling applications can be important
Engineering project management	Engineering document management systems have developed from the need to manage engineering project documents including large format drawings (e.g. up to A0 or larger) along with standard office sizes. For engineering projects such functionality as document version control, system access controls, user rights, controlled document distribution and approval and authorization are key. Hence workflow controls are normally required. Retrieval of documents is normally satisfied by structured indexing (e.g. drawing numbers). Links to creation applications for documents (e.g. word-processing) and drawings (i.e. CAD) are important as are communication links to external engineering contractors and the eventual beneficiaries of the project at the hand-over stage

Figure 9.1   Examples of application areas

9.3 Information Management Project Stages

The Technical Report that forms part 2 of the International Standard for information and documentation (ISO 15489–2 2001) outlines eight stages for undertaking a project to design and implement a records system; that is, one that manages recorded information within an organization. The stages are depicted in Figure 9.2.

In summary the stages are:

Stage A: Provides an understanding of the administrative, legal, business and social contexts in which the organization operates.

Stage B: Develops a conceptual model of what the organization does and how it does it. A key output of this stage is a Business Classification Scheme as discussed in Chapter 5.

Stage C: Identifies the requirements for record creation, receipt and retention and the regulatory environment and produces a requirements document.

Stage D: Assesses the organization's current records systems and produces a systems inventory and an outline of systems requirements.

Stage E: Identifies the strategies to satisfy the requirements taking into account the organization's vision and objectives.

Stage F: Designs the records system which takes into account the human as well as the technological aspects. The deliverables will include not only project plans, system specifications and file plans, but also procurement documentation such as tender document and tender evaluation; that is, the outputs one would expect from a formal information management project.

Stage G: Implements the selected records systems and includes working with the chosen supplier on such matters as detailed design, testing, implementation and training.

Stage H: Deals with all matters following implementation of the system including assessing the realization of expected benefits.

Its principles have been adopted by some in the public and private sectors, particularly with regard to Step B, to inform the design of function-based filing structure (file plans) and to identify a migration path from existing drive folders to those in the file plan.

The total process as detailed in the Standard has been found by some to be overly bureaucratic. Much of the work is concentrated in Step F. Even the Standard itself recognizes some problems in its use, stating 'It is sometimes difficult in practice to see where determining strategies for records systems ends (Step E) and designing systems to incorporate those strategies begins (Step F)'. As an example of the effort expended, around 5 person years spread over 6 months were needed to analyze the departmental electronic

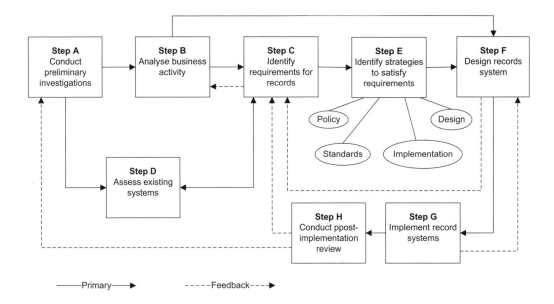

Figure 9.2 Projects stages for a records management project

Source: Permission to reproduce extracts from ISO 15489-2 2001. ISO/TE 15489-2:2001 is granted by BSI. British Standards can be obtained in PDF or hard copy formats from the BSI online shop: www.bsigroup. com/Shop or by contacting BSI Customer Services for hardcopies only: Tel: +44 (0)20 8996 9001, Email: cservices@bsigroup.com

folders of all 25 main internal departments (around 600 staff) for a UK Government Department.

Experience in using the methodology has shown that it needs to be applied pragmatically taking into account such factors as the size, type, complexity and culture of the organization. In particular it should not be followed slavishly from one stage to the next as there are many opportunities for iteration. Depending on the scope of the project it is often possible to combine the earlier stages A to D in some way as they are all address the same questions 'where are we now?' and 'where do we want to be?' while stages E to H answer the question 'how do we get there?'.

It is not uncommon for a 'green-field' project environment to commence with some form of strategy study. This is not intended to define detailed specific functional or non-functional requirements or specify specific technology solutions. Rather the aim is to identify gaps as compared with best practice or existing standards, revise or produce a policy for corporate records and establish an action plan. The output would then feed into the content of a Project Initiation Document, for example.

An example of the main elements that were used in an information management strategy study is shown in Figure 9.3. They comprise:

- project set up
- survey and analysis
- production of a Records Management Policy and (later) associated procedures
- development of a file plan and retention schedules

- identification of potential suppliers
- action plan and resources for follow-on activities.

These effectively cover stages A to D of the Standard's project stages with the output being an action plan for stages E to H.

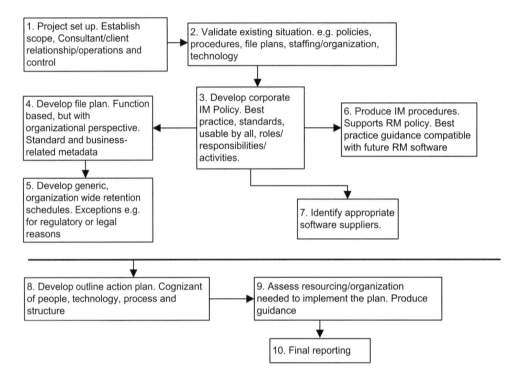

Figure 9.3   Project tasks for an IM strategy study

9.3.1 INFORMATION MANAGEMENT POLICY IN CONTEXT

An important aim of the foregoing study is to address the policy and supporting procedural framework before the introduction of any technology. The National Archives provides guidance on the formulation of a records management (RM) policy (TNA 2010a) with the sound advice to keep it short and strategic. They outline the seven steps:

- establish senior management support
- research the organization's current records management practices, resources and attitudes
- consult staff
- research the organization's legal and regulatory environment
- look at other policies
- overall policy framework
- draft the policy.

Clearly, senior management support is vital as is the need to consult staff to gain their views. Understanding the current state of information management arrangements will involve survey and analysis as discussed later in Section 9.5. The legal and regulatory environment will include laws and regulations that impact all organizations plus those that are specific to the type of organization or the business area in which it operates.

Although 'records' are the key information content in an organization, the title 'information' management (IM) policy is likely to be more readily comprehended across an organization. In fact one UK Government Department promulgated an RM policy without once mentioning the word 'record' in the document.

An IM policy will form part of a family of policies in an organization and many of these policies will need to be revised to cater for the introduction of a new system and changes in working practices. It is not unusual for some so called 'policies' to be no more than high level procedures for day-to-day activities. It is therefore important to gather details of such documents and then judge the extent to which they need to be, for example:

- incorporated in the IM policy
- revised to complement the IM policy
- referenced from the IM policy
- replaced by the IM policy
- determined as not relevant to the IM policy.

Details of all policies and any identified supporting procedures within the organization should be documented and assessments made of the changes (if any) required. The documents collected should be aligned with the appropriate level in the Strategic Planning Hierarchy (see Figure 1.4). If the project is at a departmental level, for example, there should be two sets of documents, one relating to the organizational level and one to the department level. In this way any overlap or gaps between top level and local level policies and procedures can more readily be distinguished.

While the aim should be to keep the IM Policy succinct, topics to consider for inclusion are:

- capture policy
- receipt and processing of information
- creation of information
- scanning
- systems integration and interfaces
- web-sites
- metadata policy
- access policy
- freedom of information and data protection
- security and legal admissibility policy
- retention policy
- preservation policy
- technical policy
- transition to electronic records
- communication and training.

It may well be that these topics, alone or in some combination, are better covered in separate policy documents hanging from a short policy framework document which summarizes the coverage as exemplified in Figure 9.4.

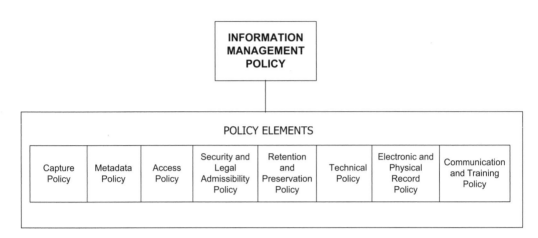

Figure 9.4   Policy framework

9.5 Survey and Analysis

In order to ensure that all 'cradle to grave' aspects are dealt with, the information gathering should involve surveying existing records and documentation types, collections and associated practices relating to the information life cycle activities. One way that has proved of value when undertaking such studies is to imagine a two-dimensional matrix relating the information activities to the organizational elements identified in Figure 3.8 in Chapter 3 – see Figure 9.5.

Clearly the entries under the heading 'Life Cycle' can be expanded according to local needs.

This, together with the questions posed in Figure 9.6, can help ensure that all the structural, process, people and tools aspects for each activity have been covered during the survey and subsequent analysis.

Where the magnitude of the investigation is substantial, as measured for example by the size of company and number of functions to be covered, there can be benefit in undertaking a scoping survey to identify key functions and issues prior to the more detailed analysis. If, however, the problem being investigated is at the task level, it tends to be self-contained and localized and can thus usually be dealt with at the detailed analytical level.

While pursuing the study, continually assess the merits and deficiencies in these organizational elements against the information activities that are undertaken, possibly applying some subjective numeric ratings in each box. Gain an overview of the flow of work, so that an awareness of the overall business processes is obtained, including any interfaces between manual and computer systems. This can help identify opportunities for improving business processes. The aim is not so much to gather extensive data at this stage, but to identify key factors. At the end of the study the completed matrix (albeit

LIFE CYCLE	Structure	People	Process	Tools
CAPTURE				
Acquisition				
Creation				
Scanning				
Data Capture				
Automatic identification and capture				
MANAGE				
Review and approval				
Editing				
Declaration				
Classification				
Applying retention				
Disposition				
Storage				
Archiving				
Retrieval				
Disposal				
UTILIZE				
Exploit				
Publish				
ORGANIZE				
MONITOR AND CONTROL				

Figure 9.5   Information activities and organizational elements

QUESTION	THE INFORMATION TO BE GATHERED
'What'	Ensures that the 'specifics' are identified, e.g. what information or data are acquired, created etc.
'Why'	The reason behind the activity. A key question for identifying redundant, inappropriate activities, documents etc.
'Who'	Identifies the people involved; ties the activity to individuals or groups of people who may be the source or recipient of the information
'How'	Determines the methods used, which may or may not involve the use of information technology
'Where'	Focuses attention on locations for the activity; locations may need to be specific, e.g. a staff member's PC, or could satisfactorily be identified more generally, e.g. a supplier's name and address
'When'	Identifies when the activity relating to the information occurs
'How many'	Gathers quantitative data about numbers and volumes for both physical and electronic records
'How often'	Ensures that variations with time are identified

Figure 9.6   Questions to pose

in the form of a written report) provides a sound basis for determining areas for future action.

9.5.1 THE RECORDS SURVEY

In addition to the activity-oriented data gathered as described above, there is the need to gather information concerning the characteristics of the records, many of which will be common to physical and electronic records.

The concept of a records series has long been important for paper records, but definitions vary depending on which authority one consults. Here a records series is defined as a group of logically-related records, irrespective of format, that support a specific activity. Many record series will exist in both physical and electronic form and there is merit in undertaking the survey simultaneously across both formats (Saffady 2009). This has the advantages of:

- minimizing the number of visits
- identifying redundancy and duplication in records across formats
- enabling the updating of retention schedules currently used only for paper.

A suitably designed inventory form should be used to log the checklist information (Figure 9.7) which for the most part covers both physical (P) and electronic (E) formats.

The record series title should reflect the name used by those who use or manage it. For example, if the organization has a computerized case management system this may hold contact details as well as individual case files. Hence two records series need to be noted 'case files' and 'contact data'. Detailed analysis of database information is discussed in Chapter 7, Section 7.4.1.

As regards describing the records it can be helpful to categorize the documents as this can indicate the level of retention and care to be taken; examples are provided in Figure 9.8.

Any inventory form used is best designed to facilitate incorporation of the collected information into a database, and may simply be created at the outset as an input screen to enable direct input on a notebook or tablet computer taken around the organization.

Consideration can be given to designing the form in such a way that it could be circulated as a questionnaire for completion by staff. Although this may save time, there is the danger that those completing the form may not fully understand what they are being asked to do, despite any prior briefing they may have had. Furthermore, they may miss noting some records which are important to the survey. Hence if this route is undertaken, it should only be used selectively, and the information should always be validated in some way, for example by visiting the staff member and their area of responsibility.

Where paper documents are to be converted to electronic form by scanning, you will need to gather additional details concerning their physical and structural characteristics. This is a pre-requisite for identifying any preparatory work needed such as removing staples, and to ensure that suitable hardware and software is chosen. Examples of the main features to consider and the types of question that arise concerning system selection are summarized in Figure 9.9.

FACTORS	P	E
Name of the department or unit whose records are being surveyed	x	x
Person undertaking the survey	x	x
Person interviewed	x	x
Date of inventory	x	x
Person responsible for the records	x	x
Title of the record series (e.g. purchase orders)	x	x
Description of records (subject, types and completeness)	x	x
Records policies and procedures (obtain copies)	x	x
Retention requirements	x	x
Regulatory or legal requirements that apply	x	x
Filing arrangements/classifications (e.g. alpha, numeric, functional)	x	x
Main users of records	x	x
Frequency & urgency of access	x	x
How vital the records are	x	x
Process which created the records	x	x
Location of records	x	x
Location of duplicates or back-ups	x	x
Earliest and latest dates in the record series (note any gaps)	x	x
Estimated growth	x	x
Identification of any form work and templates	x	x
Type of storage equipment (e.g. lateral filing, open shelf, disk storage)	x	x
Quantity – Item count	x	x
Quantity – bytes		x
Quantity – cubic or linear metres (e.g. for paper or tape storage)	x	x
Quantity – boxes, cabinets (e.g. for paper or tape storage)	x	x
Number and rate at which records are accumulated	x	x
Media characteristics – type and size		x
Media characteristics – brand and model		x
Media characteristics – recording format (e.g. DVD-R, DVD-RW)		x
File type (document, spreadsheet, PDF, image etc)		x
Technical requirements for access (e.g. software, hardware)		x
Comments	x	x

Figure 9.7   Check list for records inventory

DOCUMENT CATEGORY	EXAMPLES	LIFE CYCLE PATTERNS
Ephemeral correspondence	Sales brochures; unsolicited mail	Acquire, log, temporary store, short retention
Administrative corporate documents	Procedures; quality manuals; standards; board minutes	Create, authorize, index, communicate, revise, retain (legal requirements)
Transaction documents	Cheques; invoices; transmittals; applications	Acquire, create, authorize, index, communicate (workflow)
Reference documents	Articles; data books; reports; directories	Acquire, communicate (loans), subject/full text indexing
Design documents	Drawings; CAD designs/ models; parts lists; bill of materials	Create, approve, log/index, communicate (controlled distribution; workflow), revise (annotate; version control)
Maintenance documents	Schedules; manuals; parts lists; procedures; standards	Create, approve, index (hyperlinks to drawings), revise (annotate; version control)

Figure 9.8   Document categories

	DATA GATHERED	BACKGROUND QUESTIONS
Physical characteristics	Dimensions	Can scanner handle size range?
	Number of pages (range and average)	Can imaging system handle the volume throughput? Should the scanning of legacy documents be done in-house or by a bureau?
	Single- or double-sided printing	Is flat-bed or sheet-fed imaging system required?
	Mono or colour printing	Will mono scanning be adequate or is colour important?
	Presence of diagrams and graphics	How detailed are they, what scanning resolution is required?
	Presence of half-tone photographs	Is gray scale capture required?
	Type of paper	Can the thin or thick stock be handled in a sheet-feeder?
	Method of assembly or binding	Is it acceptable to break the binding to create single sheets, or must the document be handled in bound form?
	Condition (tears, fading, folds, dirt etc)	How much pre-preparation is required prior to scanning or filming (e.g. photocopying creased originals and scanning the copies)?
	Whether handwritten or typed	Will OCR be able to handle the typed script?
	Presence of annotations/marginal notes	Will marginal notes fit within scanning area?
	Size range of type face	What scanning resolution is necessary to ensure effective OCR?
Structure and layout	Standardization of layout	Is it a form; is the form structure consistent enough to permit its removal as a separate entity when scanning?
	Logical structure	Is key data in the same location so that it can be automatically captured for indexing?
	Mixing of non-textual with textual information	Will the scanner be able automatically to detect and OCR just the text information?
	Existence of bibliographic data	Is the data e.g. title, author, reference number, summary, publication date in locations which enable it to be captured for indexing during scanning?

Figure 9.9   Physical and structural characteristics of paper documents

9.6 Benefits from the Investment in Information Management

Justification for undertaking a project was considered in general terms in Chapter 8. Specific projects will require to be justified in their own terms based on the benefits that are expected to arise. Such benefits depend not only on technology and the functionality it delivers, but also on the changes that are made in new working practices. Such changes are often ones that should have been undertaken irrespective of the introduction of new technology, but arise as a result of users having to conform to the standardized procedures and data quality required in a database environment.

Benefits that are envisaged with the introduction of such technology as an electronic records system are exemplified in the government context by the following from the Queensland State Archives in Australia (QLD 2007):

- For the individual:
    - quicker and more convenient discovery and access to required information
    - improved administrative efficiency and effectiveness
    - facilitation of evidence-based and informed decision making
    - collaboration and avoidance of 'reinventing the wheel' when developing documentation.
- For the organization:
    - secure and systematic management of unstructured data such as emails, documents and spreadsheets
    - efficiency gains with improved quality and consistency of organizational processes
    - enhancement of an organization's recordkeeping culture and promulgation of organizational standards for recordkeeping procedures and practices
    - improved information security, through greater control over and access to corporate information
    - reduced risk of loss of records
    - reduced legal liability exposure
    - ability to integrate core business applications with the EDRMS enabling improved records capture through automation
    - facilitation of compliance with legislative obligations and standards.
- For society:
    - improved accountability and transparency of government administration
    - improved customer service
    - evidence of the authenticity, integrity and reliability of electronic public records.

Taking a broader view, a study focusing on Enterprise Content Management (ECM) examined Return On Investment (ROI) factors quantifying the improvements that a well-implemented system can provide, and indicating the potential costs of compliance and security lapses (AIIM 2011b). It also reported on the experiences of those who have such systems in use.

Of the key findings, the following are noteworthy:

- eight per cent of the working day is spent filing, maintaining and searching for information

- productivity of professional staff would be improved by 30 per cent if they could find internal information and documents as quickly and as easily as they find information on the web
- productivity of administrative staff can be increased on average by 33 per cent by work-flowing processes using scanned forms and automated data capture
- office space allocated to filing storage could be reduced by 60 per cent by changing to a culture of electronic-only filing
- the size of server farms dedicated to unstructured content and emails could be reduced by between a third and a half if each document or email attachment was stored only once
- a collaborative, widely accessible team-site environment is likely to improve project delivery by 23 per cent on average in terms of timescales and project costs
- although the technologies are immature as yet, respondents consider that Social Business Systems or Enterprise 2.0 applications (developments in Web 2.0 technology to improve business processes) can improve staff productivity and engagement by around 18 per cent.

Based on the actual experience of using ECM systems, estimates for workflow productivity gains and project delivery improvements were higher than projections by non-users, indicating results that are better than expected. On the other hand, information finding and remote access improvements were overestimated by non-users.

In a separate study (AIIM 2009b), the benefits of adopting scanning to capture paper documents in electronic form were investigated. It was concluded that in addition to improving access to information, savings in process time, staff costs and storage space could provide a payback in 12 to 18 months. Such projects were believed to be much more likely to meet or exceed benefit realization expectations compared to other IT investments.

The benefits of electronic records management were reported by Sprehe (2005) for The Defense Advanced Research Projects Agency (DARPA) and the Nuclear Regulatory Commission (NRC). For DARPA the EDRMS supported the Executive Information System (EIS) by providing transparent access via the EIS to key procurement documentation holding data on disbursements. An Agency-wide Document Access and Management System (ADAMS) in the NRC provided record management functions but also has electronic signature capability, published documents to a public website, managed the web content and has made more efficient the NRC's adjudicatory and rulemaking processes.

For the UK a range of case studies is available at http://www.aiim.org.uk/casestudies. asp . Examples include:

- Northern Ireland Office – the introduction of an EDRMS eliminated the need to create and store separate paper trails and to store information on anything other than the system itself. Particular emphasis was placed on the need to be able to manage the internal publication and dissemination of information in a cost effective manner, while ensuring that the organization must have access to information published electronically by other providers, particularly other government departments.
- Norton Rose legal practice – improved efficiency and reduced in-house scanning costs by introducing high speed scanners capable of creating large quantities of

eBibles for electronically storing all the documentation associated with any corporate transaction.

- The Ipswich Hospital NHS Trust – to manage more than half a million case notes housed both on and off site, it implemented high speed scanning and an EDRMS integrated with the hospital's Patient Administration System and Clinical Management Systems with a customized portal for access.

9.7 Requirements Specification

An organization will not necessarily require all the functionality that can be provided by a commercial system, although the initial application area may be viewed as a pilot for possible roll-out and extension of functionality to other business areas.

Consideration of the generic information life cycle presented earlier in Figure 3.8 can inform discussions on functionality. An alternative presentation is provided in Figure 9.10 covering:

- secure store for indexed documents
- acquisition of documents from outside the immediate organization
- creation of documents within the organization
- retrieval of documents
- distribution of documents
- support for business processes using workflow
- additional modules such as records management and e-Discovery.

The functions cited, and others, can be used in the Requirements Specification as headings under which the requirements can be spelt out in more detail. The following specifications provide a checklist for the detailed content:

- Modular Requirements for Records Systems (MoReq10 2010) – from the Document Lifecycle Forum (DLM), Europe
- Electronic Records Management Software Applications Design Criteria Standard (DoD 2007) – from Department of Defense, United States
- EDRMS Functional Specification (SAU 2009), Australia
- Functional Requirements for Electronic Records Management Systems – from The National Archives, UK (TNA 2007b)

The requirements specification must include non-functional as well as functional requirements. Within the former category may be included:

- access controls – relating to users and security protected documents or folders
- data loading and exchange – for legacy data and ongoing interfaces to existing systems. Guidance on transfer between EDRM systems is provided by The National Archives (TNA 2010b)
- auditing – ability to monitor and report on all access and changes to the content
- performance – ability to meet defined response times given expected volumes and system architecture

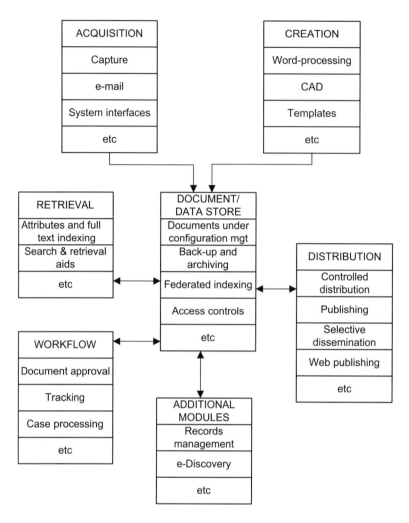

Figure 9.10 Content management functionality

- user interface – definitions of the desired user experience such as menus and ease of use
- technical design – defining the type of hardware and software with which the product must operate.

9.7.1 SYSTEM SOLUTIONS

System solutions addressing the foregoing specifications provide, or often form part of a wider product suite that delivers a greater range of functionality. These may variously be called content management (CM) or Enterprise Content Management (ECM) systems. These, along with Document Management (DM), Electronic Records Management (ERM) and Electronic Document and Records Management (EDRM) systems, present a somewhat confusing array of products. The acronyms often end with 'S' denoting 'System'. EDRM also stands for the Electronic Discovery Reference Model which is discussed in Section 6.8.7.

Intending users should consider to what extent the chosen product may have to satisfy any future needs over and above their immediate requirements as this will have a bearing on the type of solution procured at the outset.

The specifications noted above provide a checklist against which suppliers can test the conformance of their products, although not all the authorities currently operate a formal testing regime. The DoD does, for example, publish a list of products conforming to records management requirements, available at http://jitc.fhu.disa.mil/recmgt/register.html.

Profiles of possible suppliers are contained in published software vendor surveys, examples being ones on Electronic Records Management and Capture software (AIIM 2001c), Content Management (CM 2011), Enterprise Content Management (ECM 2011) and Document Management (DM 2011).

9.8 Implementation and Change Management

Detailed consideration of systems implementation and change management is beyond the scope of this book. Nevertheless, it is noteworthy that the experience of those adopting information management technology shows that some form of pilot offers the greatest chance of achieving a successful implementation. The initial knowledge gained from a pilot with well-defined functionality experienced by a chosen group of users provides the foundation for additional functionality or roll out to more users, or a combination of the two.

Thus the phasing may involve the successive provision of:

- storage and retrieval of documents accompanied by the necessary indexes including initial file plan – a 'vanilla' system' – then
- document review and approval, either newly created or under revision, possibly supported by simple, ad-hoc workflow or groupware procedures, followed by
- more complex workflow to support a variety of business processes.

This phasing addresses at the outset the basic requirements of most users who seek access to and ready communication of documents. It enables users to build up confidence in the system from simple beginnings and avoids the risks associated with one-time implementation of all functionality.

In addition, a model office may be constructed to replicate on a small scale the intended technical and business environment.

Whether a pilot or a model office, or both, are used the following need to specified and agreed at the outset:

- functionality to be piloted
- technical environment; workstations, network, storage, and so on
- users to be involved
- technical staff to be involved; in-house and supplier
- test data

- test scripts including expected results
- training
- timescales
- budget
- project management and plan for this stage.

Useful guidance on implementing an EDRMS is provided by the Joint Information Systems Committee (http://www.jiscinfonet.ac.uk/InfoKits/edrm) which supports the UK education and research communities.

All this work needs to proceed in the context of a strategy to manage the change arising within the organization from the introduction of new technology and ways of working.

Harding (2004) suggests there are four key factors for success when implementing change:

- pressure for change – demonstrated senior management commitment is essential
- a clear, shared vision – this is a shared agenda that benefits the whole organization
- capacity for change – the resources of time and finance must be available
- action and performance – adopt a 'plan, do, check, act' approach and keep communication channels open.

The progress of an organization in identifying and plotting its status and progress can be charted using a change management matrix (Harding 2004) as shown in Figure 9.11.

A further way to look at change is provided by the Change Factory (2011) which cited seven deadly sins of change management:

Underestimation

ERDM roll-outs always take longer, due to lack of training and management of expectations. Better to recognize that users will not like giving up some of their control over 'records'; therefore introduce stronger change management.

Ignorance

The degree of change is acknowledged but too much store is placed in a single approach to change. The change strategy is either all carrot, concentrating on getting engagement; or all stick, relying on compliance and directives from executive management to drive uptake. A range of tactics needs to be applied rather than extremes.

Centralization

Continuing with highly centralized records management leaves the user community remote from the benefits and ignorant of good practice. Better to devolve responsibility, but still retain central control.

CHANGE MANAGEMENT MATRIX

Plot in each column where the organization stands and then try to make progress by moving up the matrix in a straight horizontal line, targeting the weaker areas first.

Awareness ⟹ *Interest* ⟹ *Desire* ⟹ *Action*

Pressure for change	Clear shared vision	Capacity (resources)	Action (and performance)
3 Policy and action plan in place Regular reviews Active commitment from top management	3 High level of awareness and support at all levels Staff highly motivated	3 Resources (staff and funding) routinely committed Cost savings re-invested for further improvements	3 Action being taken and embedded throughout the organization Monitoring and reporting of progress
2 Policy agreed and communicated to all staff	2 Representatives from all levels of management chain involved in planning process and drawing up action plan(s) All staff given opportunity to make an input	2 Key staff working on plans and projects. Staffing and funding needs identified and resources becoming available	2 Wider engagement across the organization 'Low-cost' and more 'no-cost' measures implemented
1 Board level 'champion' appointed Drafting of policy	1 Key and supportive staff identified for assisting in drafting policy, taking action, and driving the process	1 'Champion' appointed at middle management level (to support the Board's 'Champion'). Training and development needs assessment	1 Commencement of action at some levels of the organization. Some 'no-cost' measures implemented
0 No explicit policy 'Business as usual', no forward planning Lack of consistent leadership & responsibility (buck passing)	0 De-motivated staff kept in the dark No communication. General mistrust	0 No investment. High stress levels in over-worked and under-valued staff No training & development	0 Zero action (or limited to crisis management)

Figure 9.11 Change management matrix

Source: Reproduced with permission of Phil Harding www.oursouthwest.com

Hopefulness

Technology is the main the vehicle of change with emphasis on technical training and the hope is that this is all that is needed. Insufficient attention is given to individuals and teams.

Overestimation

Overestimation may apply to a number of factors including users' computer literacy, management commitment and users commitment to training and good records management practice.

Disengagement

The hierarchy within the organization is not engaged from top to bottom. Engagement tactics must ensure each level of management through to the frontline is addressed appropriately and consistently.

Incongruence

Deciding the change strategy in isolation to the training strategy and training model is a recipe for an unsuitable motivational environment resulting in little or no change in behaviours.

9.9 Conclusion

According to Burnett et al. (2008), as of that year Enterprise Content Management (ECM) had a market penetration of over 80 per cent with more than 40 per cent of organizations planning to invest in new ECM systems or expand their solution in the next two years. This exemplified the continued and growing interest in better management and exploitation of enterprise content. Because of the importance of information as an organizational resource, it is vital to have:

- a clear and agreed information strategy in place with senior management ownership and leadership
- a plan for fulfilling the strategy, managing change and engaging stakeholders, including any external suppliers
- a robust survey and analysis of existing information management arrangements
- agreed future direction supported by prioritized functional and non-functional requirements
- an organization-wide information management policy framework and supporting procedures
- assigned coordinated responsibilities for information management covering structured and unstructured information.

Considerable benefits can accompany the introduction of information management technologies, but technology alone is not enough. The other levers of change – process, structure and people – introduced first in Chapter 1 (Figure 1.1) will be affected by the appearance of new technology and need to adapt accordingly. It is clearly preferable for such adaptation to take place in a culture where all those affected have been fully involved in the process of change and are therefore best placed to reap any benefits.

Bibliography

AACR2 2005. *Anglo-American Cataloguing Rules Second Edition, 2002 Revision: 2005 Update.* London: Chartered Institute of Library and Information Professionals.

ACM 1998. *The ACM Computing Classification System.* [Online: Association for Computing Machinery]. Available at: http://www.acm.org/about/class/1998 [accessed: 29 June 2011].

Aguilar, F.J. 1967. *Scanning the Business Environment.* New York: Macmillan.

AIDC 2011. *Automatic Identification and Data Capture Fact Sheets.* [Online: University of Glamorgan]. Available at: http://fat.glam.ac.uk/consultancy/AIDC/publications/ [accessed: 19 June 2011].

AIIM 2006. *Web Content Management.* [Online: Association for Image and Information Management]. Available at: http://www.aiim.org/Resources/Publications/ECM-Toolkits/1722 [accessed: 15 August 2011].

AIIM 2009a. *Records Management – Who is Taking Responsibility?* [Online: Association for Image and Information Management]. Available at: http://www.aiim.org/Research/AIIM-White-Papers/records-management-who-is-responsible [accessed: 15 August 2011].

AIIM 2009b. *Extending Capture Capabilities – Measuring the ROI.* [Online: Association for Image and Information Management]. Available at: http://www.aiim.org/pdfdocuments/36743.pdf [accessed: 17 July 2011].

AIIM 2011a. *Social Business Roadmap 2011.* [Online: Association for Image and Information Management]. Available at: http://www.aiim.org/~/media/Files/AIIM%20White%20Papers/Social-Business-Roadmap/Social-Business-Roadmap-Paper.ashx [accessed: 19 July 2011].

AIIM 2011b. *Capitalizing on Content: A Compelling ROI for Change.* [Online: Association for Image and Information Management]. Available at: http://www.aiim.org/Research/AIIM-White-Papers/Capitalizing-on-Content [accessed: 14 July 2011].

AIIM 2011c. *New Electronic Records Management (ERM) Software Product Study.* [Online: Association for Image and Information Management]. Available at: http://www.aiim.org/Research/Product-Studies [accessed: 7 December 2011].

AIM 2011. *Association for Automatic Identification and Mobility.* [Online]. Available at: http://www.aimglobal.org/technologies/ [accessed: 19 June 2011].

Ambler, S.W. 2004. *The Object Primer.* New York: Cambridge University Press.

Ang, J. and Pavri, F.A. 1994. Survey and Critique of the Impacts of Information Technology. *International Journal of Information Management,* 14(2), 122–133.

Antoniou, G. and van Harmelen, F. 2009. Web Ontology Languages: OWL, in *Handbook on Ontologies,* edited by Staab, S. et al. London: Springer. 91–110.

ASQ 2004. *Plan–Do–Check–Act Cycle.* [Online]. Available at: http://asq.org/learn-about-quality/project-planning-tools/overview/pdca-cycle.html [accessed 1 August 2011].

Baym, N.K. 2010. *Personal Connections in the Digital Age.* Cambridge: Polity Press.

Berners-Lee, T and Calliau, R 1990. *WorldWideWeb: Proposal for a HyperText Project.* [Online]. Available at: http://www.w3.org/Proposal.html [accessed: 17 June 2011].

Bessant, C. (Ed.) 2009. *Information Sharing Handbook.* London: The Law Society.

BIP 0008 2008. *BIP 0008–1:2008 Evidential Weight and Legal Admissibility of Information Stored Electronically. Code of Practice for the Implementation of BS 10008; BIP 0008–2:2008 Evidential*

Weight and Legal Admissibility of Information Transferred Electronically. Code of Practice for the Implementation of BS 10008; BIP 0008–3:2008 Evidential Weight and Legal Admissibility of Linking Electronic Identity to Documents. Code of Practice for the Implementation of BS 10008. London: British Standards Institute.

BIP 0009 2008. *BIP 0009:2008 Evidential Weight and Legal Admissibility of Electronic Information. Compliance Workbook for Use with BS 10008.* London: British Standards Institute.

Birkinshaw, P. 2010. Freedom of information and its impact in the United Kingdom. *Government Information Quarterly,* 27, 312–321.

Bott, E. 2010. *Paper or Pixels? Which Book Format Do You Prefer?* [Online]. Available at: http://www.edbott.com/weblog/2010/10/paper-or-pixels-which-book-format-do-you-prefer/ [accessed: 9 July 2010].

Bourne, L. 2008. *Stakeholder Relationship Management.* London: Gower.

Bourne, M. et al. 2008. *The Impact of Investors in People on People Management Practices and Firm Performance.* [Online: Cranfield University School of Management]. Available at: http://www.som.cranfield.ac.uk/som/dinamic-content/research/cbp/IIP_Impact_StudyReport.pdf [accessed: 25 November 2010].

Bradford, P. 2011. Reported in: *How Is Japan's Nuclear Disaster Different?* [Online: National Geographic]. Available at: [http://news.nationalgeographic.com/news/energy/2011/03/1103165-japan-nuclear-chernobyl-three-mile-island/ [accessed: 9 July 2010].

Bradley, G. 2010. *Benefit Realisation Management.* London: Gower.

BS 6079 1996. *BS 6079 1996 Guide to Project Management.* London: British Standards Institute.

BS 6079 2010. *BS 6079–1 2010. Project Management. Principles and Guidelines for the Management of Projects.* London: British Standards Institute.

BS 6529 1984. *BS 6529:1984 Recommendations for Examining Documents, Determining their Subjects and Selecting Indexing Terms.* London: British Standards Institute.

BS 10008 2008. *BS 10008:2008 Evidential Weight and Legal Admissibility of Electronic Information.* London: British Standards Institute.

Burnett, S., Clarke, S., Eager, A., Ganesh, B. and Kellett, A. 2008. *Document and Records Management.* Hull: Butler Direct Ltd.

Burns, C. 1985. Three Mile Island: the Information Meltdown. *Information Management Review,* 1(1), 19–25.

Chainey, S. 2010. *Information Sharing for Community Safety. Guidance and Practice Advice.* [Online: Home Office]. Available at: http://www.homeoffice.gov.uk/publications/crime/info-sharing-community-safety/guidance?view=Binary [accessed: 1 July 2010].

Change Factory 2011. *The seven deadly sins of EDRMS Change Management.* [Online]. Available at: http://www.changefactory.com.au/articles/edrms/the-seven-deadly-sins-of-edrms-change-management/ and http://www.linkedtraining.com.au/view_article.aspx?article=The%20seven%20deadly%20sins%20of%20EDRMS%20Change%20Management [accessed: 3 February 2012].

Charlesworth, I., David, M. and Holden, J. 2003. *Workgroup and Enterprise Collaboration.* Hull: Butler Direct Ltd.

Checkland, P. 1981. *Systems Thinking, Systems Practice.* London: John Wiley.

Checkland, P and Scholes, J. 1990. *Soft Systems Methodology in Action.* London: John Wiley.

Chowdhury, G.G. 2010. *Introduction to Modern Information Retrieval.* London: Facet Publishing.

CIPD 2010a. *SWOT Analysis.* [Online: Chartered Institute of Personnel and Development]. Available at: http://www.cipd.co.uk/subjects/corpstrtgy/general/swot-analysis.htm [accessed: 13 November 2010].

CIPD 2010b. *PESTLE Analysis*. [Online: Chartered Institute of Personnel and Development]. Available at: http://www.cipd.co.uk/subjects/corpstrtgy/general/pestle-analysis.htm?IsSrchRes=1 [accessed: 13 November 2010].

CM 2011. *Top 10 Content Management Software Vendors Revealed*. [Online]. Available at: http://www.business-software.com/crm-reports/content-management.php [accessed: 18 July 2011].

Codling, S. 1992. Benchmarking, in *The Gower Handbook of Management*, edited by D. Lock. Aldershot: Gower, 182–198.

Craig, C. and Graham, R. 2003. Rights Management in the Digital World. *Computer Law & Security Report*, 19(5), 356–362

Crowther, D. and Green, M. 2004. *Organizational Theory*. London: Chartered Institute of Personnel and Development (CIPD).

DAMA 2008. *DAMA-DMBOK Functional Framework v3.02* [Online: Data Management Association]. Available at: http://www.dama.org/files/public/DAMA-DMBOK_Functional_Framework_v3_02_20080910.pdf [accessed: 2 June 2011].

Davenport, T. 1995. *The Fad That Forgot People*. [Online: Fast Company]. Available at: http://www.fastcompany.com/magazine/01/reengin.html [accessed: 24 November 2010].

Delgado, A. 1979. *The Enormous File: A Social History of the Office*. London: John Murray.

Deming, W.E. 1986. *Out of the Crisis*. Cambridge: MIT Press.

Deng, Li, Wang, K. and Guido, R.C. 2010. *A Semantic and Detection-Based Approach to Speech and Language Processing*. In *Semantic Computing*, edited by Phillip C.-Y Sheu. Hoboken: John Wiley, 49–68.

Desouza, K.C. and Paquette, S. 2011. *Knowledge Management – An Introduction*. London: Facet Publishing.

Dewey, 2011. *Dewey Decimal Classification, DDC 23* [Online: Online Computer Library Center]. Available at: http://www.oclc.org/uk/en/info/ddc23/uk-en.htm [accessed: 29 June 2011].

DM 2011. *Top 10 Document Management Vendors Revealed*. [Online]. Available at: http://www.business-software.com/content-management/document-management/document-management-software.php [accessed: 18 July 2011].

DoD 2007. DoD 5015.02-STD *Electronic Records Management Software Applications Design Criteria Standard*. [Online: Department of Defense]. Available at: http://jitc.fhu.disa.mil/recmgt/p50152stdapr07.pdf [accessed: 17 July 2011].

DTP 2011. 2011 *Desktop Publishing Software Review Product Comparisons*. [Online: TopTenReviews]. Available at: http://desktop-publishing-software-review.toptenreviews.com/ [accessed: 13 May 2011].

Dublin Core 2010. *Dublin Core Metadata Element Set, Version 1.1*. [Online: Dublin Core Metadata Initiative]. Available at: http://dublincore.org/documents/dces/ [accessed: 29 June 2011].

e-GMS 2004. *e-GMS-e-Government Metadata Standard Version 3.0*. [Online]. Available at: http://www.esd.org.uk/standards/egms/ [accessed: 29 June 2011].

EAD 2002. *Encoded Archival Description*. [Online: Library of Congress]. Available at: http://www.loc.gov/ead/ [accessed 29 June 2011].

EBM 2011. *The Espresso Book Machine*. [Online: Blackwell's]. Available at: http://bookshop.blackwell.co.uk/jsp/editorial/browse/espresso.jsp [accessed: 20 July 2011].

ECM 2011. *Top 10 Enterprise Content Management Vendors Revealed*. [Online]. Available at: http://www.business-software.com/crm-reports/enterprise-content-management.php [accessed: 18 July 2011].

EDIDEV 2011. *EDI vs XML*. [Online]. Available at: http://www.edidev.com/XMLvsEDI.html [accessed: 6 July 2011].

EMC 2011. *EMC Captiva ISIS vs TWAIN.* [Online: EMC]. Available at: http://www.emc.com/collateral/software/data-sheet/h3556-isis-vs-twain-ds.pdf [accessed: 13 May 2011].

EPUB3 2011. *EPUB 3 Overview Proposed Specification 23 May 2011.* [Online: International Digital Publishing Forum]. Available at: http://idpf.org/epub/30/spec/epub30-overview-20110523.html [accessed: 2 July 2011].

Fresko, M. 2011. Searching for Solutions. *Information and Records Management Bulletin,* 160, 18–23.

Friedland, G. and Van Leeuwen, D. 2010 *Speaker Recognition and Diarization.* In *Semantic Computing,* edited by Phillip C.-Y Sheu. Hoboken: John Wiley, 115–129.

GBN 2010. *Global Survey on Business Improvement and Benchmarking.* [Online: Global Benchmarking Network]. Available at: http://www.globalbenchmarking.org/images/stories/PDF/2010_gbn_survey_business_improvement_and_benchmarking_web.pdf [accessed: 11 November 2010].

Graham, I., Lloyd, A.D., Slack, R.S. and Williams R.A.: *Uptake of BPR in the UK.* [Online: University of Edinburgh July 2000]. Available at: http://omni.bus.ed.ac.uk/adl/workp6.pdf [accessed: 24 November 2010].

Graves, M and Batchelor, B. 2003. *Machine Vision for the Inspection of Natural Products.* London: Springer-Verlag.

GSA 1998. *Performance-based Management.* [Online: General Services Administration]. Available at: https://www.acquisition.gov/sevensteps/library/GSAeightsteps.pdf [accessed: 12 July 2011].

Hamer, C. 2011. *The ICSA Guide to Document Retention.* London: ICSA Publications.

Hammer, M. 1990. Reengineering Work: Don't Automate, Obliterate. *Harvard Business Review,* July–August 107.

Hammer, M. and Champy, J. 2003. *Reengineering the Corporation: A Manifesto for Business Revolution.* New York: HarperCollins.

Handy, C. 1993. *Understanding Organizations.* 4th edition. London: Penguin.

Harding, P. 2004. *Managing Change.* [Online]. Available at: http://www.oursouthwest.com/SusBus/mggchange.html [accessed: 8 August 2011].

Hatten, J.H. and Rosenthal, S.R. 1999. Managing the Process-centred Enterprise. *Long Range Planning,* 32 (3), 293–310.

Haughey, D. 2009. *Waterfall v Agile: How Should I Approach My Software Development Project?* [Online]. Available at: http://www.projectsmart.com/articles/waterfall-v-agile-how-should-i-approach-my-software-development-project.html [accessed: 27 May 2011].

Healy, S. 2007. *Code of practice for archivists and records managers under Section 51(4) of the Data Protection Act 1998.* [Online: The National Archives]. Available at: http://www.nationalarchives.gov.uk/documents/information-management/dp-code-of-practice.pdf [accessed: 2 April 2012].

Higgins, N.J. and Cohen, G. 2010. *Investors in People: An Emperor with no Clothes?* [Online: International School of Human Capital Management]. Available at: http://www.ishcm.com/pdf/IIP_EmperorWithNoClothes_040406.pdf [accessed: 25 November 2010].

Hrebiniak, L.G. 2006. Obstacles to Effective Strategy Implementation. *Organizational Dynamics,* 35(1), 12–31.

ICO 2007. *Freedom of Information Good Practice Guidance.* [Online: Information Commissioner's Office]. Available at: http://www.ico.gov.uk/upload/documents/library/freedom_of_information/practical_application/using_the_cop_v2_10_07_07.pdf [accessed: 24 May 2011].

ICO 2011. *Guide to Data Protection.* [Online: Information Commissioner's Office]. Available at: http://www.ico.gov.uk/for_organisations/data_protection/the_guide.aspx [accessed: 24 May 2011].

IDC 2008. *The Diverse and Exploding Digital Universe.* Framingham, MA: IDC.

IIS 2008. *Institute of Information Scientists IIS – Celebrating 50 years.* [Online]. Available at: http://www.slis.indiana.edu/news/story.php?story_id=1784 [accessed: 25 April 2011].

IMechE 2010. *Model Forms of General Conditions of Contract*. London: Institution of Mechanical Engineers.

IRMS 2005. *Retention Guidelines for Local Government* – currently under review. [Online: Information and Records Management Society]. Available at: http://www.irms.org.uk/resources/91 [accessed: 22 May 2001].

ISAD(G) 1999. *ISAD(G): General International Standard Archival Description*. [Online: International Council on Archives]. Available at: http://www.icacds.org.uk/eng/ISAD(G).pdf [accessed: 29 June 2011].

i-Sight 2011. *How to Secure Customer Loyalty*. [Online]. Available at: http://www.customerexpressions.com/cex/cexweb.nsf/(GetPages)/ffd7cd76aa05d6c985257012004b6404 [accessed: 4 April 2011].

ISO 1004 1995. *ISO 1004:1995 Information processing – Magnetic ink character recognition – Print specification*. Geneva: International Organization for Standards.

ISO 2788 1986. *ISO 2788:1986 Documentation – Guidelines for the establishment and development of monolingual thesauri*. Geneva: International Organization for Standards.

ISO 3200 2008. *ISO 3200–1:2008. Document management – Portable document format –Part 1: PDF 1.7*. International Organization for Standards. [Online]. Available at: http://www.adobe.com/content/dam/Adobe/en/devnet/acrobat/pdfs/PDF32000_2008.pdf [accessed: 13 May 2011].

ISO 7813 2006. *ISO/IEC 7813:2006 Information technology – Identification cards – Financial transaction cards*. Geneva: International Organization for Standards.

ISO 7816 2011. *ISO/IEC 7816–1:2011 Identification cards – Integrated circuit cards – Part 1: Cards with contacts – Physical characteristics* Geneva: International Organization for Standards.

ISO 8601 2000. *ISO 8601:2000 Data elements and interchange formats – Information interchange – Representation of dates and times*. Geneva: International Organization for Standards.

ISO 8632 1999. *ISO/IEC 8632–1:1999 Information technology – Computer graphics – Metafile for the storage and transfer of picture description information – Part 1: Functional specification*. Geneva: International Organization for Standards.

ISO 9001 2008. *ISO 9001:2008 Quality management systems – Requirement*. Geneva: International Organization for Standards.

ISO 9001 2010. *ISO9001 for Small Businesses – What to do: Advice from ISO/TC 176*. Geneva: International Organization for Standards.

ISO 9660 1988. *ISO 9660:1988 Information processing – Volume and file structure of CD-ROM for information interchange*. Geneva: International Organization for Standards.

ISO 10149 1995. *ISO/IEC 10149:1995 Information technology – Data interchange on read-only 120 mm optical data disks (CD-ROM)*. Geneva: International Organization for Standards.

ISO 10180 1995. *ISO/IEC 10180:1995 Information technology – Processing languages – Standard Page Description Language (SPDL.)* Geneva: International Organization for Standards.

ISO 10303 1994. *ISO 10303–1:1994 Industrial automation systems and integration – Product data representation and exchange – Part 1: Overview and fundamental principles*. Geneva: International Organization for Standards.

ISO 10918 1994. *ISO/IEC 10918–1:1994 Information technology – Digital compression and coding of continuous-tone still images: Requirements and guidelines*. Geneva: International Organization for Standards.

ISO 10995 2011. ISO/IEC 10995:2011 *Information technology – Digitally recorded media for information interchange and storage – Test method for the estimation of the archival lifetime of optical media*. Geneva: International Organization for Standards.

ISO 11179 2004. *ISO/IEC 11179–1:2004 Information technology – Metadata registries (MDR)* Geneva: International Organization for Standards.

ISO 11693 2005. *ISO/IEC 11693:2005 Identification cards – Optical memory cards – General characteristics.* Geneva: International Organization for Standards.

ISO 11694 2005. *ISO/IEC 11694–2:2005 Identification cards – Optical memory cards – Linear recording method – Part 2: Dimensions and location of the accessible optical area.* Geneva: International Organization for Standards.

ISO 12639 2004. *ISO 12639:2004 Graphic technology – Prepress digital data exchange – Tag image file format for image technology (TIFF/IT).* Geneva: International Organization for Standards.

ISO 14001 2004. *ISO 14001:2004 Environmental management systems – Requirements with guidance for use* Geneva: International Organization for Standards.

ISO 15438 2006. *ISO/IEC 15438:2006 Information technology – Automatic identification and data capture techniques – PDF417 bar code symbology specification.* Geneva: International Organization for Standards.

ISO 15489–1 2001. *ISO 15490–1:2001. Information and documentation – Records management – Part 1: General.* Geneva: International Organization for Standards.

ISO 15489–2 2001. *ISO/TE 15489–2:2001, Information and documentation – Records management – Part 2: Guidelines.* Geneva: International Organization for Standards.

ISO 15948 2004. *ISO/IEC 15948:2004 Information technology – Computer graphics and image processing – Portable Network Graphics (PNG): Functional specification.* Geneva: International Organization for Standards.

ISO 17341 2006. *ISO/IEC 17341:2006 Information technology – Data Interchange on 120 mm and 80 mm Optical Disk using +RW Format – Capacity: 4,7 Gbytes and 1,46 Gbytes per Side (Recording speed up to 4X).* Geneva: International Organization for Standards.

ISO 17342 2004. *ISO/IEC 17342:2004 Information technology – 80 mm (1,46 Gbytes per side) and 120 mm (4,70 Gbytes per side) DVD re-recordable disk (DVD-RW)* Geneva: International Organization for Standards.

ISO 17344 2006. *ISO/IEC 17344:2006 Information technology – Data Interchange on 120 mm and 80 mm Optical Disk using +R Format – Capacity: 4,7 and 1,46 Gbytes per Side (Recording speed up to 16X)* Geneva: International Organization for Standards.

ISO 17592 2004. *ISO/IEC 17592:2004 Information technology – 120 mm (4,7 Gbytes per side) and 80 mm (1,46 Gbytes per side) DVD rewritable disk (DVD-RAM).* Geneva: International Organization for Standards.

ISO 17594 2004. *ISO/IEC 17594:2004 Information technology – Cases for 120 mm and 80 mm DVD-RAM disks.* Geneva: International Organization for Standards.

ISO 18921 2008. *ISO 18921:2008 Imaging materials – Compact discs (CD-ROM) – Method for estimating the life expectancy based on the effects of temperature and relative humidity.* Geneva: International Organization for Standards.

ISO 18925 2008. *ISO 18925:2008 Imaging materials – Optical disc media – Storage practices.* Geneva: International Organization for Standards.

ISO 18926 2006. *ISO 18926:2006 Imaging materials – Information stored on magneto-optical (MO) discs – Method for estimating the life expectancy based on the effects of temperature and relative humidity.* Geneva: International Organization for Standards.

ISO 18927 2008. *ISO 18927:2008 Imaging materials – Recordable compact disc systems – Method for estimating the life expectancy based on the effects of temperature and relative humidity.* Geneva: International Organization for Standards.

ISO 18933 2006. *ISO 18933:2006 Imaging materials – Magnetic tape – Care and handling practices for extended usage.* Geneva: International Organization for Standards.

ISO 18934 2006. *ISO 18934:2006 Imaging materials – Multiple media archives – Storage environment.* Geneva: International Organization for Standards.

ISO 19005 2005. *ISO 19005–1 2005, Document management – Electronic document file format for long-term preservation – Part 1: Use of PDF 1.4 (PDF/A–1).* Geneva: International Organization for Standards.

ISO 19503 2005. *ISO/IEC 19503:2005 Information technology – XML Metadata Interchange (XMI).* Geneva: International Organization for Standards.

ISO 20563 2001. *ISO/IEC 20563:2001 Information technology – 80 mm (1,23 Gbytes per side) and 120 mm (3,95 Gbytes per side) DVD-recordable disk (DVD-R)* Geneva: International Organization for Standards.

ISO 23912 2005. *ISO/IEC 23912:2005 Information technology – 80 mm (1,46 Gbytes per side) and 120 mm (4,70 Gbytes per side) DVD Recordable Disk (DVD-R).* Geneva: International Organization for Standards.

ISO 24724 2011. *ISO/IEC 24724:2011 Information technology – Automatic identification and data capture techniques – GS1 DataBar bar code symbology specification.* Geneva: International Organization for Standards.

ISO 25434 2007. *ISO/IEC 25434:2007 Information technology – Data interchange on 120 mm and 80 mm optical disk using +R DL format – Capacity: 8,55 Gbytes and 2,66 Gbytes per side (recording speed up to 8x).* Geneva: International Organization for Standards.

ISO 25964. *ISO 25964–1 Information and documentation – Thesauri and interoperability with other vocabularies – Part 1: Thesauri for information retrieval – status (*under development). Geneva: International Organization for Standards.

ISO 26300 2006. *ISO/IEC 26300:2006, Open Document Format for Office Applications (OpenDocument) v1.0.* Geneva: International Organization for Standards.

ISO 27002 2005. *ISO/IEC 27002 2005 Information technology – Security techniques – Code of practice for information security management.* Geneva: International Organization for Standards.

ISO 32000 2008. *IS0 32000–1:2008 Document management Portable document format – Part 1: PDF 1.7.* Geneva: Geneva: International Organization for Standards.

ISO Mgt Sys 2004. Taking the first steps towards a quality management system. *ISO Management Systems,* 4(4), 19–25.

JISC 2011. *Controlling your Language: A Directory of Metadata Vocabularies.* [Online]. Available at: http://www.jiscdigitalmedia.ac.uk/crossmedia/advice/controlling-your-language-links-to-metadata-vocabularies/ [accessed: 20 May 2011].

Johnson, L. K. 2004. Execute your strategy – without killing it. *Harvard Management Update,* December 3–5.

Kaplan, R.S. and Norton, D.P. 1996. *The Balanced Scorecard.* Boston: Harvard Business School Press.

Kaplan, R.S. and Norton, D.P. 2004. *Strategy Maps.* Boston: Harvard Business School Press.

Kaplan, R.S. and Norton, D.P. 2005. The office of strategy management. *Harvard Business Review,* 83(10), 72–80.

Lake, C. 2009. What *is Social Media? Here are 34 Definitions.*[Online: eConsulltancy]. Available at: http://econsultancy.com/uk/blog/3527-what-is-social-media-here-are-34-definitions [accessed: 2 May 2011].

Leavitt, H.H., Dill, W.R. and Eyring H.B. 1973 *The Organizational World – A Systematic View of Managers and Management.* New York: Harcout Brace Jovanovich.

LGCS 2007. *Local Government Classification Scheme v2.03* [Online: Information and Records Management Society]. Available at: http://www.irms.org.uk/resources/92 [accessed: 21 May 2011].

MacLeod, A. and Baxter, L. 2001. The Contribution of Business Excellence Models in Restoring Failed Improvement Initiatives. *European Management Journal,* 19(4), 392–403.

Macmillan, H. and Tampoe, M. 2000. *Strategic Management – Process, Content and Implementation.* London: Oxford University Press.

MARC 1999. *MARC 21 Format for Bibliographic Data.* [Online: Library of Congress]. Available at: http://www.loc.gov/marc/bibliographic/ecbdhome.html [accessed: 29 June 2011].

McIver, V. 2011. Connecting to the Network. *IOD News* May 2011.

McLuhan, M. 1964. *Understanding Media Part 1, Chapter 1.*

McManus, J. and Wood-Harper T. 2008. *A Study in Project Failure.* [Online: BCS]. Available at: http://www.bcs.org/content/ConWebDoc/19584 [accessed 20 September 2011].

Mell, P and Grance, T. 2011 *The NIST Definition of Cloud Computing (Draft).* Gaithersburg: National Institute of Standards and Technology.

Mercer, H. 2004. *Appraisal Policy – Version 1.* Kew: The National Archives.

MOJ 2009. *Lord Chancellor's Code of Practice on the management of records issued under section 46 of the Freedom of Information Act 2000* [Online: Ministry of Justice]. Available at: http://www.justice.gov.uk/guidance/docs/foi-section-46-code-of-practice.pdf [accessed: 24 May 2011].

Monks 2010. *John Monks' Speech to Investors in People Conference.* [Online: Unionlearn organization]. Available at: http://www.unionlearn.org.uk/initiatives/learn-179-f0.cfm [accessed: 25 November 2010].

Moon, B.M., Hoffman, R.R., Novak, J.D. and Cañas, A.J. 2011. *Applied Concept Mapping.* Boca Raton: CRC Press.

MoReq10 2010. *MoReq2010: Modular Requirements for Records Systems – Volume 1: Core Services & Plug-in Modules.* [Online: Document Lifecycle Forum]. Available at: http://moreq2010.eu/pdf/MoReq2010-Core+Plugin(v1-0).pdf [accessed: 4 July 2010].

Niven, P.R. 2003. *Balanced Scorecard Step-by-Step for Government and Nonprofit Agencies.* Hoboken: John Wiley.

NLM 2011. *National Library of Medicine Classification..* [Online: National Library of Medicine]. Available at: http://www.nlm.nih.gov/class/ [accessed: 29 June 2011].

Nonaka, I. 1991. The Knowledge-Creating Company. *Harvard Business Review,* November–December 96–104.

Nørreklit, H. 2000. The balance on the balanced scorecard – A critical analysis of some of its assumptions. *Management Accounting Research,* 11, 65–88.

NSW 2011a 2011. *Keyword AAA.* New South Wales Government State Records. [Online]. Available at: http://www.records.nsw.gov.au/recordkeeping/keyword-products/keyword-aaa [accessed: 20 May 2011].

NSW 2011b 2011. *Keyword for Councils.* New South Wales Government State Records. [Online]. Available at: http://www.records.nsw.gov.au/recordkeeping/keyword-products/keyword-for-councils [accessed: 20 May 2011].

Oakland, J.S. 1992. Quality Assurance, control and Improvement, in *The Gower Handbook of Management,* edited by D. Lock. Aldershot: Gower, 681–702.

Oakland, J.S. 2003. *TQM: Text with Cases.* London: Butterworth Heinemann.

OECD 2002. *OECD Guidelines for the Security of Information Systems and Networks.* [Online: Organization for Economic Co-operation and Development]. Available at: http://www.oecd.org/dataoecd/16/22/15582260.pdf [accessed: 19 July 2011].

OED 2001. *Shorter Oxford English Dictionary.* Oxford: Oxford University Press.

OJEC 2011a. *European and UK Procurement Regulations.* [Online: Official Journal of the European Union]. Available at http://www.ojec.com/Directives.aspx [accessed: 3 February 2012].

OpenOffice.org 2011. *Open Office.* [Online: OpenOffice.org]. Available at: http://www.openoffice. org/ [accessed: 12 May 2011].

Open Source 2011. *Open Source Initiative.* [Online: OSI]. Available at: http://www.opensource.org/ [accessed: 12 May 2011].

OU 1980. *M352 Block II A. Conceptual Modelling B. Logical Modelling.* Milton Keynes: Open University.

Pande, P. and Holpe, L. 2002. *What is Six Sigma?.* London: McGraw Hill.

Paul, R. 2011. *Oracle gives up on OpenOffice after Community Forks the Project.* [Online: Ars Technica]. Available at: http://arstechnica.com/open-source/news/2011/04/oracle-gives-up-on-ooo-after-community-forks-the-project.ars [accessed: 12 May 2011].

Polanyi, M. 1966. *The Tacit Dimension.* Chicago: University of Chicago Press.

ProjectConnections 2008. Plan and Schedule Development – Create a Work Breakdown Structure (WBS Completion Checklist). Available at: http://www.projectconnections.com/templates/detail/plan-development-work-breakdown.html. [accessed: 20 September 2011].

QLD 2007. *Realising the benefits of implementing an eDRMS.* [Online: Queensland State Archives]. Available at: http://www.archives.qld.gov.au/Recordkeeping/GRKDownloads/Documents/eDRMSbenefits.pdf [accessed: 29 March 2012].

Ranganathan, S.R. 2006. *Colon Classification.* Ess Ess Publications.

Saffady, W. 2009. *Managing Electronic Records.* London: Facet Publishing.

Salton. G. 1989. *Automatic Text Processing: the Transformation, Analysis and Retrieval of Information by Computers.* Reading, MA: Addison Wesley.

SAU 2009 *EDRMS Specification.* [Online: Government of South Australia]. Available at: http://www. archives.sa.gov.au/files/management_EDRMS_functionalcompliance.pdf [accessed: 17 July 2011].

Shepherd, E. and Yeo, G. 2003. *Managing Records – A Handbook of Principles and Practice.* London: Facet Publishing.

Sprehe, J.T. 2005. The positive benefits of electronic records management in the context of enterprise content management. *Government Information Quarterly*, 22, 297–303.

Smedinghoff, T.J. 2008. *Information Security – The Emerging Standard for Corporate Compliance.* Ely: IT Governance Publishing.

Stark, H. and Lachal, L. 1995. *Ovum Evaluates Workflow.* London: Ovum Ltd.

Tague, N.R. 2005. *The Quality Toolbox.* Milwaukee: American Society for Quality.

Tate, M.A. 2010. *Web Wisdom.* Boca Raton: CRC Press.

TNA 2007a. *Requirements for Electronic Records Management Systems. 3 Reference Document.* [Online: The National Archives]. Available at: http://collections.europarchive.org/tna/20080108102455/http://www.nationalarchives.gov.uk/documents/referencefinal.pdf [accessed 17 July 2011].

TNA 2007b. *Requirements for Electronic Records Management Systems 1. Functional Requirements.* [Online: The National Archives]. Available at: http://collections.europarchive.org/tna/20080108102455/http://www.nationalarchives.gov.uk/documents/requirementsfinal.pdf [accessed 17 July 2011].

TNA 2008. *Guidance – Freedom of Information Publication Schemes.* [Online: The National Archives]. Available at: http://www.nationalarchives.gov.uk/documents/information-management/freedom-of-information-publication-schemes.pdf [accessed: 3 April 2012].

TNA 2010a. *Guide 3 Records Management Policy.* [Online: The National Archives]. Available at: http://www.nationalarchives.gov.uk/documents/information-management/rm-code-guide3.pdf [accessed: 13 July 2011].

TNA 2010b. *Migrating Information between EDRMS.* [Online: The National Archives]. Available at: http://www.nationalarchives.gov.uk/documents/information-management/edrms.pdf [accessed: 1 August 2011].

Todd, M. 2003. *Business Classification Design*. Kew: The National Archives.

TWAIN 2009. *TWAIN Organization*. [Online: TWAIN Working Group]. Available at: http://www.twain.org/ [accessed: 3 April 2012].

UDC 2005. *Universal Decimal Classification. Standard edition*. London: BSI.

UIMA 2009: *Unstructured Information Management Architecture (UIMA) Version 1.0*. [Online: Organization for the Advancement of Structured Information Standards]. Available at: http://docs.oasis-open.org/uima/v1.0/uima-v1.0.html [accessed: 20 July 2011].

Uschold, M. and Gruninger, M. 2004. Ontologies and Semantics for Seamless connectivity. *SIGMOD Record* 33(4), 58–64.

W3C 2004. *RDF Primer W3C Recommendation*. [Online]. Available at: http://www.w3.org/TR/2004/REC-rdf-primer-20040210/ [accessed: 1 July 2011].

W3C 2008. *Extensible Markup Language*. [Online]. Available at: http://www.w3.org/XML/ [accessed: 3 April 2012].

W3C 2009. *OWL 2 Web Ontology Language Document Overview W3C Recommendation 27 October 2009* [Online]. Available at: http://www.w3.org/TR/owl2-overview/ [accessed: 1 July 2011].

W3C 2010. Compound Document by Reference Framework 1.0. [Online]. Available at: http://www.w3.org/TR/2010/NOTE-CDR-20100819/#definitions [accessed: 26 April 2010].

W3C 2011. CGM Open specification – WebCGM 2.0 – WebCGM Profile. [Online]. Available at: http://www.w3.org/Submission/WebCGM20/WebCGM20-Profile.html [accessed: 21 June 2011].

WFMC 2009. *Terminology & Glossary* Issue 3.0. Winchester: Workflow Management Coalition. [Online]. Available at: http://www.wfmc.org/Download-document/WFMC-TC-1011-Ver-3-Terminology-and-Glossary-English.html [accessed: 03 April 2012].

Wikipedia 2007. *Computer Storage Types*. [Online: Wikipedia]. Available at: http://en.wikipedia.org/wiki/File:Computer_storage_types.svg [accessed: 17 August 2011].

Wikipedia 2011a. *List of Social Networking Websites*. [Online: Wikipedia]. Available at: http://en.wikipedia.org/wiki/List_of_social_networking_websites [accessed: 25 May 2011].

Wikipedia 2011b. *Comparison of e-book Formats*. [Online: Wikipedia]. Available at: http://en.wikipedia.org/wiki/Comparison_of_e-book_formats [accessed: 26 May 2011].

Wikipedia 2011c. *XML Schema Comparison*. [Online: Wikipedia]. Available at: http://en.wikipedia.org/wiki/XML_Schema_Language_Comparison [accessed: 8 August 2011].

Wikipedia 2011d. *Information Quality*. [Online: Wikipedia]. Available at: http://en.wikipedia.org/wiki/Information_quality [accessed: 8 August 2011].

Wilson, T.D. 2002. The Nonsense of 'Knowledge Management'. *Information Research*. [Online], 8(1). Available at: http://informationr.net/ir/8-1/paper144.html#non95 [accessed: 10 December 2010].

About the Author

Bob graduated with an honours metallurgy degree but soon realized that working with blast furnaces was not his forte. So he chose the more stimulating atmosphere of information work, qualifying as an information scientist from City University. After working in the Research Department of The Metal Box Company supplying evaluative literature and patent surveys for research staff, he moved from packaging to gas as head of the Information Group at the British Gas Engineering Research Station developing information, computing and administrative services for scientists and engineers dealing with the conversion of the United Kingdom to natural gas. Still feeling energized, he was recruited by oil and moved to BP where he headed the group's corporate information services as Information Resources Manager, was responsible for the central data and records management consultancy teams and introduced one of the first major corporate text retrieval systems. He later moved to Scicon, then the IT consultancy arm of BP, where he conducted a range of consultancy assignments, many centred around a records management programme he developed. In 1990 he established Cura Consortium with like-minded independents since when he has undertaken over 60 assignments in the UK and abroad. He has run courses on records and document management, published and presented many papers and authored 'Document Imaging' published by Meckler in 1994 prior to writing the first two editions of this current volume. He is a member of the Information and Records Management Society, Professional Member of AIIM and past Fellow of the Institute of Management Consultants, the Institute of Information Scientists and the Chartered Institute of Library and Information Professionals. He is also Assistant Editor of the 'International Journal of Information Management' published by Elsevier.

Index

If you have found this book useful you may be interested in other titles from Gower

**Accelerating Business and IT Change:
Transforming Project Delivery**
Alan Fowler and Dennis Lock
Hardback: 978-0-566-08604-5
CD-ROM: 978-0-566-08742-4

**Advising Upwards:
A Framework for Understanding and Engaging
Senior Management Stakeholders**
Edited by
Lynda Bourne
Hardback: 978-0-566-09249-7
e-book: 978-1-4094-3430-6

**Buying Information Systems:
Selecting, Implementing and Assessing
Off-The-Shelf Systems**
David James
Hardback: 978-0-566-08559-8
e-book: 978-0-7546-8285-1

GOWER

Leading Complex Projects
Kaye Remington
Hardback: 978-1-4094-1905-1
e-book: 978-1-4094-1906-8

Leading Successful PMOs:
How to Build the Best Project Management
Office for Your Business
Peter Taylor
Hardback: 978-1-4094-1837-5
e-book: 978-1-4094-1838-2

Making Knowledge Visible
Elizabeth Orna
Hardback: 978-0-566-08562-8

Strategic Review:
The Process of Strategy Formulation
in Complex Organisations
Robert F. Grattan
Hardback: 978-1-4094-0728-7
e-book: 978-1-4094-0729-4

Visit **www.gowerpublishing.com** and

- search the entire catalogue of Gower books in print
- order titles online at 10% discount
- take advantage of special offers
- sign up for our monthly e-mail update service
- download free sample chapters from all recent titles
- download or order our catalogue